A TIME AND PLACE
CHRISTIAN MOELLER
MEDIA ARCHITECTURE
1991–2003

A TIME AND PLACE
CHRISTIAN MOELLER
MEDIA ARCHITECTURE
1991–2003

LARS MÜLLER PUBLISHERS

Für Martina, Maria und Anna

Foreword

Since the early nineties, Christian Moeller has occupied an important position in the international media art scene. His ongoing artistic deployment of the most recent media technologies tells an almost seamless story of the infant genre of Media Arts. Christian Moeller's pioneering experiments have ranged from room-filling video projection, to the inspired re-purposing of scientific software. Over the course of his career, he has translated technological developments into artistic interventions and architectural installations showing us a spectacularly new aesthetic for interactive experiences. Because almost all of these elaborate projects were temporary installations, recorded in photographs and on video, an accessible survey of the work is urgently needed so as to properly anchor Christian Moeller within current Media Art discourses.

Taking account of the work's particular qualities and of the formal limitations of the printed book, he and I have jointly devised an innovative means to present this work. The print publication uses the artist's authentic language and photographic documentation to create a continuous and complete overview of his work. But the experience of space and action that makes this work so engaging can be better conveyed cinematically than with words alone. Thus for each project in the book, we also offer a link to a corresponding video clip at http://www.christian-moeller.com. This interactive combination of analogue and digital resources is entirely in keeping with the times and has been developed in an exemplary fashion by Daniel Sauter.

Lars Müller

Introduction

A blind child, given sight with the help of an operation, was only able to see white noise. He was unable to build a bridge to the world of things he'd known by feeling and hearing, and saw instead a thunderstorm of dashes, static and angry patterns coming down on him, an incomprehensible image world without order. He kept his eyes shut to escape this noise of light, and wished himself back to the orderly sensorium he had inhabited before. We, with our vision trained to make sense of what we perceive, can't imagine the world as he must see it, a maximum image so totally undecodable.

But with our acoustic perception, we live more comfortably with chaos, in a world of signals that we ignore, and barely listen to or process. When we find this unpleasant we call it noise. Sometimes we listen to noise but don't hear it; sometimes we hear it but don't listen. For an audio environment consisting of numerous different noises, the greater the complexity, the more tolerable the event becomes. Not that it would be particularly pleasant to have to listen to 20 radio stations at the same time in one room, but surely 20 is more bearable than just 3. And so, unlike visual cognition, in the state of auditory non-attentiveness undecodable chaos is more pleasant than an almost manageable complexity.

My art and architecture explores such conditions and differences, not in the laboratory, but as they work themselves out at the level of the city. The weirdly beautiful ambience of the city pulsing with neon light is not a conscious, deliberately created event. The electronic city is a flood of potentially decodable signs, tolerable only by someone who has given up on reading it. In the city, we become like the blind child, dropped in an ocean of optical signification. Amazingly, we learn to see the city by borrowing from how we've learned to hear it. As we tune out acoustic blur, we also let the city slide into visual noise, a more pleasant, manageable buzz than the overwhelming accumulation of legible signs.

For me signs applied to architecture must not be too decipherable or comprehensible. It is much more interesting to give the sign characteristics and teach it to react and change, to intelligently insert the necessary interfaces into urban spaces. At the scale of the city, the abstract installation is a form of urban design, one that because of its constructional dimensions and the manipulability of its performance, does more and enables more than a flashing Coca-Cola symbol. As modern display and projection techniques develop, the architectural dimension of moving images will continue to overtake the urban landscape. While this poses incredible artistic opportunities, it is also certain to bring a ridiculous and tragic media sprawl.

Whereas advertising attempts the impossible goal of "communication", our goal for the moving image at the architectural scale is the creation of event. In this way, the event is a time and place for which sensation itself is the content of the composition. This is inevitably a strategy of mediation, but one by no means unique to modern times and its technologies. Even the most "technical" of my projects is not about technology itself, but about people, their ability to manipulate and be manipulated by

its environment. Today and always, the spaces we inhabit are designable, as sensation, as technology, and as cognition. To explore the beauty of this condition is the first and last problem of media architecture.
One seemingly unsuccessful project will make this point clear. The installation, *Sound of the Growing Grass*, is about a willfully unrealistic attempt, as the name would indicate, to hear the sound of grass blades growing. Contact microphones are mounted on a hollow wooden structure onto which a small field of grass is planted. The inspiration for this project did not come from advanced surveillance media, astrophysical optics, or any other modern device. The idea is based on a historical drawing of marble chairs in ancient Roman gardens. These chairs were upholstered with a thin layer of herbs growing on them. According to the description, sitting in the chairs and pressing down on the herbs perfumed the air. To me, this was a very successful example of early media architecture, one that I wanted to work with, but by addressing people's sense of sound rather than smell.
The idea of listening to grass grow is bit naïve, but deliberately so and needless to say, the project didn't literally work. Part of the beauty in the approach was the consistent and conscientious undertaking of something that was known in advance to be unachievable. In this, the important point was not really even knowing what the actual goal was, but following this road there might be a moment along the way that would provide an interesting surprise. For me, as for many before me, the open pursuit of the *event* is the only way we can find out something new, can learn to see in new ways, to hear in new ways, and to build cities in new ways.
You see then how the printed publication of these event-projects poses problems. Not only must they be appreciated physically, but they occur in time as much as space, and are thus poorly suited to still photography and textual description. For this "book" we hoped to find a form of publication particularly suited to withstand the same demands I place on the works that it presents. In discussions with publisher Lars Mueller, we devised a solution that would allow printed matter and time-based elements to mix by linking printed and broadband internet content to form a whole that would make the best use of both media with minimum redundancy. The result is *A Time and Place*, a book that asks to be read in front of an on-line computer. Texts, drawings, and photographs that appear in the book form a complement to the digitized sequences of image, sound and video on the web.

I originally trained as an architect and practiced until the late 1980s. While I enjoyed it, today the architect is a lonely figure. He is often the only one who gives much thought to the quality of the project and defends it. But by necessity, there are many others involved. Too many times they prevent the architect from achieving what would be the optimal result. This can be due to cost or regulatory limits, or can simply be because the mind-set of the people involved in building these days does not allow them to aspire to do anything extraordinary. This has made the architect

something of a “lonesome warrior;” he surrounds himself with other architects, which hardly improves his situation. Architects marry architects, and they have children who become architects. This fate would not have made me very happy.
Around 1990, I got to know Peter Weibel, then in the process of founding the Institute of New Media at the Städel School in Frankfurt. Before I had even noticed it myself, Weibel saw very clearly the directions that my work could take. At a point in time when I did not yet know how to turn a computer on and off, he invited me to become involved in building the Institute as a guest artist. This was my first introduction to computer technology and electronic media.
As a result of this collaboration, I became the first architect to have a media laboratory of my own within my studio, a place where various creative people with many different talents met and worked together, not just to jointly complete outstanding projects, but also to simply have a good time. Work takes up such a considerable part of our lives, that an inspiring social ambience is important. The sign outside read “Architect’s Office”, but inside, computer scientists, musicians; all sorts of people were at work, and eventually not a single “architect.” Very quickly we realized that our main focus was the border between architecture and the electronic media. We wanted to make architecture capable of dialogue, and to integrate electronic media into the urban context. Unexpectedly, we found there was a lot of demand for this type of thinking.
The pages that follow are a map of events that took place over the subsequent 13 years. Because we still know very little about how we make sense of our spaces and the time we spend there, these questions hold my continuing interest.

Christian Moeller

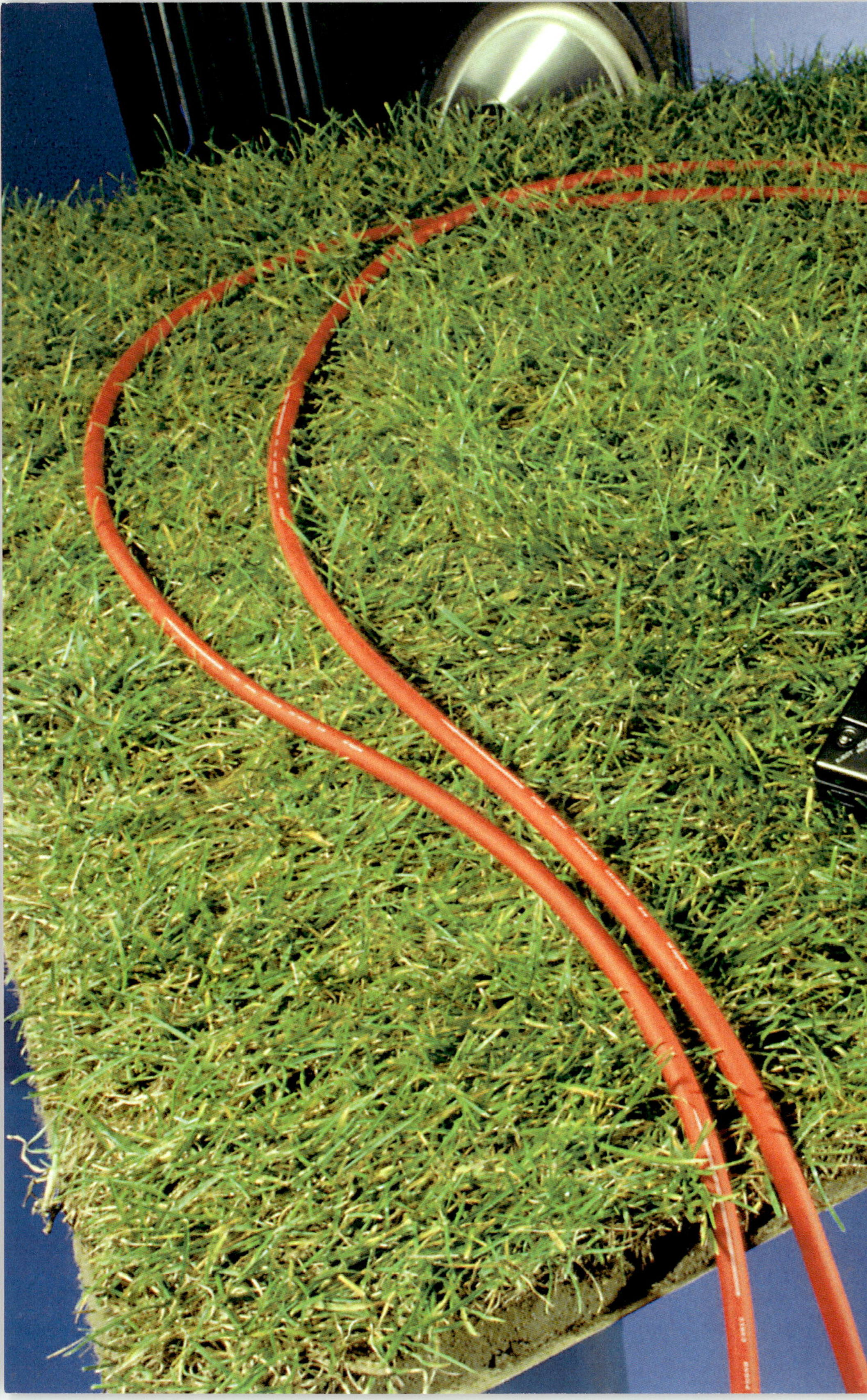

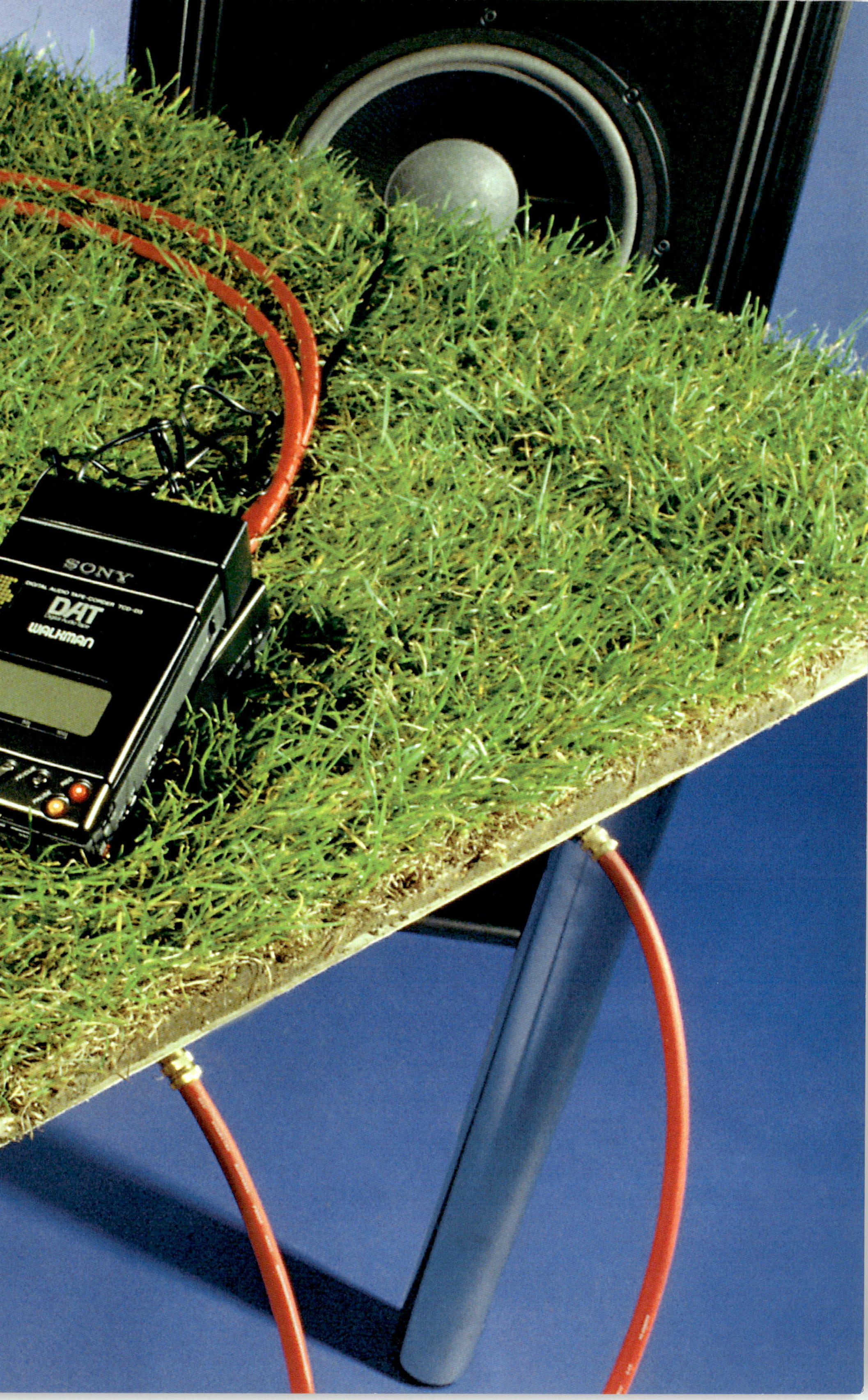
SONY
DAT
WALKMAN

PROJECTS 1991–2003

The following text is based on a lecture given in Basel on November 15, 2001.

CAMERA MUSIC/ KINETIC SHADOWS

1997
www.christian-moeller.com/camera_music
Sound Garden, Spiral/Wacoal Art Center, Tokyo

Curators: Yukiko Shikata, Kazunao Abe
Producer: Fumihiko Sumitomo
Sound: Hubert Machnik
Programming: Sven Thöne

In 1997 I was invited to do a series of sound installations for the Spiral Gallery/Wacoal Art Center in Aoyama, Tokyo, an unusual building designed by the architect Fumihiko Maki. These installations were experimental in nature and they did not have to be integrated into a particular given theme. An installation entitled Camera Music was set up in the lobby. My intention was to provoke certain actions by the visitors in this part of the building. People walking by would find themselves and their movements reflected as sparkling cluster of dynamic pixel rods on a rear projection screen. This abstract reflection system resulted in their doing strange things and gesticulating while being watched through the glass façade by passers-by outside on the sidewalk. The passers-by could not see the moving digital imagery, but only saw people in the lobby waving their arms about and were thus encouraged to enter the gallery to find out what was causing such strange behavior.

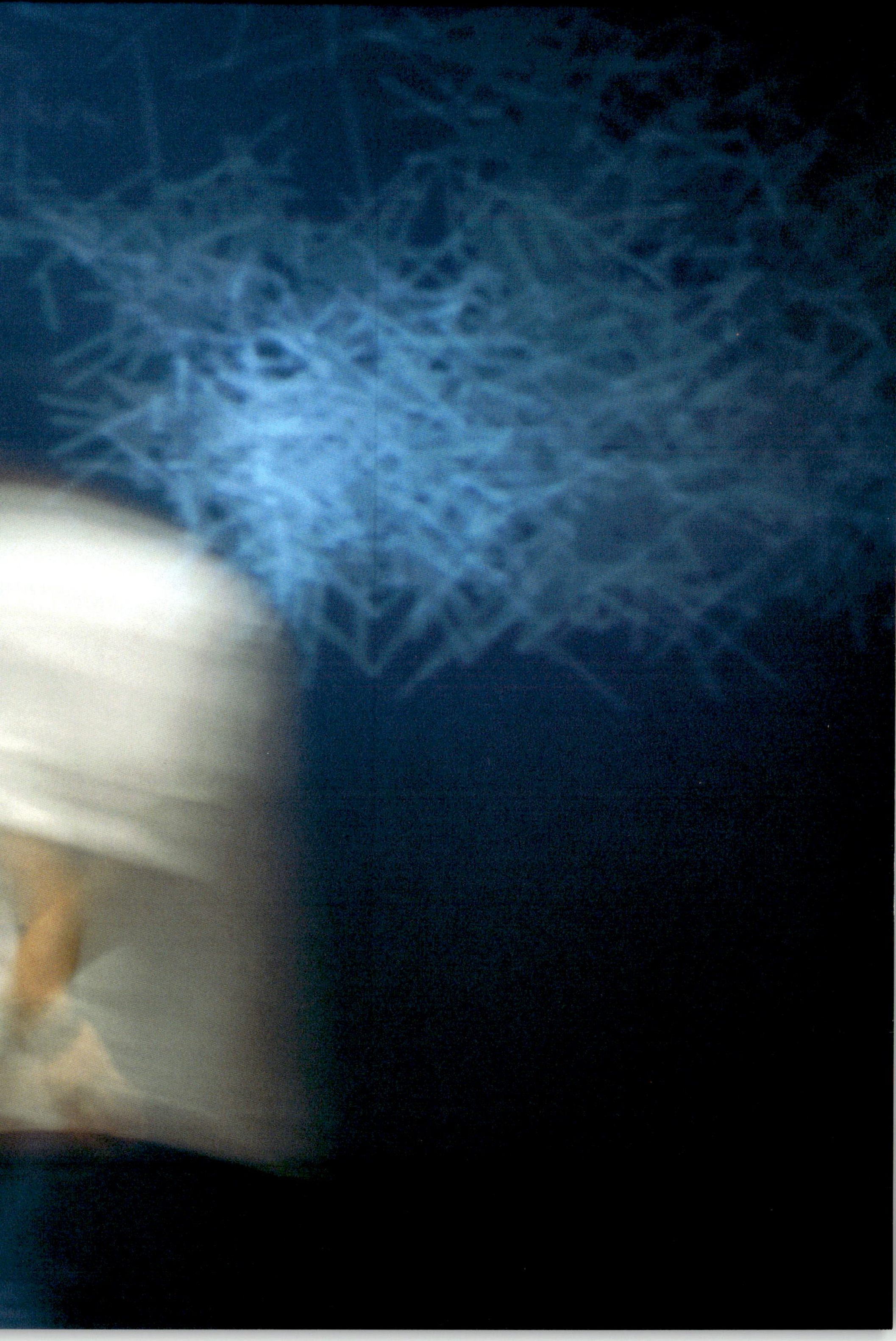

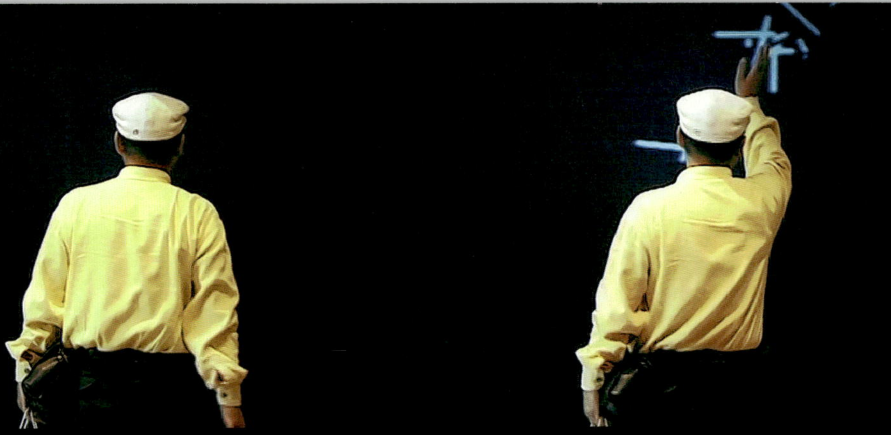

www.christian-moeller.com/camera_music

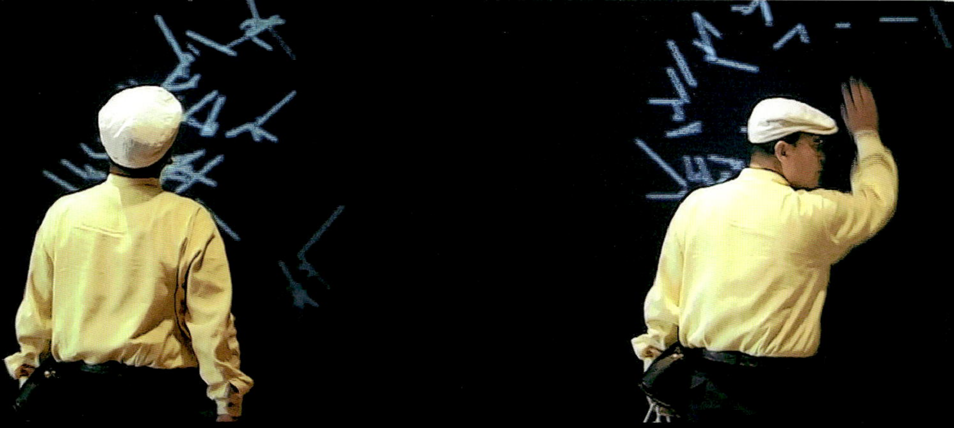

Abstract kinetic representation of passers-by, captured by video camera and rear projected on screen.

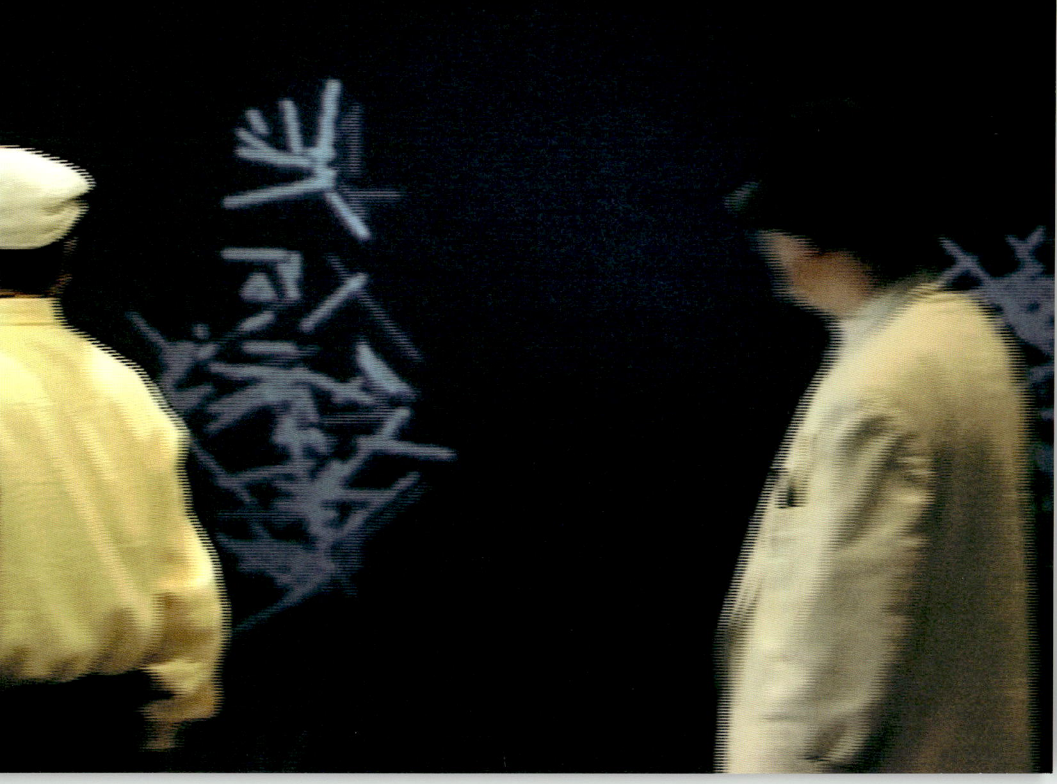

VIRTUAL TRAIN

1997
www.christian-moeller.com/virtual_train
Sound Garden, Spiral/Wacoal Art Center, Tokyo

Curators: Yukiko Shikata, Kazunao Abe
Producer: Fumihiko Sumitomo
Light design: Nathan Thompson
Sound technician: Willi Bopp
Programming: Daniel Schmitt

Virtual Train was a video installation that created an underground train running through the gallery. The tremendous volume was exactly the same as you would hear if you stood next to a train passing by in an underground tunnel. Through the change in location—the sound of the train now oriented inside a gallery—it became evident just how much our perception of place is dependent on the context of noise. It is not the sheer volume of the sound source alone which determines how loud we perceive it to be. Whereas the clatter of a train approaching the platform is almost ignored, the same noise imported into the gallery space becomes an unbearable din. A stretch of 8-channel audio equipment attached to the ceiling produced a spatial simulation of the train running through the gallery.

These trains passed by in irregular intervals, between 15 or 30 minutes each. The rest of the time, the monitors displayed green pixelated, flickering patterns. As a matter of fact, the train never needed longer than six or eight seconds to pass through the 30m of gallery space. The majority of the visitors missed the event, or saw only a bit of it. One interesting reaction was that exhibition visitors would remain standing in front of the installation for the next train to come before they would leave the gallery, just like passengers waiting at a station.

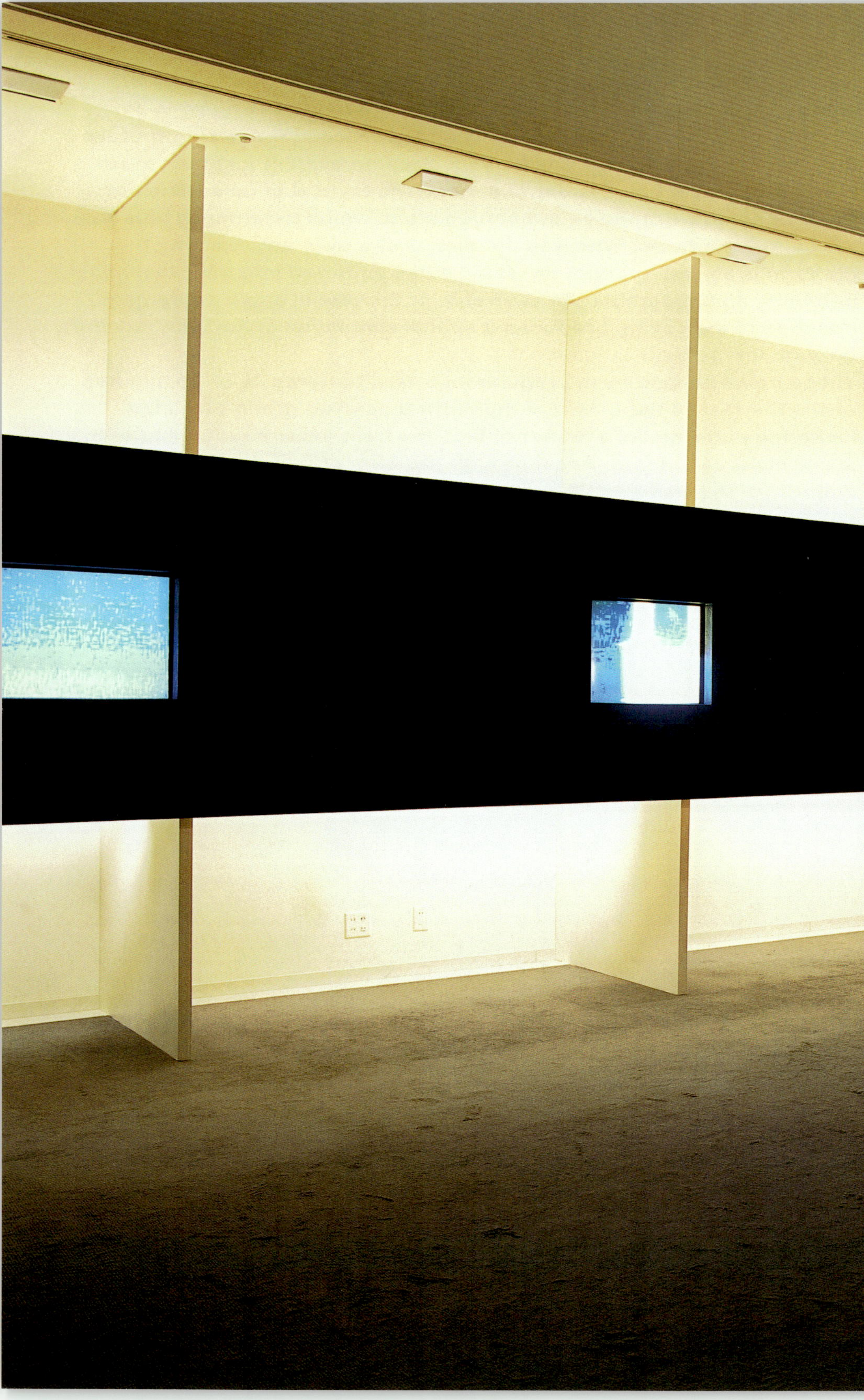

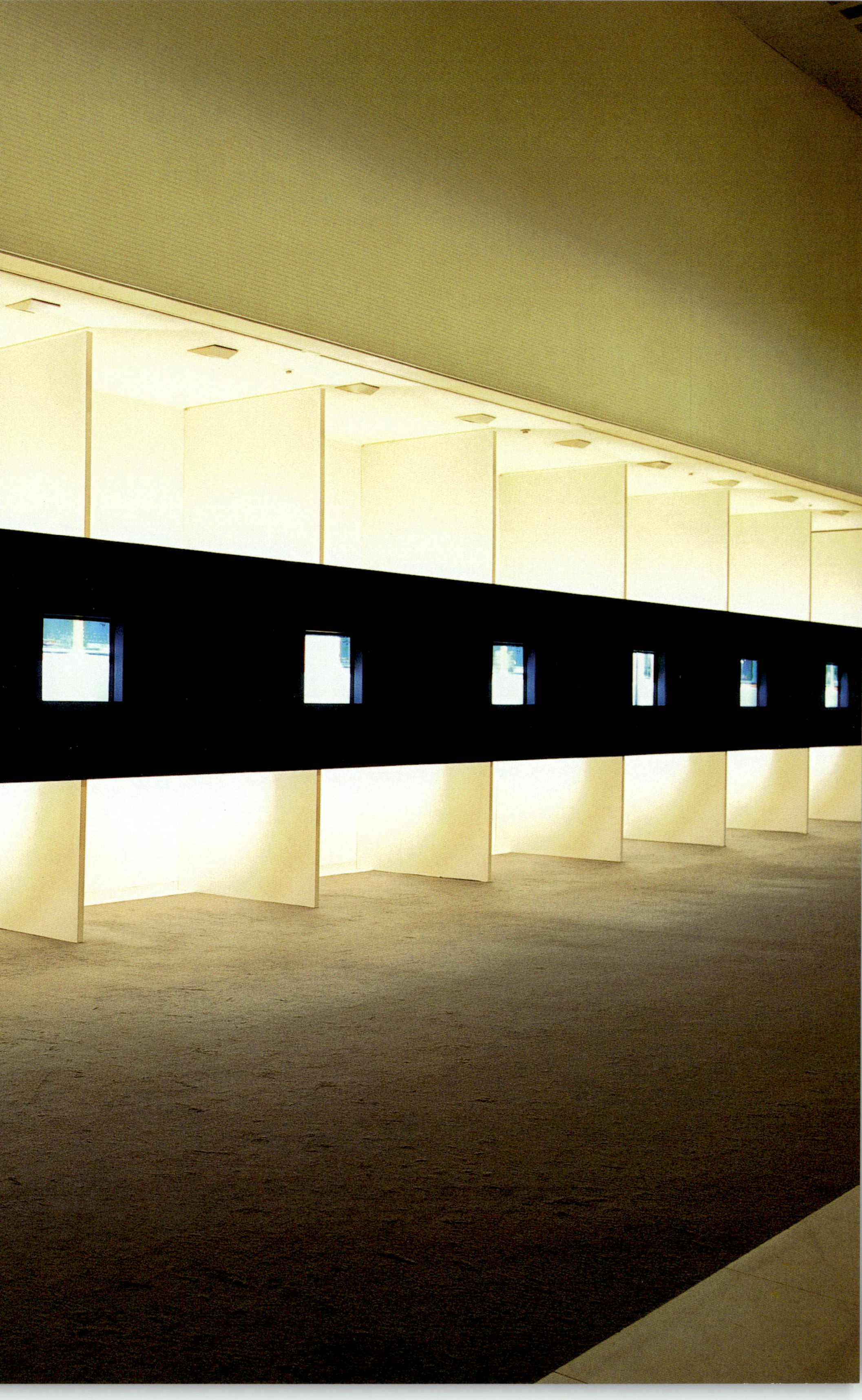

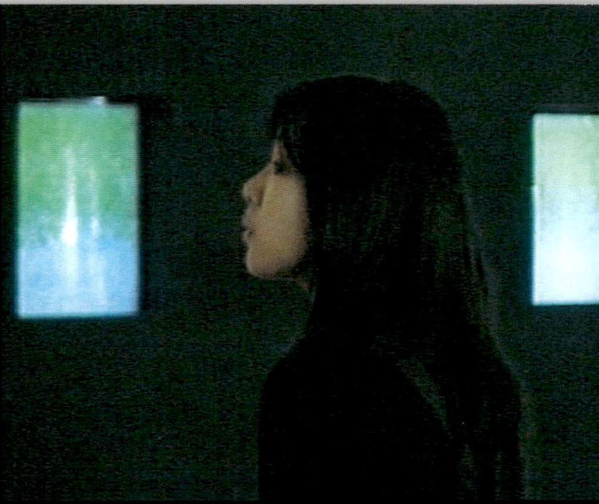

www.christian-moeller.com/virtual_train

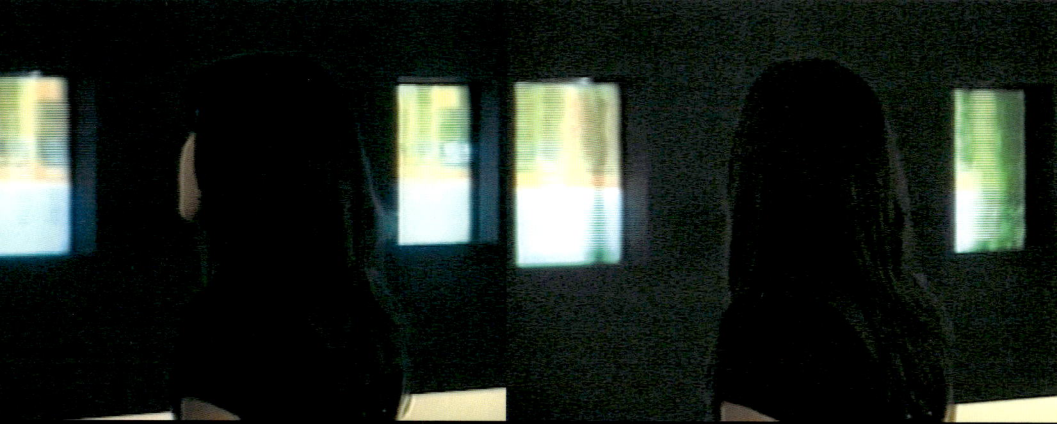

Segmentation of the video, to be displayed on 9 horizontally aligned video monitors.

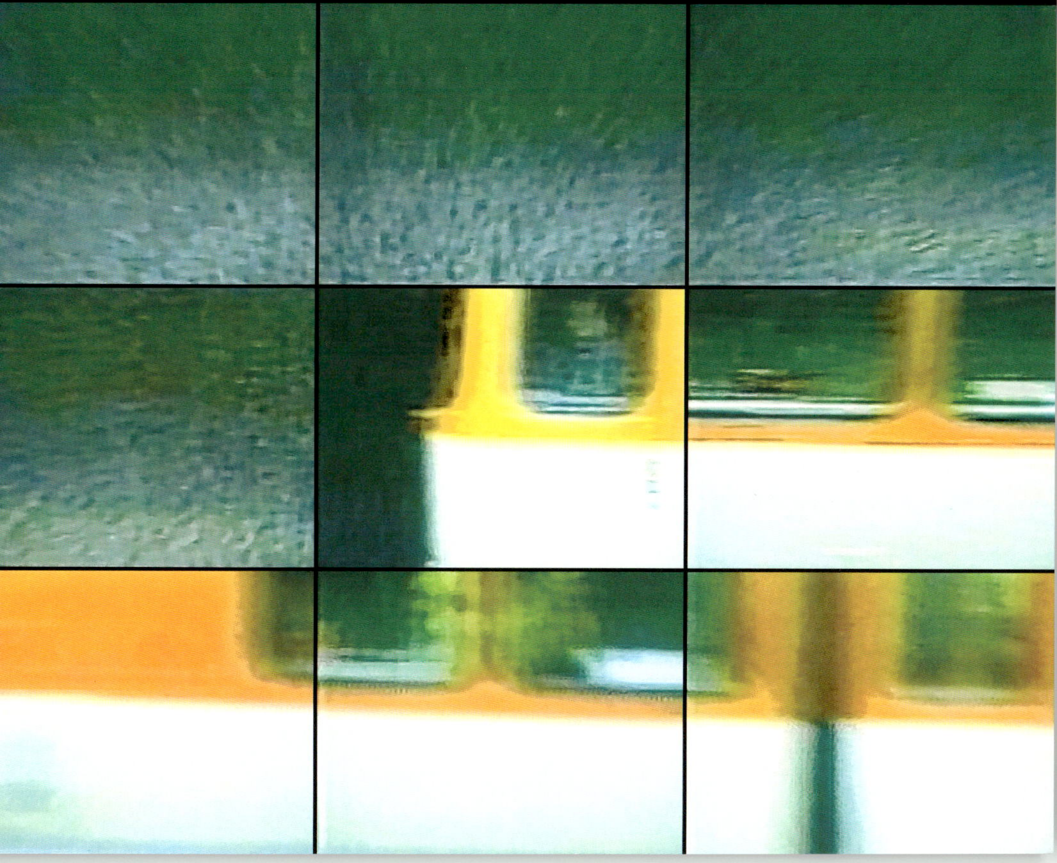

AUDIO GROVE

1997
www.christian-moeller.com/audio_grove
Sound Garden, Spiral/Wacoal Art Center, Tokyo;
Cyber 98, Centro Cultural de Belém, Lisbon, Portugal

Curators: Yukiko Shikata, Kazunao Abe
Producer: Fumihiko Sumitomo
Sound: Ludger Brümmer
Light design: Nathan Thompson
Programming: Sven Thöne
Hardware: Wolfgang Schemmert
Sound technician: Willi Bopp
Curator (Lisbon): Rui Trindade
Construction management (Lisbon): Petra Trefzger

Audio Grove is an installation consisting of 64 upright, almost six-meter-high iron poles. These are linked to touch-sensitive electronic sensors and are capable of emitting sounds when touched.
The first step was to build a 1:20 scale model of the installation, but not because we required it for testing proportions, as is customary. Instead it functioned as the interface for our composer, Ludger Brümmer, who needed to be able to efficiently distribute his sound structures into the three-dimensional sculpture, which he couldn't achieve by using a keyboard.
Audio Grove represents a very important step regarding the musical potential of interactive, and non-linear music in an installation context. The problem created by this situation is imaginable as a concert without a conductor, one in which every musician is playing for himself, independent of his colleagues. The result becomes sonic confusion. To avoid this in the past, we used pentatonic or natural scales to create the necessary harmonic potential. But here, there was a new way. Ludger uses a physical modeling system to create his sound elements. Using very advanced computer systems, he engineers virtual objects as instruments, locates them in a mathematically constructed virtual world and designs the attack to create a particular sound. In this way, he is generating families of sounds which harmonize almost independent of their individual frequencies, regardless of the sequence in which they are activated.
The interface on the touch-sensitive steel poles recognized two different events to trigger the audio system. A simple touch activates one sound, and the simultaneous touch of two poles by the same person moves the overall audio up or down by one octave. Just these two operations were enough to create a surprising amount of sonic varation but also an unexpected problem on the day of our opening. We didn't take into account that almost everybody instinctively wandered within this forest of steel poles, continously touched two poles at the same time, which overwhelmed and corrupted the quality of the sound performance. We only realized this little conceptual mistake at the opening night with so many people playing simultaneously in the installation. The way we found to control this problem makes me smile a little bit, even today. With no time to spare, we wrote a one-page, almost banal user manual on how to "use" the installation. We xeroxed a huge number of these and handed them out to visitors. Now everybody had a piece of paper to carry in one hand, and all of a sudden the visitors touched the steel poles only with their free hand, like they were supposed to do. It seems that the many years of work with interactive phenomena and the behavior of exhibition visitors affords some wisdom in its own right.
For the installation lighting, we integrated further visual complexity. During the day, the rotunda of the gallery was lit from a large skylight and the room was flooded with diffuse light.
At night, the installation was surrounded by 25 profile spotlights, all projecting the same square of light carefully aligned into the installation. When the poles were touched by the visitor, the lights went on and off alternately, generating a light-shadow texture on the floor of the installation.

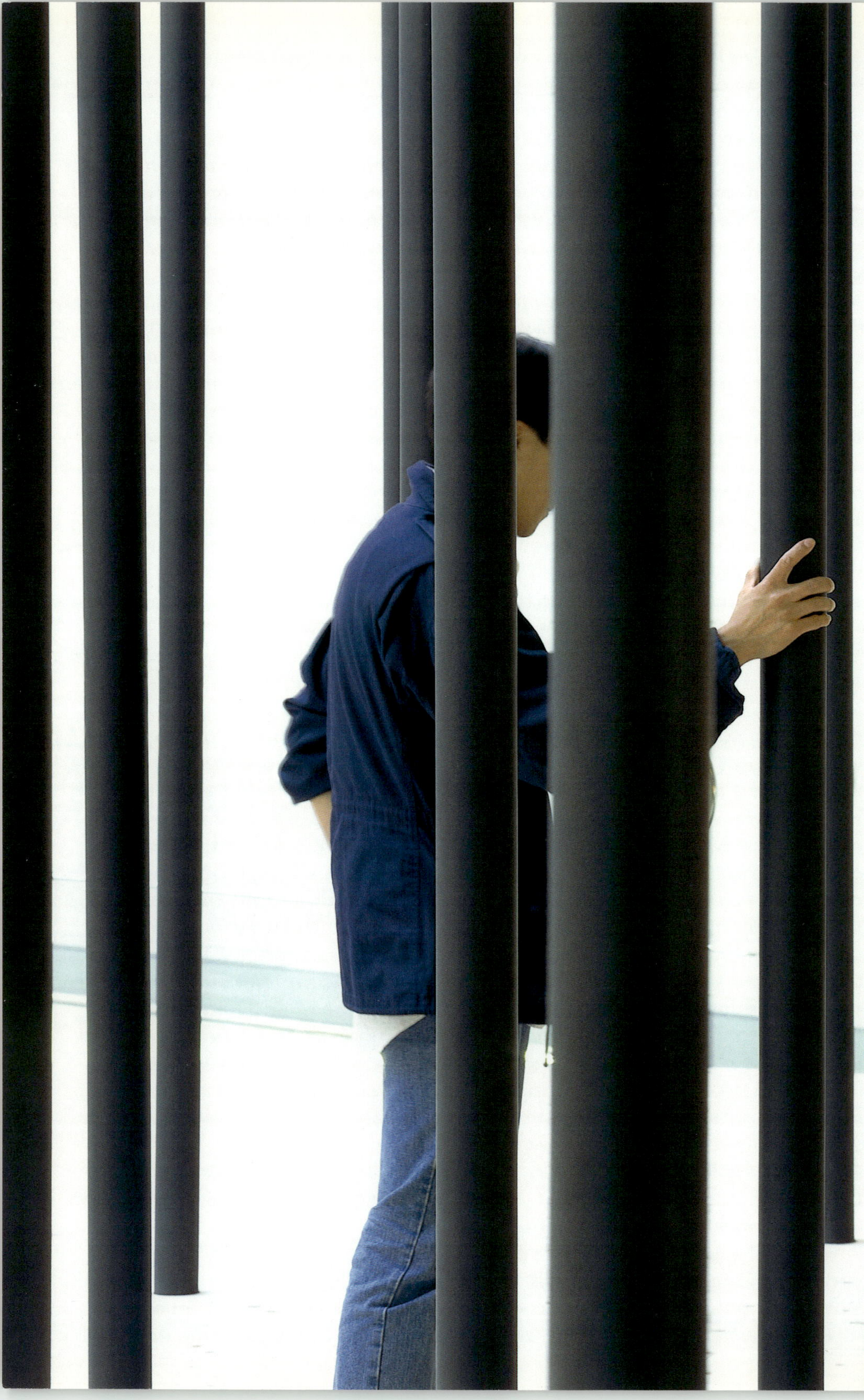

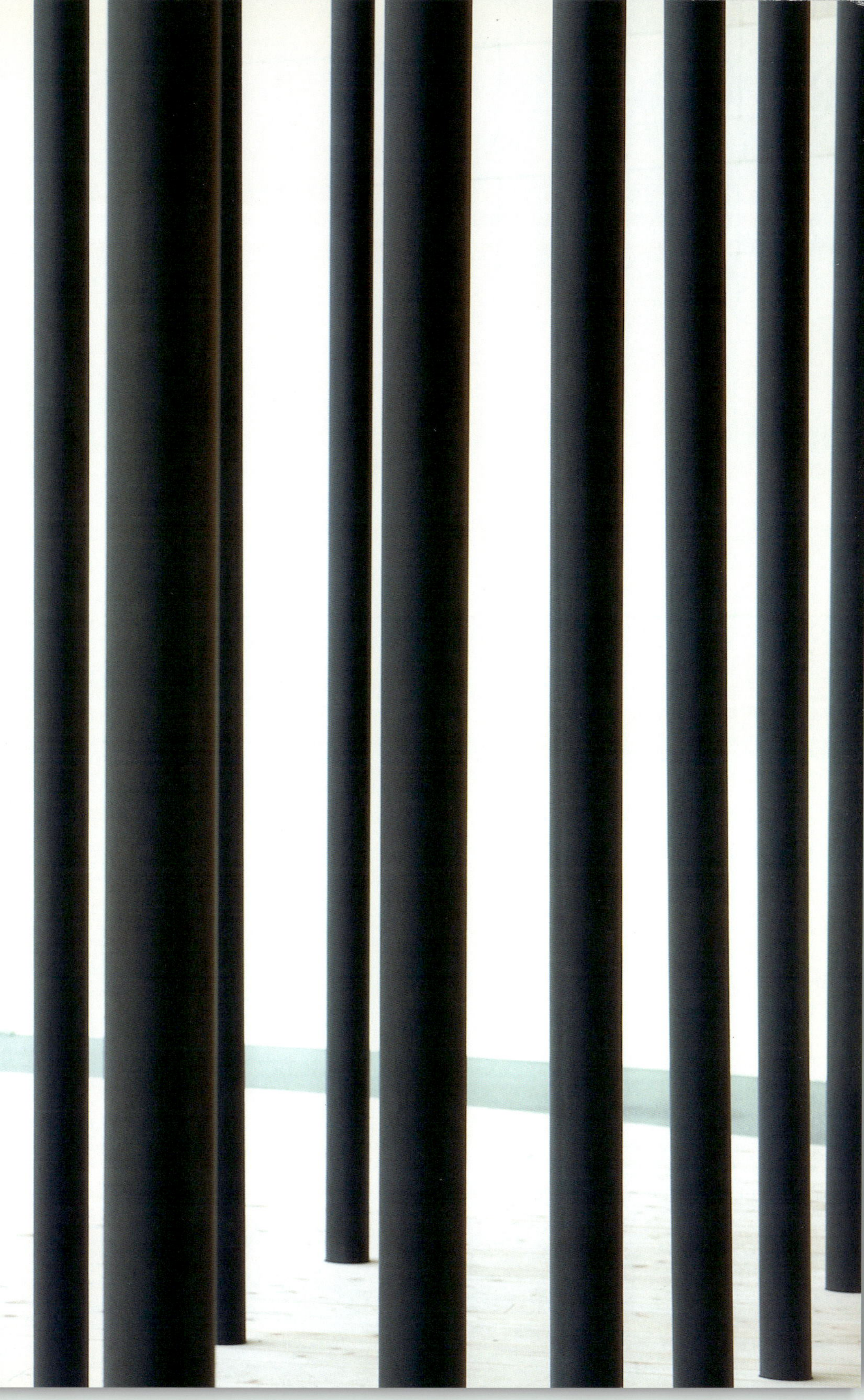

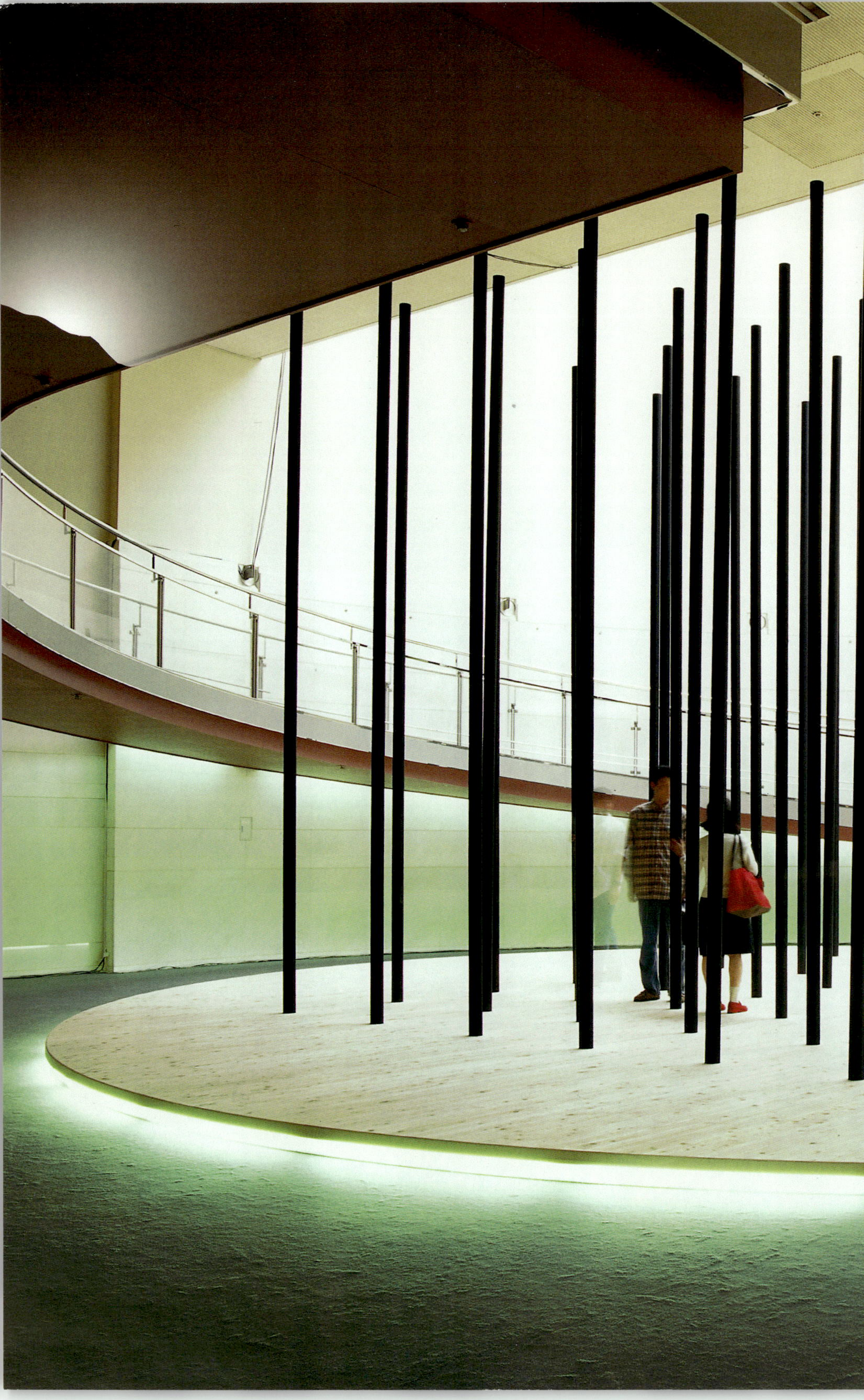

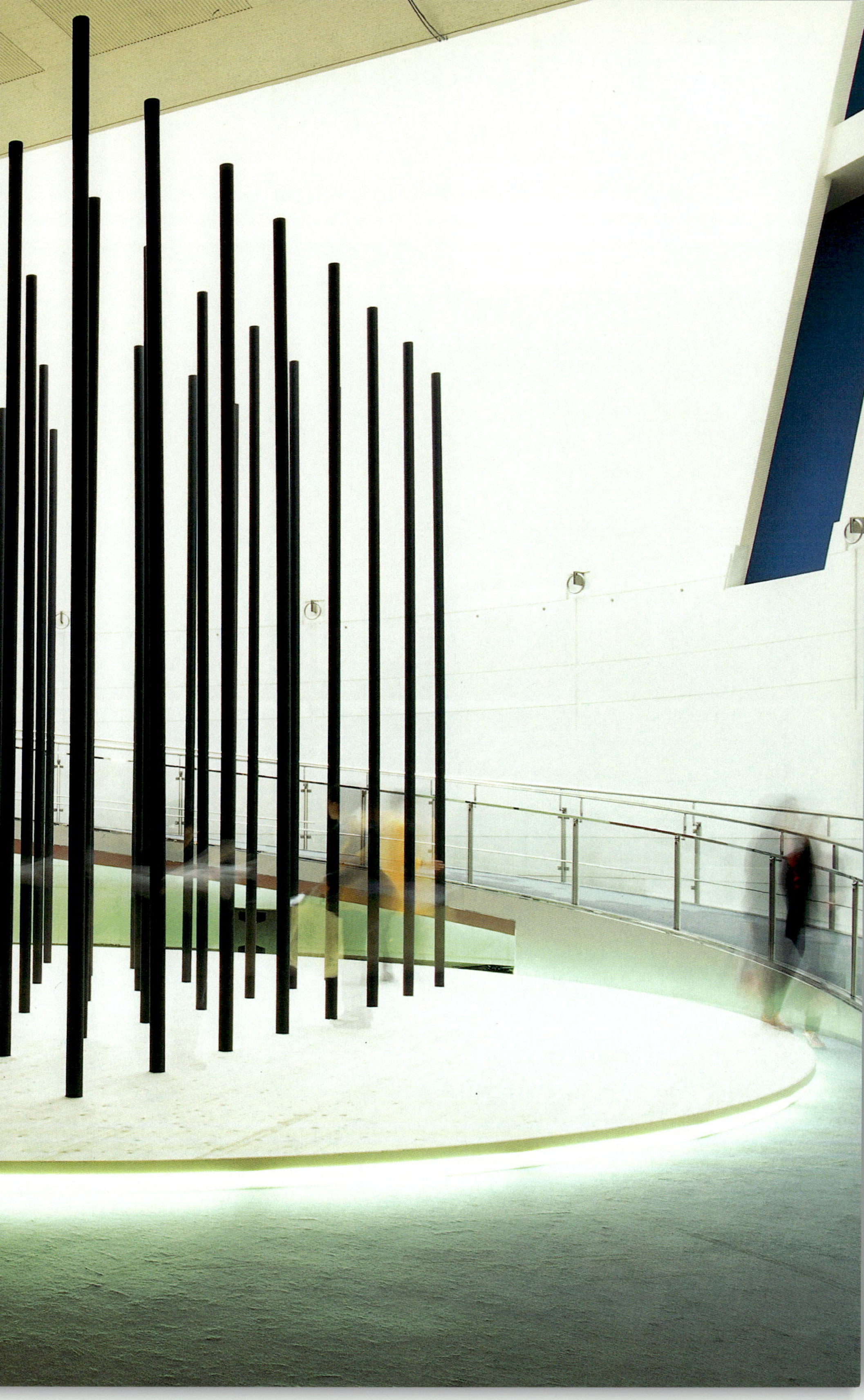

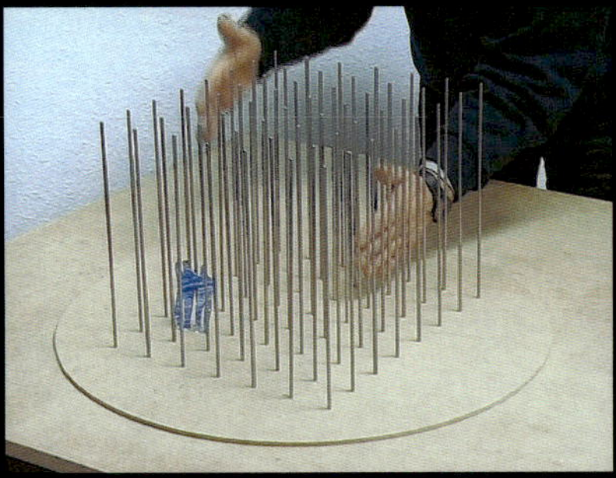

1:5 scale fully-functional interface for the spatial composition of the sound.

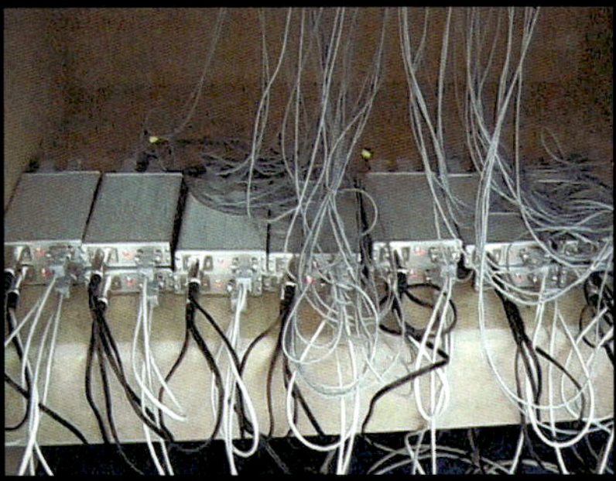

64-channel touch sensor electronics.

www.christian-moeller.com/audio_grove

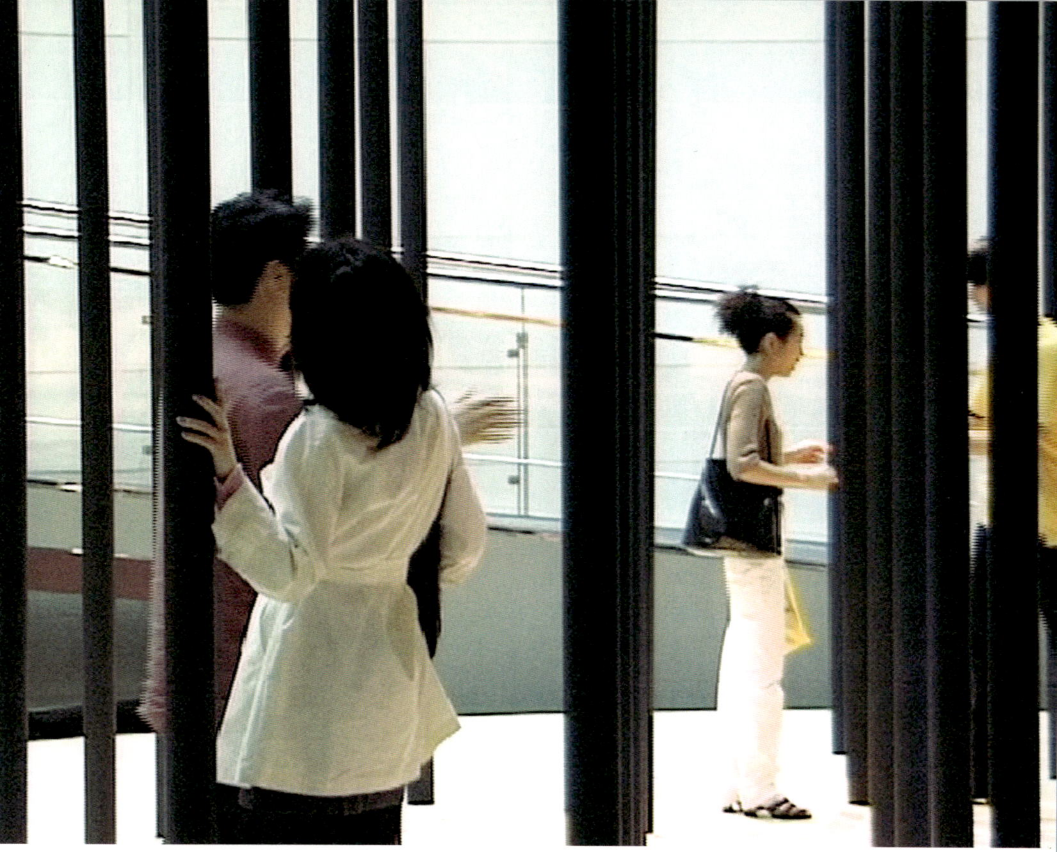

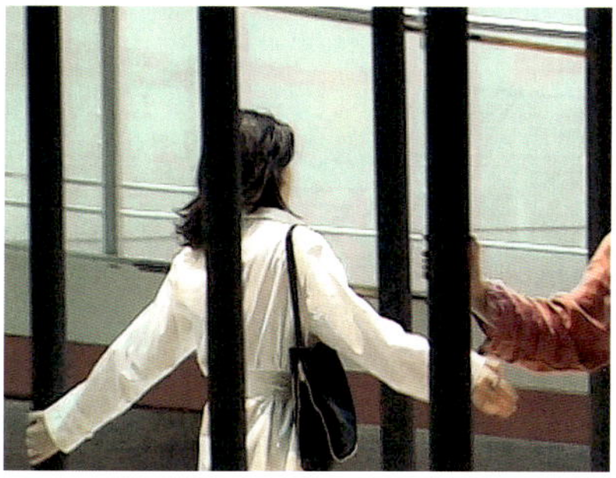

Visitors play music by interacting with
the touch sensitive steel poles.

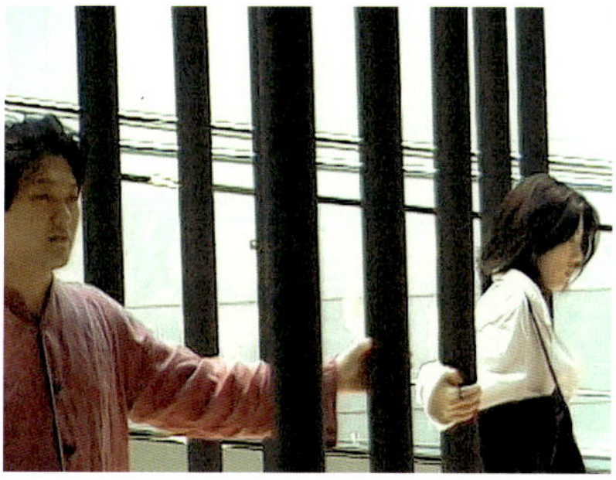

At night, the play of interactive lights and shadows.

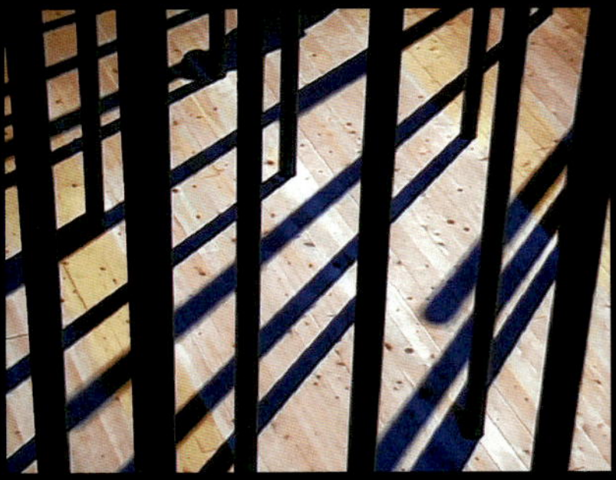

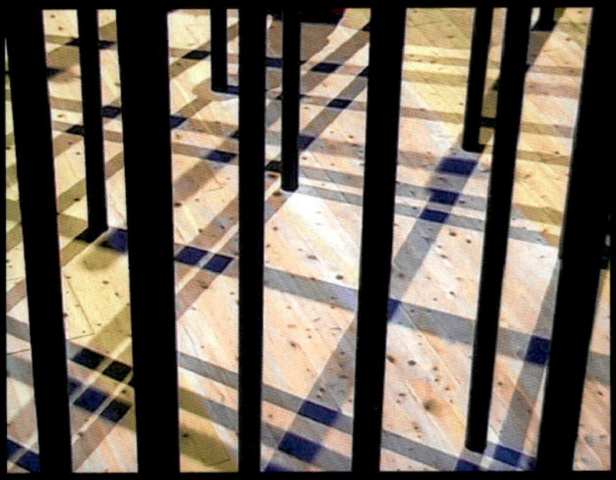

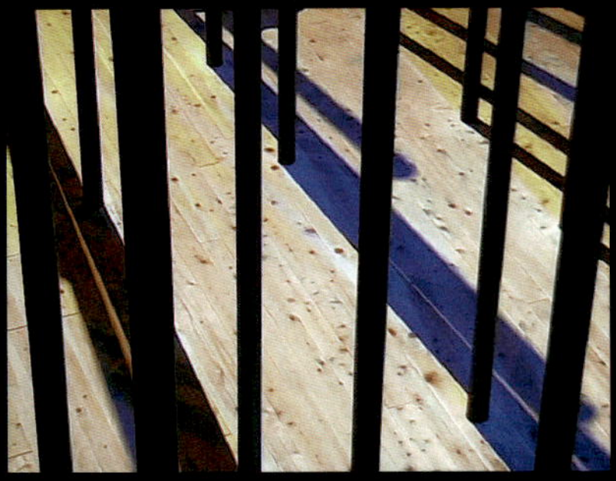

www.christian-moeller.com/audio_grove

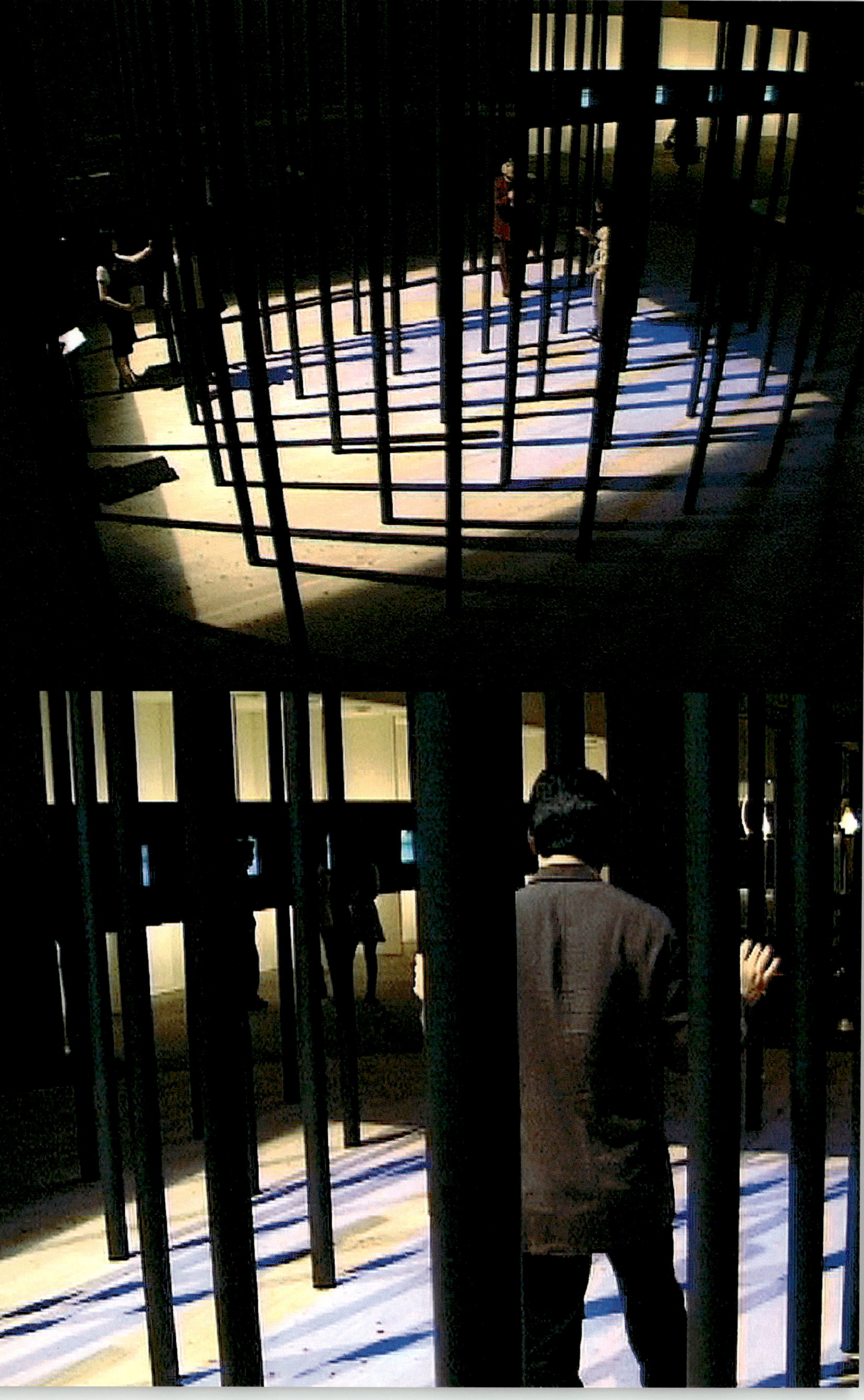

VOICE OF THE PEOPLE

1998
www.christian-moeller.com/voice_of_the_people
1848 Aufbruch zur Freiheit, Kunsthalle Schirn, Frankfurt/Main
In collaboration with: Hellmut Seemann

Editing: Susanne Craemer
Sound recording/technik: Willi Bopp and Jo Schlosser
Programming: Sven Thöne
Hardware: Wolfgang Schemmert
Lighting: Stefan Zimmermann
Construction management: Ronald Kammer

The project was made possible through the kind support of the lawyers' offices Oppenhoff & Rädler, and Pfünder, Volhard, Weber & Axner; as well as of the sound archives of the West German Broadcasting Corporation (WDR), and of the German Federal Parliament.

In 1848 the first German parliament was convened in the Paulskirche (St. Paul's Church) in Frankfurt under the presidency of Heinrich von Gagern. "150 years of German Parliamentarism" was reason enough for an extensive exhibition in Frankfurt to celebrate that important anniversary. Hellmut Seemann, then the director of Frankfurt's Schirn Kunsthalle, was well aware of the potential dryness of the theme and recognized the need for a contribution with a hint of irony. I made a piece for the exhibition "Aufbruch zur Freiheit 1848" (Towards Freedom 1848).
What was required was an installation for an exterior public space, a roofed rotunda, accessible 24-hours a day in the entrance area of the Kunsthalle Schirn.
Hellmut Seemann called the installation "Voice of the People". Sixty touch-sensitive poles were used, each engraved with the name of a German parliamentarian, whom we jointly selected from the parliament of 1848. Fortunately, because the taking of minutes in stenographic form was just becoming an established custom at the time, all the speeches made by those first parliamentarians have been fully recorded. In accordance with Wilhelm Stolze's Theoretisch-praktisches Lehrbuch der deutschen Stenographie A theoretical and practical handbook of German stenography, written in 1841, every word ever spoken in a German parliament has been documented.
The selected speeches made in 1848 were then recorded at my studio, spoken by actors. Perhaps "actor" is not the right term in this case. When considering how to best create the project, I had made a careless mistake. I was used to calling on drama school students for sound and video recordings. I only realized later that students could not plausibly imitate the voices of more mature speakers, and immature voices would compromise the quality of the work in an unnacceptable manner.
We didn't have a budget for professional actors, but our recording engineer, Willi Bopp, came up with a brilliant idea. Frankfurt is the city of bankers and lawyers and the first parliamentarians were all members of these professions. No sooner said than done, we wrote to the big lawyers' offices and to the boards of banks requesting, unusually enough, not money, but the direct involvement of their employees, as speakers in our recording studio. The response was overwhelming. A few days later we were able to choose the speakers according to accent and age.
The other 30 politicians' voices were taken from a recording of a recent last parliamentary debate, at that time in Bonn, held before the opening of the Frankfurt exhibition. The aim was to mix these in with the old parliamentarians. An important aspect of this installation was that it enabled you to hear how rhetoric and language culture have changed in the course of the past 150 years.
When one of the poles, or "voices of the people", in this sound forest was touched, the respective politician began to speak. And when several people touched several poles simultaneously, the gentlemen, and the few ladies, all spoke at the same time, sometimes even about one another. This resulted in an interesting verbal confusion from which the listener could filter out a single voice with astonishing ease, as it was he who determined

its presence. This is an interesting phenomenon which we call the "party effect", (something that is being particularly closely examined by engineers and scientists involved in trying to provide machines with artificial intelligence.) What is the party effect? You are at a party, and hundreds of people are standing around with you in a room. They all have a glass in their hands, and they are all talking. Everybody is familiar with this kind of chatter or din. Now just imagine that someone at the far end of the room, at a distance of say forty metres, mentions your name and maybe even says something impertinent. You will notice that you are immediately able to grow an "elephant's ear" and effortlessly filter out exactly what that person is saying about you, good or bad, from this "verbal noise". The Voice of the People also achieves this effect. As long as I am the one who turns a spoken contribution on or off, I can hear that particular voice despite the noise.

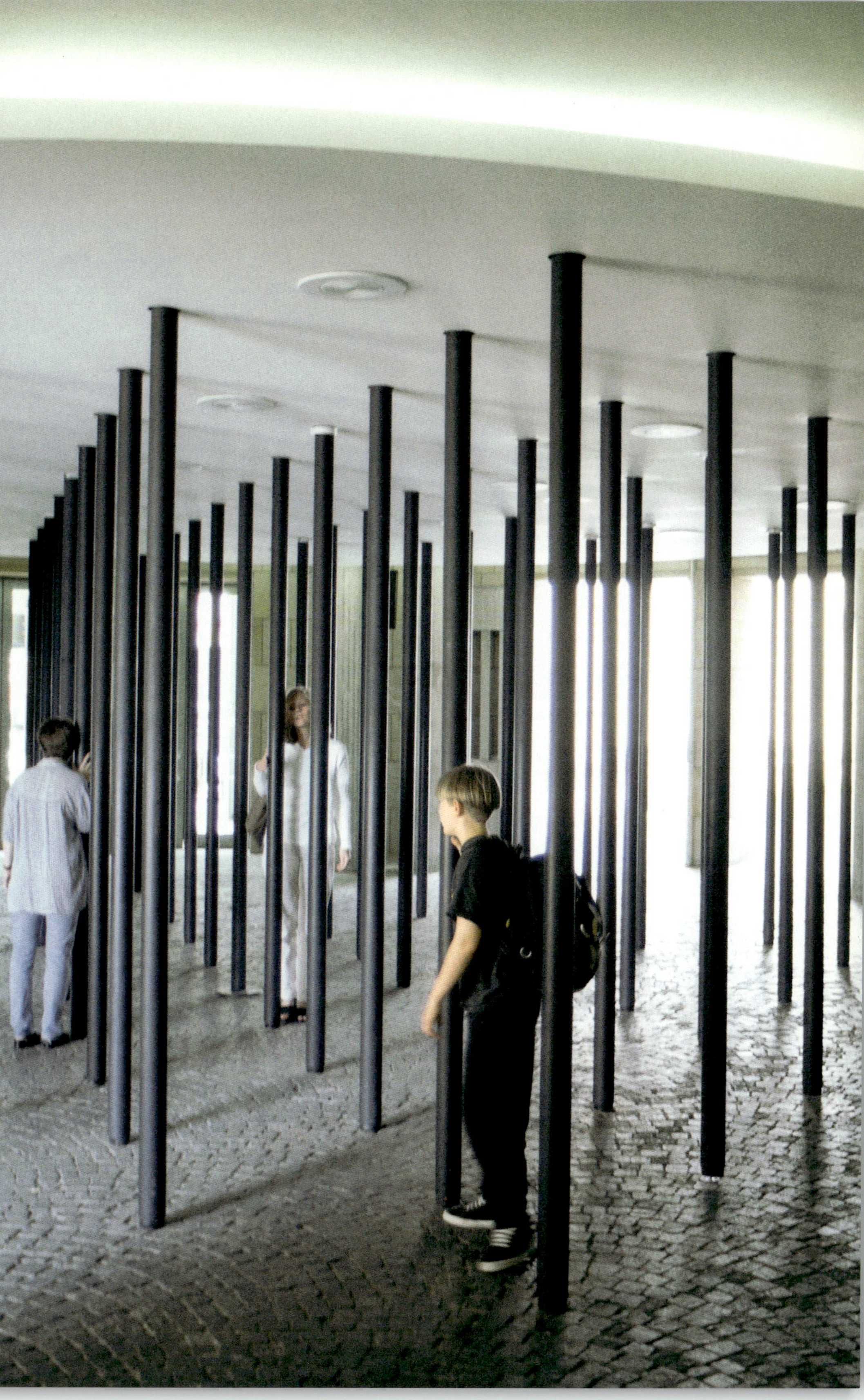

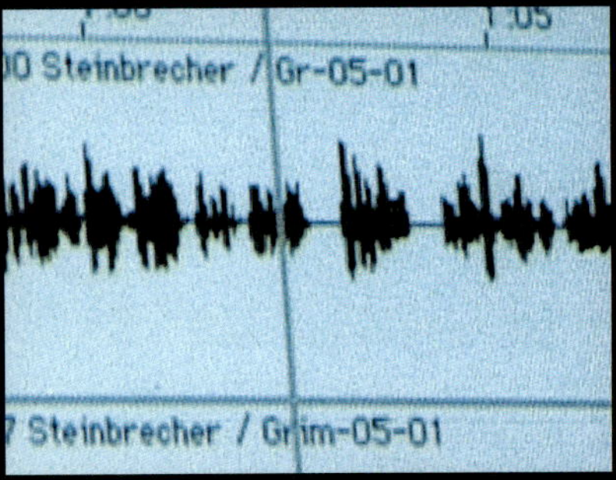

The recording of 30 historic speeches originally from the German Parliament of 1848.

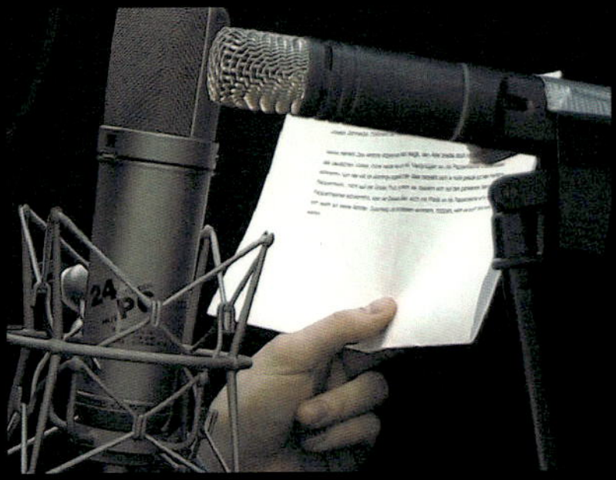

www.christian-moeller.com/voice_of_the_people

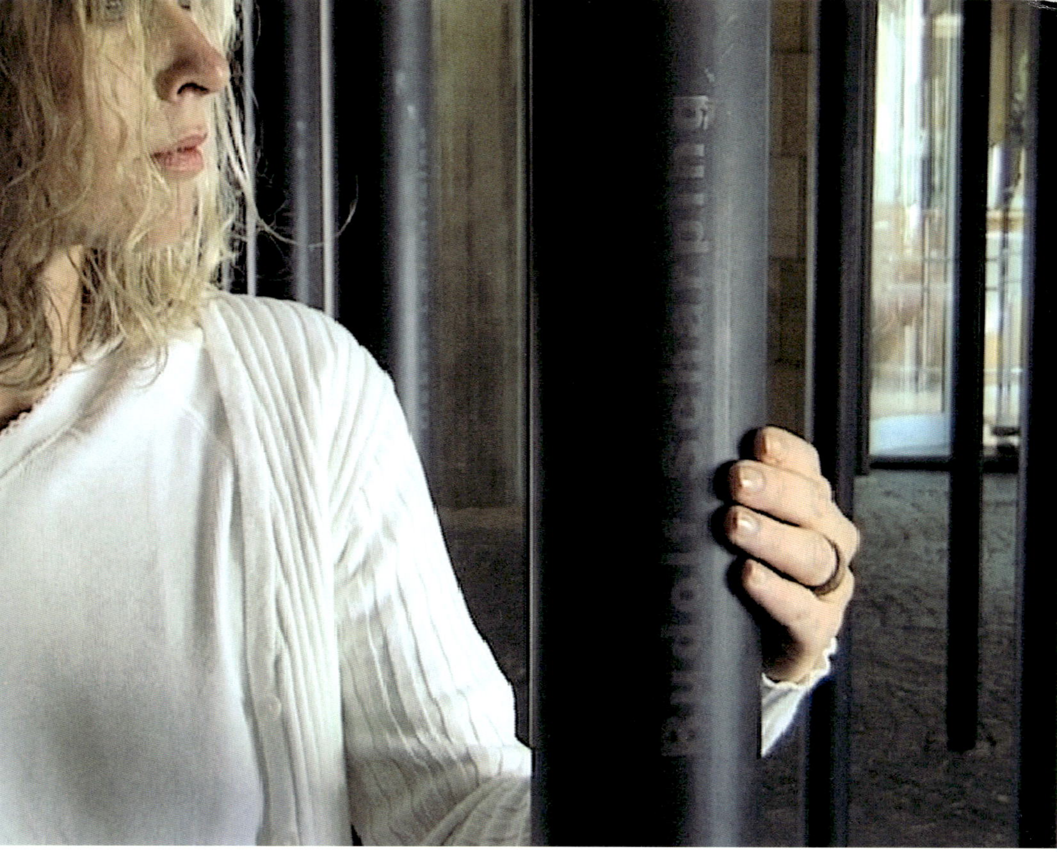

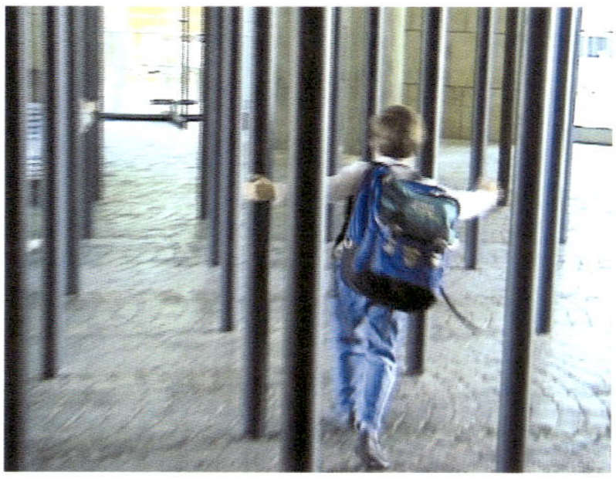

Touch sensitive steel poles engraved with the names of German politicians.

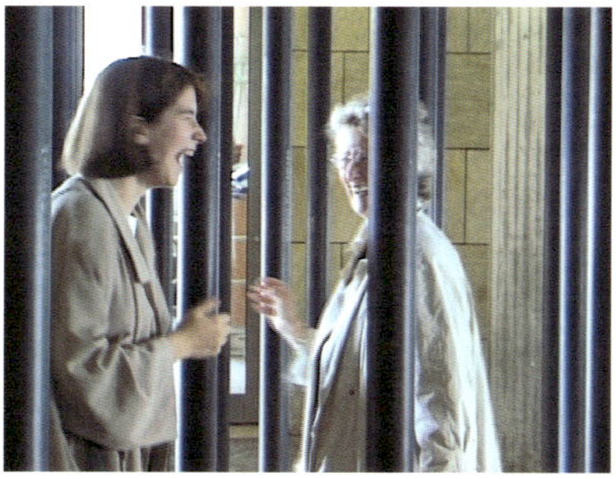

Following The Voice of the People, I was invited by the President of the House of History in Bonn, Hermann Schäfer, to consider an installation for the Reichstag in Berlin, more precisely, for the glass dome on the roof designed by Norman Foster. A difficult challenge. Hermann Schäfer was responsible for the concept of the permanent exhibition on the history of parliamentarism and his problem was how to exhibit "the third symbol of state". What I learned on that occasion was that there are three state symbols: the national colors, the flag; the nation's heraldic beast—the eagle; and then the third state symbol, the national anthem. How can you "exhibit" a national anthem, and particularly in such a symbolically charged place? Even the most patriotic Christian Democrat back-bencher would concede that to have the national anthem broadcast day in day out over loudspeakers would be neither worthy, nor humanly bearable.
I was also certain that Norman Foster would surely not be amused if some strangely "expressive" installation was set up in one of his most prominent achievements. I proposed an object that would be no more conspicuous than a manhole cover, a metal plate inserted flush with the existing cast stone floor in the entrance area of the dome. I designed a concept for a perforated round plate made of quality metal such as bronze bearing the title of the anthem, Das Lied der Deutschen **by Haydn and Fallersleben.**
The idea was to have this metal plate rest on rubber-metal springs. These are used in mechanical engineering to absorb the vibrations of heavy production machinery, and to keep factory buildings from constantly vibrating. At the center of this metal plate is an electromagnetic device capable of vibrating computer-controlled frequencies between 0 and 200 Hz, variable in real time. Imagine if you will, a loudspeaker that cannot be heard. A regular loudspeaker has an electromagnetically driven paper or textile membrane that moves and thus makes the air vibrate. In my system, instead of the paper membrane, a very heavy weight is moved so that instead of the air, the solid surrounding, in this case a person's body, is made to vibrate.
This technology was originally developed as a sound cancelling system to eliminate vibrations and other associated noises from the German ICE high speed train. An interesting and very unexpected problem arose with the ICE. If one is particularly meticulous, too well-meaning as it were, it can have negative effects. It is not hard to imagine that in "precision focused" Germany the sleepers under the tracks are actually placed at exactly the same distance from one another, to a tenth of a millimeter, which they need not be. This exactness creates problems. The tiny but existing sags in the tracks cause a constant up-and-down movement which, in its regularity, tends to grind the steel wheels of the train into a triangular form. Needless to say, we are talking here about very tiny dimensions, but these are still large enough to produce a kind of melody on this track. A melody in the form of a vibration which—and this is the problem—at a certain speed becomes the same as the resonance frequency of the train's aluminium body so that this congruence is greatly amplified.

The resulting noise is not just irritating, it is loud enough to make your teeth fillings fall out. One idea for combating this problem, once it had arisen, was to resort to these body-sound transducers. Positioned at the right points in the train, they measure the vibrations that arise, build them up artificially, then cause them to vibrate into the train, shifted at the exact half amplitude which effectively cancels out the sound 100%. This technology was never implemented in the trains, but when I heard about it, I approached its inventor, Tillmann Freudenberg, whom I have known since I was young, and asked him if we might try to use it in reverse, that is to cause vibrations.

The first prototype was developed at the Hochschule für Gestaltung in Karlsruhe, where I was teaching at the time. We made a serious mistake in choosing wood for the surface of the active plate, because this closed surface caused the air to vibrate. The result was a walk-in loudspeaker, an interesting thing, but not what we had intended. Later we used perforated metal which produced the desired silence.

The metal plate created for the Reichstag was to be inserted inconspicuously into the floor surface below the dome where it would vibrate continually but completely soundlessly, to the melody of the German national anthem. Nothing could be heard, as not enough air would be moved through the perforations. By contrast, the visitor who stood on the plate would receive the German national anthem vibrated directly into his or her body! The transmitted frequencies would travel up the skeleton, the skull would become a resonance chamber, and if the visitor put his hands over his ears, with his inner ear he could hear the melody reflected from the top of his head. We all surely know this phenomenon; it is how sound is perceived in the bath if your ears are under water. I was and still am very taken by the concept of building a musical interpretation of the German national anthem which would literally move the “hearer” physically but without creating any pathos.

I presented this project to the Committee for Art and Cultural Affairs in the German parliament. After a heated debate, during which feelings ran high, the project eventually received approval. However, I must admit to never having such negative feedback, especially from the considerable number of the deputies, and the nominated art experts who were present. But “approval” here meant that it was agreed to pursue the project, and that is how things still stand: the actual commission has not been given.

Within the same context I have worked on a project called “Vibra Lounge”, which I hope to be able to realize sooner or later. Like the Reichstag proposal, it is based on the transmission of sound by means of physical vibration. The idea is to create a music lounge that is apparently silent. The central area, instead of being a dance floor, will be an “activated floor” on which music and rhythm are physically perceived through the vibrations. As we all know, the younger ones among us probably best, the experience of contemporary dance music is becoming more and more physical. Vibra Lounge might be an extreme experiment, but it would be interesting to see the social interaction within such a setting.

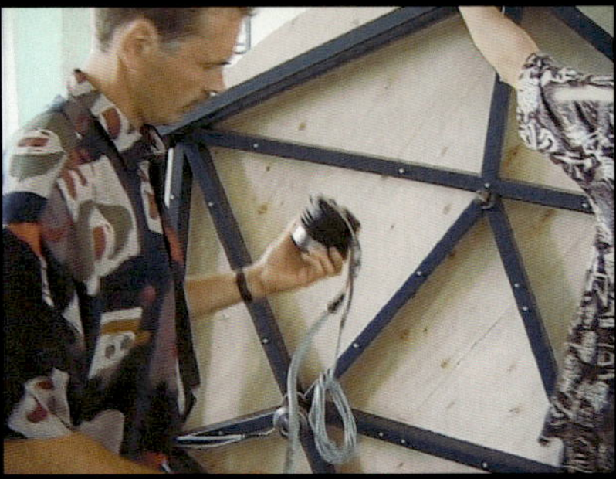

Electro mechanical actuators from a sound canceling system by Tillmann Freudenberg adapted to create controlled vibrations.

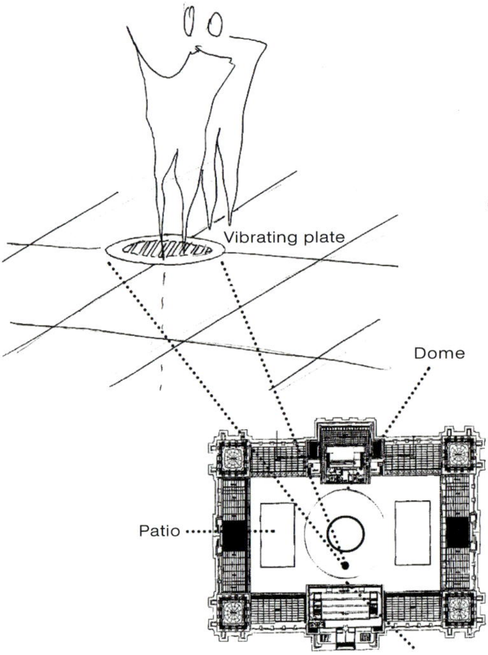

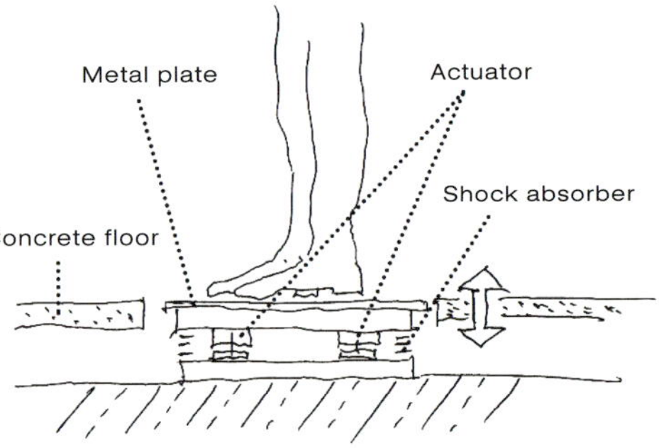

www.christian-moeller.com/insound_out

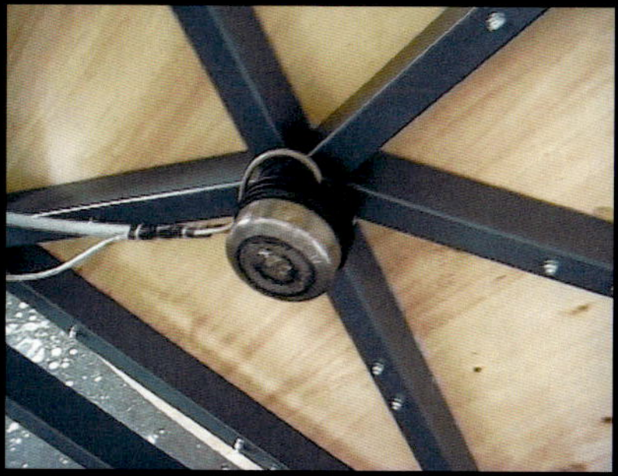

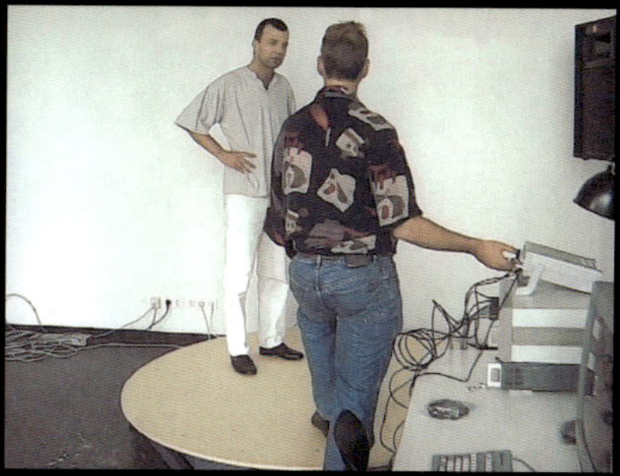

Mounting detail of an actuator underneath the floor structure.

The first test of an activated floor unit, using sinusoidal sounds at various frequencies.

Visualization for Vibra Lounge, an installation for the physical perception of electronic music proposed for the Expo 2000, Hannover.

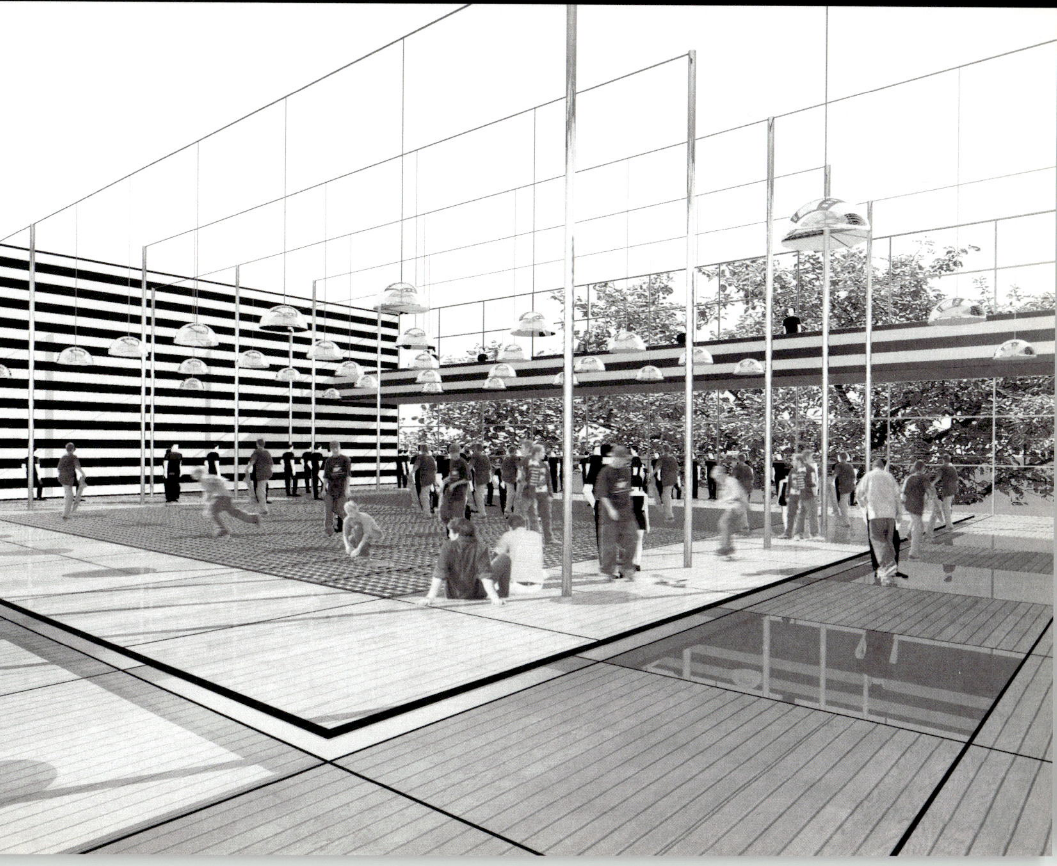

INSOUND OUT

2000
www.christian-moeller.com/insound_out
Digitopolis, Wellcome Wing, Science Museum, London

Curator: Hannah Redler
Sound: Ludger Brümmer
Programming: Thomas Lauerbach
Mechanical enineering and construction: Tillmann Freudenberg, and Hans-Jürgen Diekmann, Freudenberg KG, Weinheim
Exhibition design: Roger Mann

A year later I was invited by Hannah Redler to create a work for Science Museum, London. The brief was to come up with a piece that would allow people to play with electronic sound through an interactive installation. Based on my experience of working with vibration technology, I proposed that it would be more interesting to build a situation where sound would play the people. "Insound Out" uses 2 vibrating panels built into the gallery floor, a camera-motion recognition system, and a pair of parabolic sound projectors which enable sound to be focused at very specific points in the space. Sound elements created by Ludger Brümmer and composed by the movements of the visitor in front of the video camera, and then played back into **his body. Lower musical frequencies are transmitted through the floor while the higher ones are projected directly onto the visitor's head with the aid of the sound projectors.**

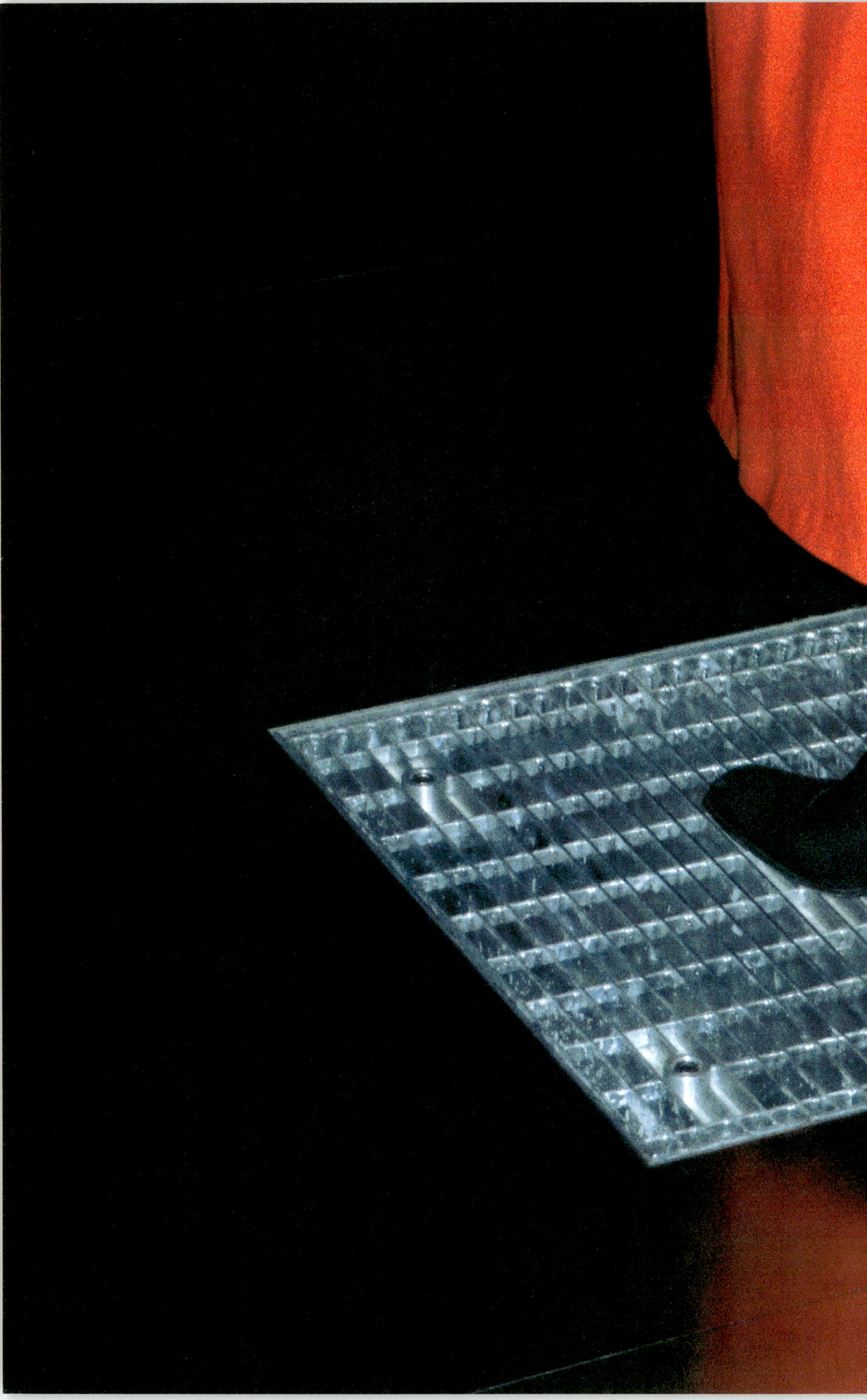

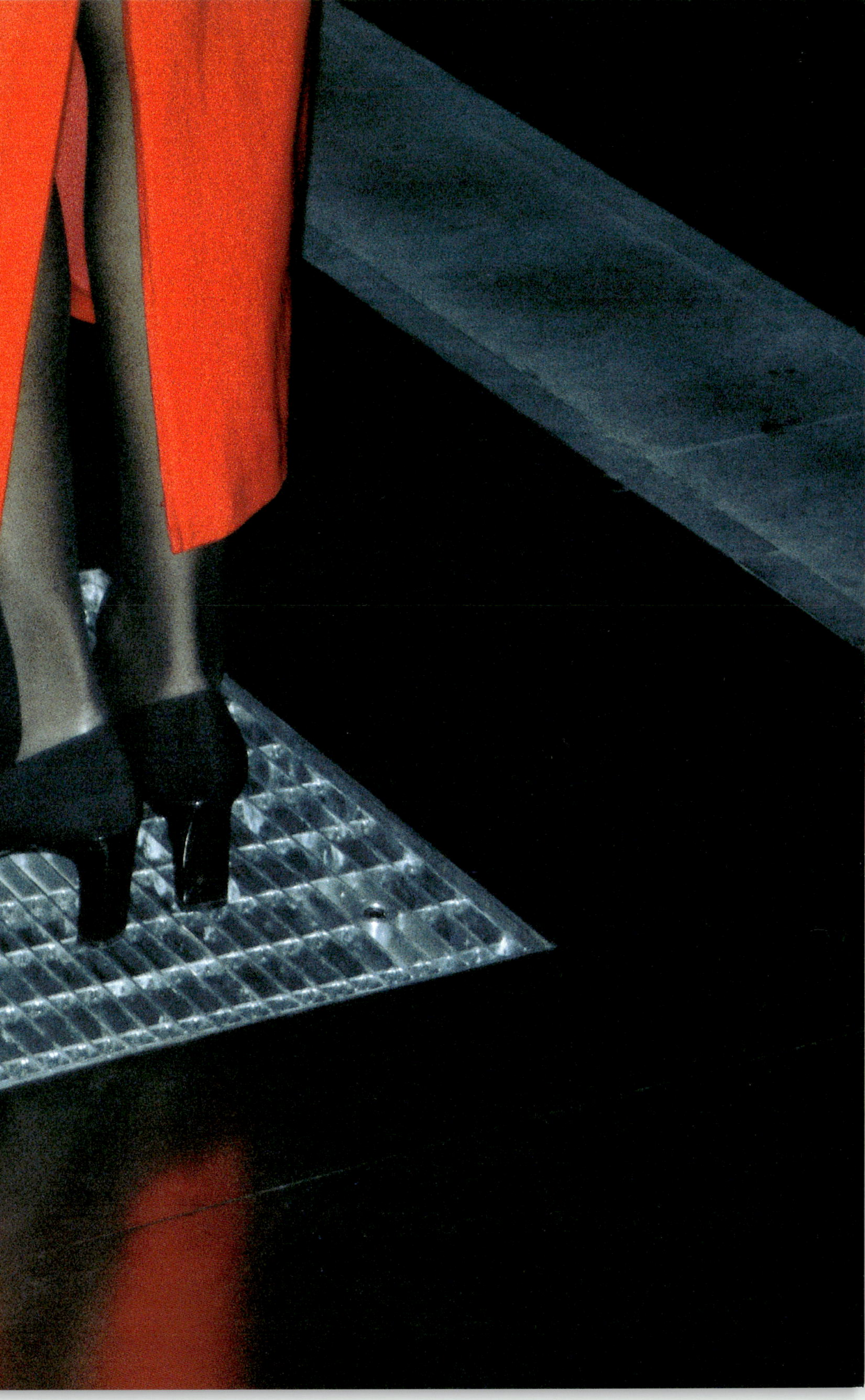

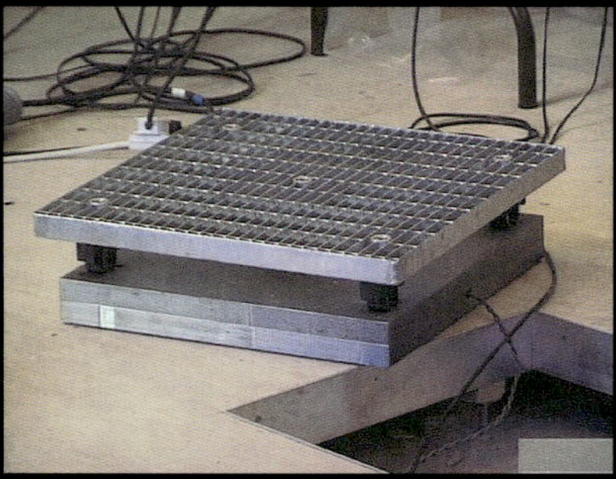

Active floor element that vibrates low musical frequencies.

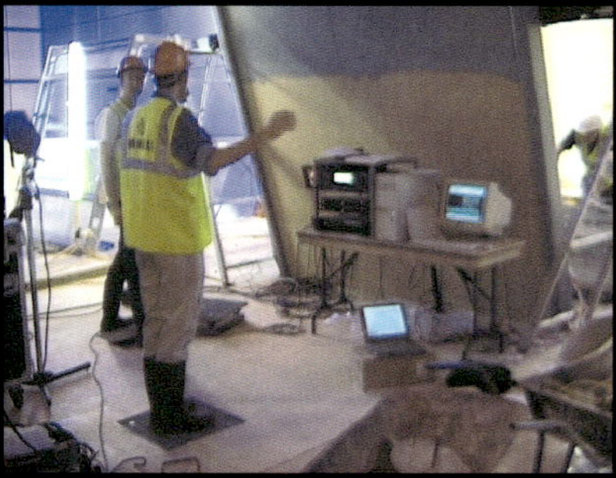

Ludger Brümmer adjusting the video motion-capturing system that triggers tactile feedback.

Visitors create music by their movement in front of a hidden video camera, and experience the sound physically through the active floor element.

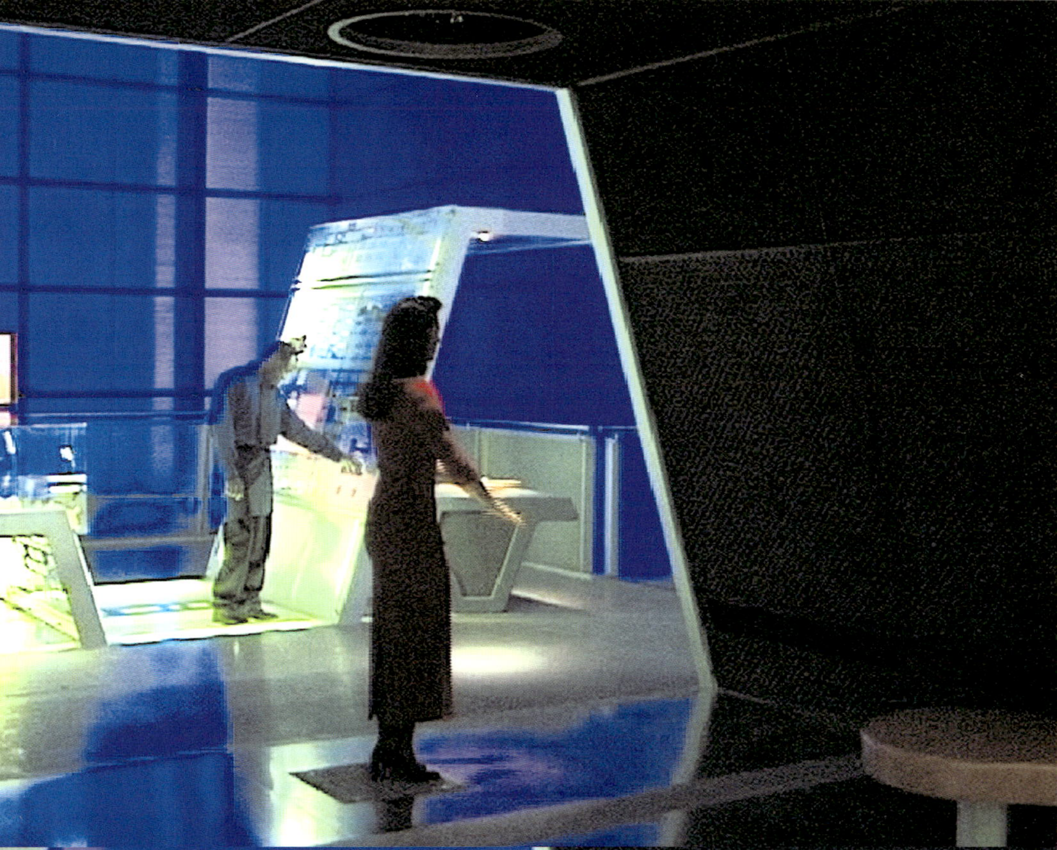

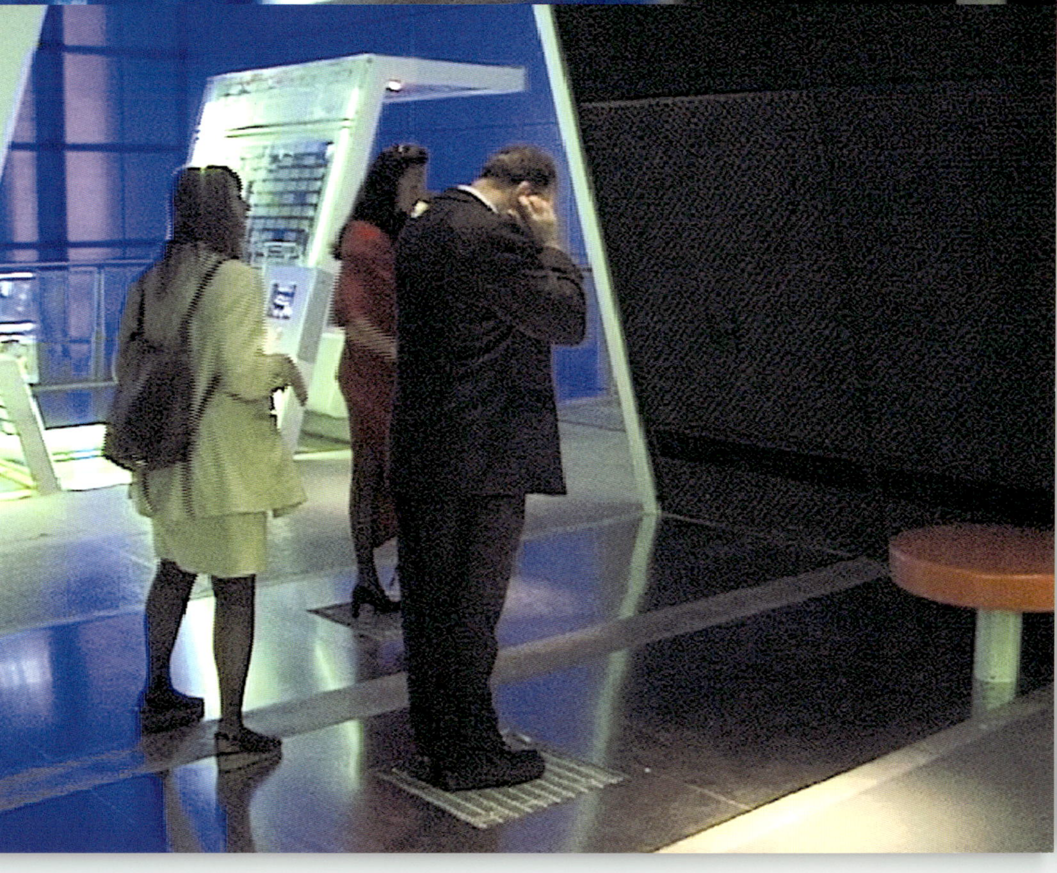

MOZART'S FUGUE FOR PIANO OP. 154

1995
www.christian-moeller.com/mozarts_fugue_for_piano
Figaro-Haus, Vienna
In collaboration with: Elsa Prochazka and Herbert Lachmayer

Pianists: Werner Eder and Ernst Kronsteiner
Programming: Christian Gusenbauer
Hardware: Hermann Gruber
Architecture: Elsa Prochazka
Production: Archimedia, Institute for Arts and Technology,
University for Art and Industrial Design, Linz, Austria

The “Figaro House” in Vienna’s First Quarter, was once the apartment of Wolfgang Amadeus Mozart. Mozart is supposed to have composed more works here than at any of his other Viennese addresses, including the opera “Le Nozze di Figaro.”
Elsa Prochazka, the architect responsible for the design of the exhibition, approached me and asked to see if we could imagine a computer installation which would complement the exhibition. Not a bad task, and I was delighted to have been offered it, but it was clearly a difficult commission begging several questions, not the least of which is “what for?” I was unsure that what I could contribute would be of relevance. Then it occurred to me that a memorial to a musician involves an interesting contradiction, that between the important documents on display, in particular the composer’s handwritten scores, and the visitors’ ability or inability to appreciate them. After all, most people cannot read music and so are at a complete loss when confronted with these scores (except of course that they can appreciate the composer’s writing style or discover a red wine stain on an important piece of paper). My idea was to make the music come alive. I took one of Mozart’s manuscripts for Fugue op. 154 for piano and placed it under a sheet of glass, coated with an invisible layer of metal and linked to an analogue-capacitive electronic sensor system.
By touching on a note on the original score, through the glass, visitors can make it resound electro-acoustically. If they draw their finger along the line of notes, they hear the melody as composed, but at a speed which they dictate, deliberately or casually, forwards or backwards.
The question arose whether it was legitimate to treat the legacy of a great composer, and thus the cultural legacy of the City of Vienna, in such a way.
Sometimes such ethical questions can be difficult to answer and you look for some truth which confirms that what you are doing is right. Help came in the form of the opinion of a wise and worthy advisor who had devoted his life to music. He said: “Let’s consider the problem this way. If Mozart were in a position to look down from heaven, so to speak, and peer into his former apartment, how would he like to see a group of tourists standing around his sheet of music and playing this little score forward and backward, backward and forward, but always at the wrong tempo?” We came to the conclusion that he would appreciate it a lot.
We thus felt justified in continuing the work, but would probably not have done so if it were a Brahms Museum.

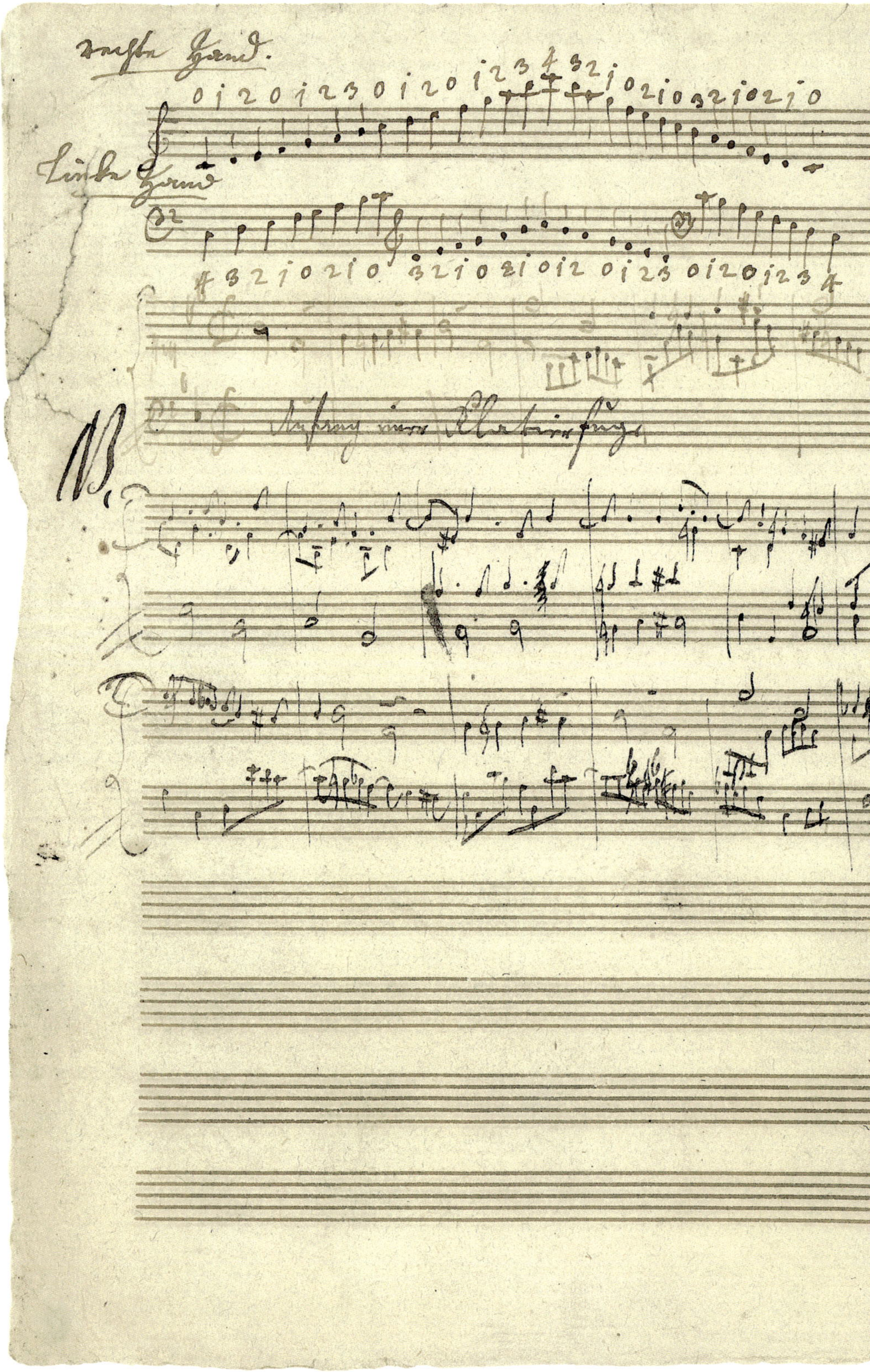

rechte Hand
linke Hand
Anfang einer Clavierfuge

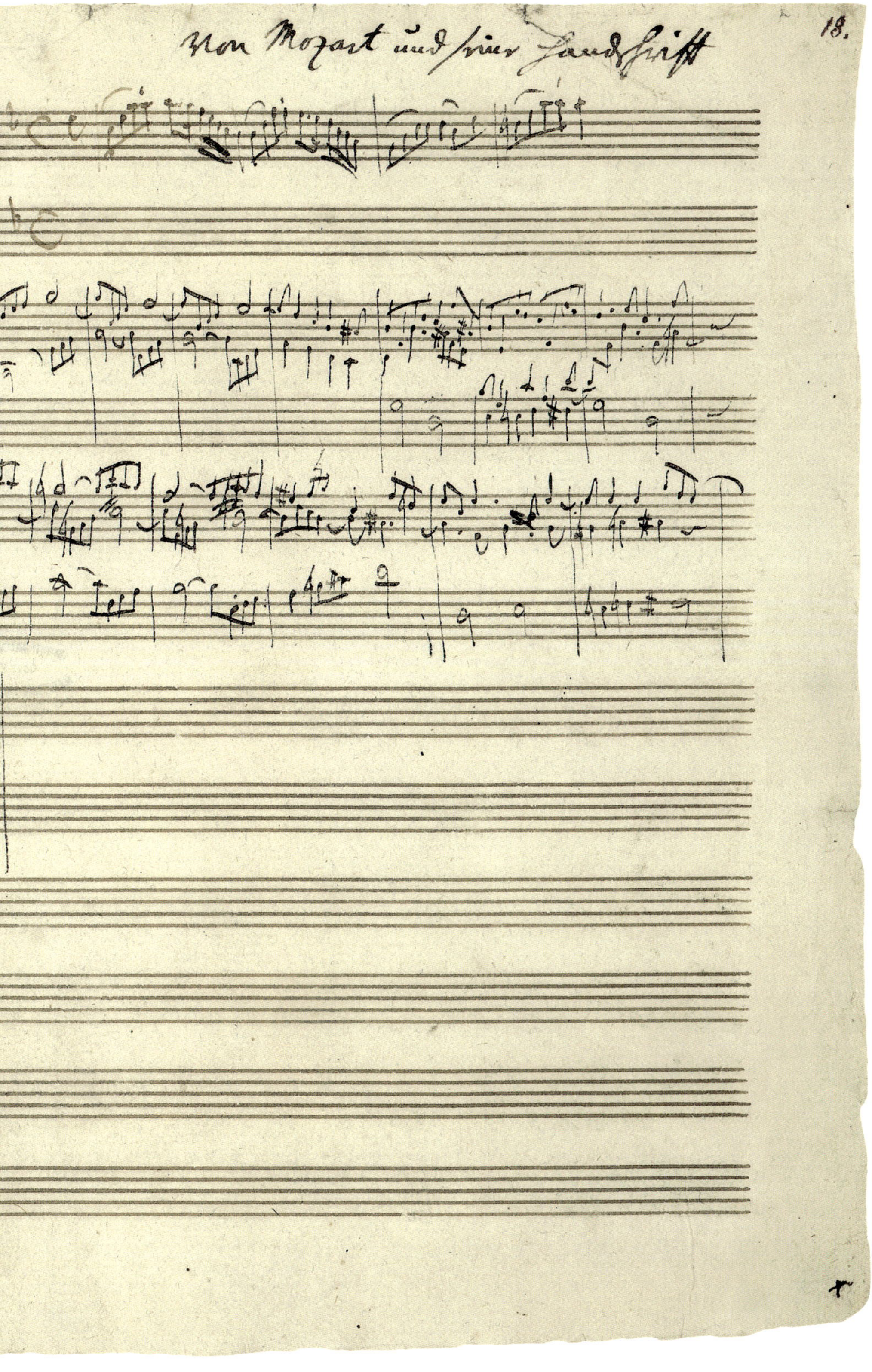
Von Mozart und seiner Handschrift
18.

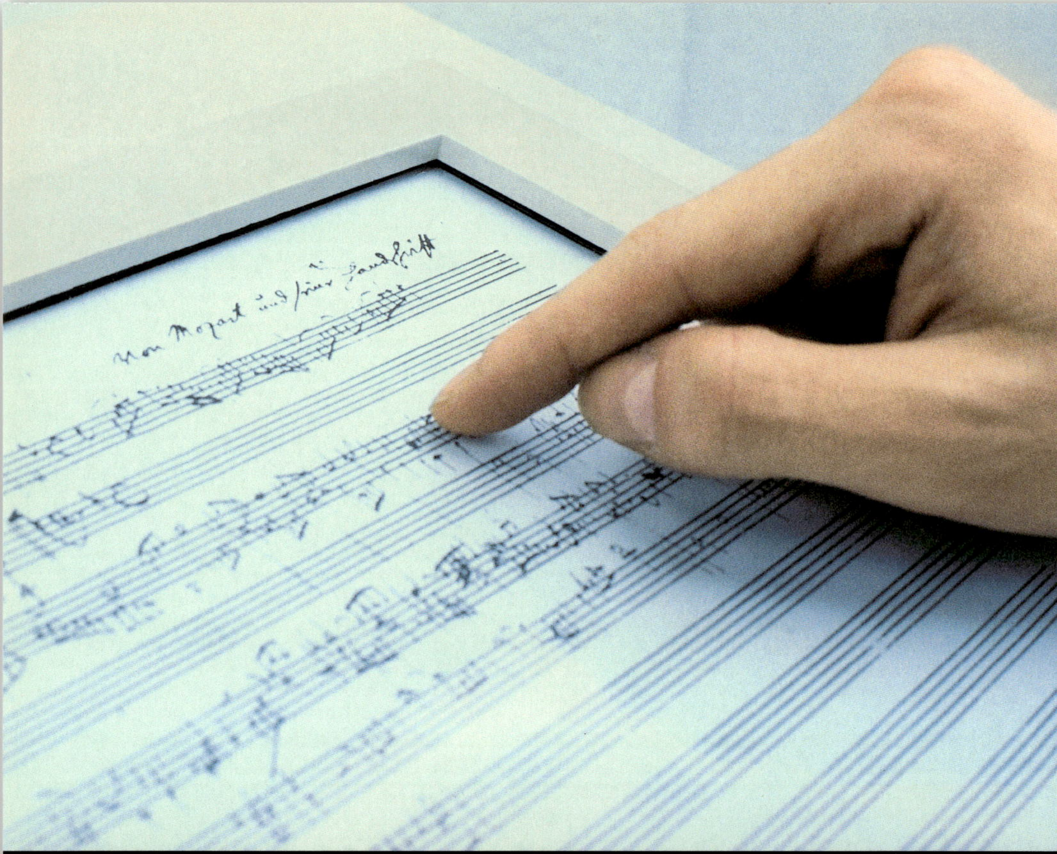

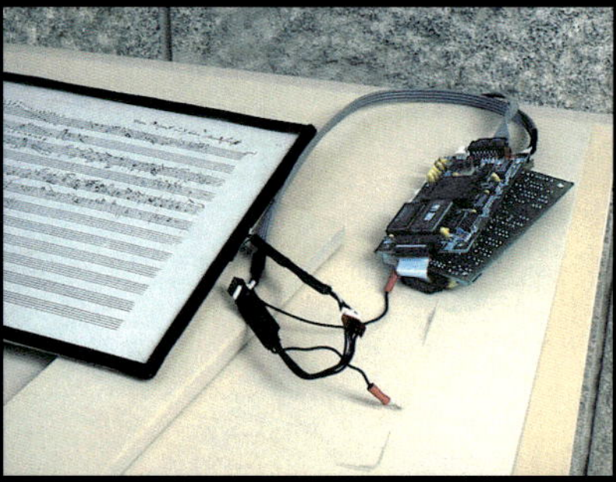

Touch sensitive glass pane with electronic interface overlaying sheet music.

www.christian-moeller.com/mozarts_fugue_for_piano

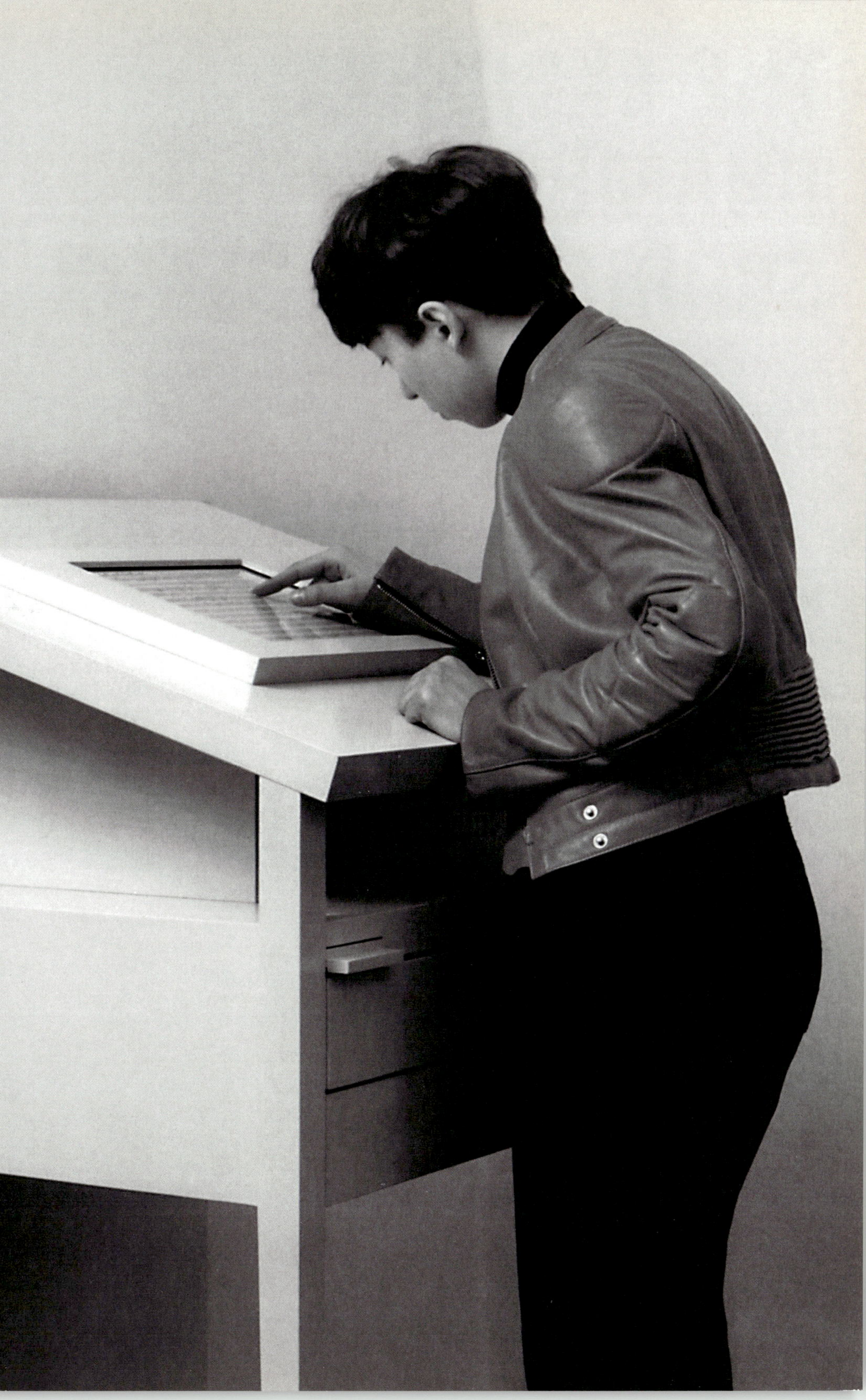

THE EXPANDED CHAMBER: SCORING THE DEMIX

1996
www.christian-moeller.com/expanded_chamber_scoring_the_demix
Botschaft der Musik, Kunsthistorisches Museum Vienna, Palais Harrach, Vienna
In collaboration with: Wilfried Seipel

Music: Mutare Ensemble
Conductor: Gerhard Müller-Hornbach
Recording and sound: Willi Bopp
Video: Anna Saup
Digitalization and synchronization: Hubert Machnik
Programming: Sven Thöne
Hardware: Wolfgang Schemmert
Screen design: Paul Claessen
Exhibition design: Hans Hoffer
Music software: Logic Audio, Emagic

Music selection: Thomas Trabitsch
Die sieben letzten Worte unseres Erlösers am Kreuz (String quartet, Haydn)
Kegelstatt-Trio (for Clarinet, Viola and Piano, Mozart)
Bei Männern welche Liebe fühlen (Variations for Violoncello and Piano, Beethoven)
Chineser-Galopp (Quartet for 3 Violins and Contrabass, Strauss)
Forellen-Quintet (for Piano, Violin, Viola, Violoncello and Contrabass, Schubert)
Verklärte Nacht (String sextet, Schoenberg)

We were approached by the Kunsthistorisches Museum in Vienna and asked to collaborate on the exhibition “The Message of Music”. We were asked to develop an installation concept for a space in which to listen to chamber music. Wilfried Seipel, director of the Kunsthistorisches Museum, knew from experience that a successful space for listening to chamber music requires more than simply selecting important compositions and then placing them at people’s disposal in the form of a series of CD players and headphones. Visitors, especially younger people, are not going to have the stamina to sit down and absorb this music attentively. It is a form of reception which is unlikely to satisfy today’s, let us say, “visually spoiled” audiences.

Only experienced musicians are able to pick out individual instruments from an entire orchestra. As a lay-person it is very difficult to do so for more than a short period of time, because one quickly becomes carried away or distracted by the music as a whole. We made it possible to extricate musicians and their individual instruments from the orchestra to curious effect. We selected compositions to be performed and re-recorded by the Mutare Ensemble conducted by Gerhard Müller-Hornbach. We made a separate sound and video recording of each instrument being played.

Once a piece has been chosen a new interface of slide controls appears on the touch screen monitor allowing the visitor to raise and lower the volume at which each individual musician plays. People could, for example, listen to only the double-bass in the Chinese Gallop by Strauss, an extraordinary musical experience in its own right.

When selected, a piece of music on a touch screen monitor starts playing as the rear wall of the space is completely “electronically wallpapered” with a visual representation of the musical score, synchronized with the music in real time.

Unlike MTV, the point was not to invent visual elements additional to the music, but rather to use the existing signs and images which already appear in the context of making and playing music.

Monitors, with screens facing downwards, show the video portraits of the musicians. These images are reflected in a sheet of glass at a 45 degree angle. The visual impression, something achieved unintentionally by the decision to display the video sequences in black-and-white, is that the musicians standing in the middle of the room fade in and out like ghosts.

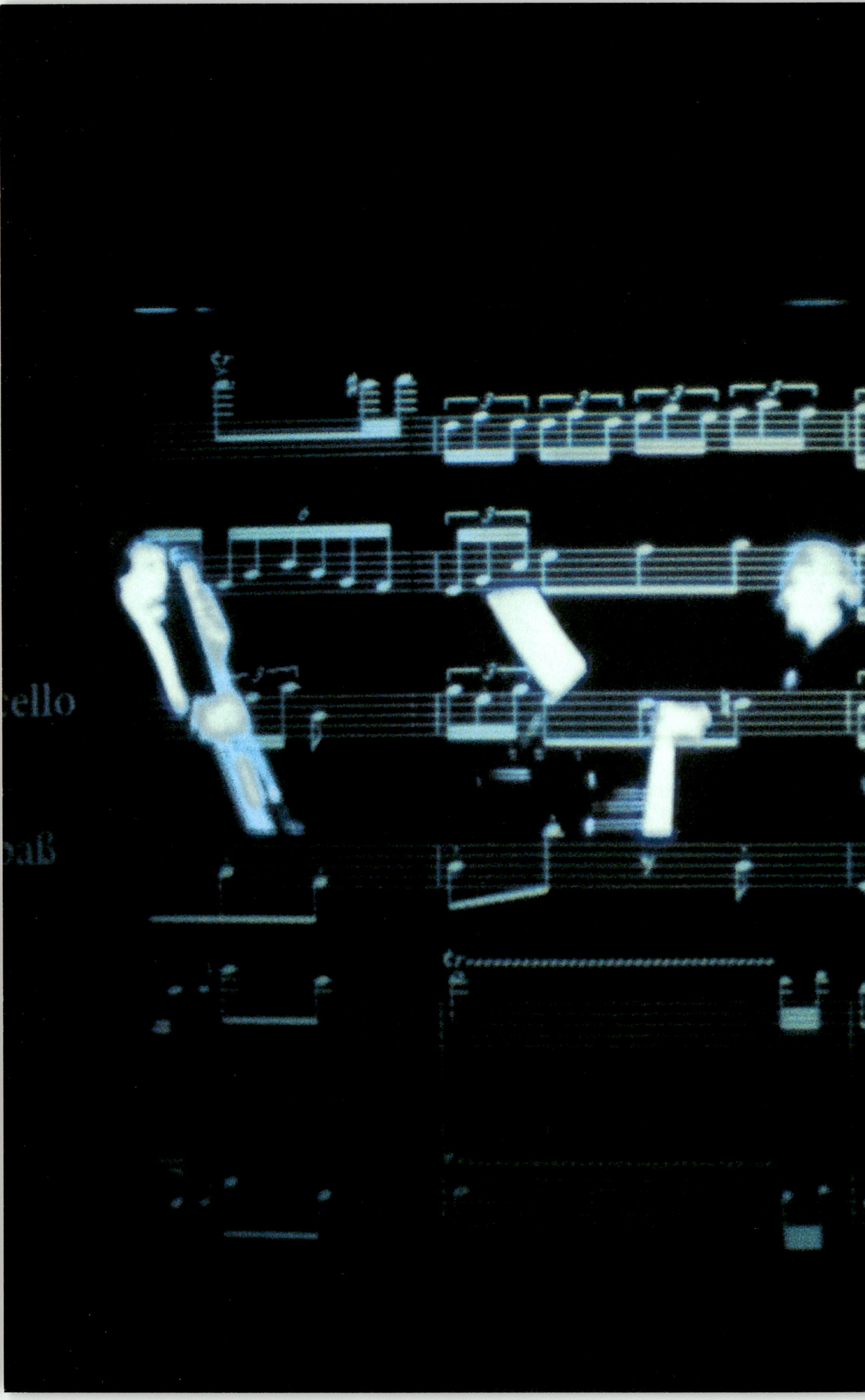

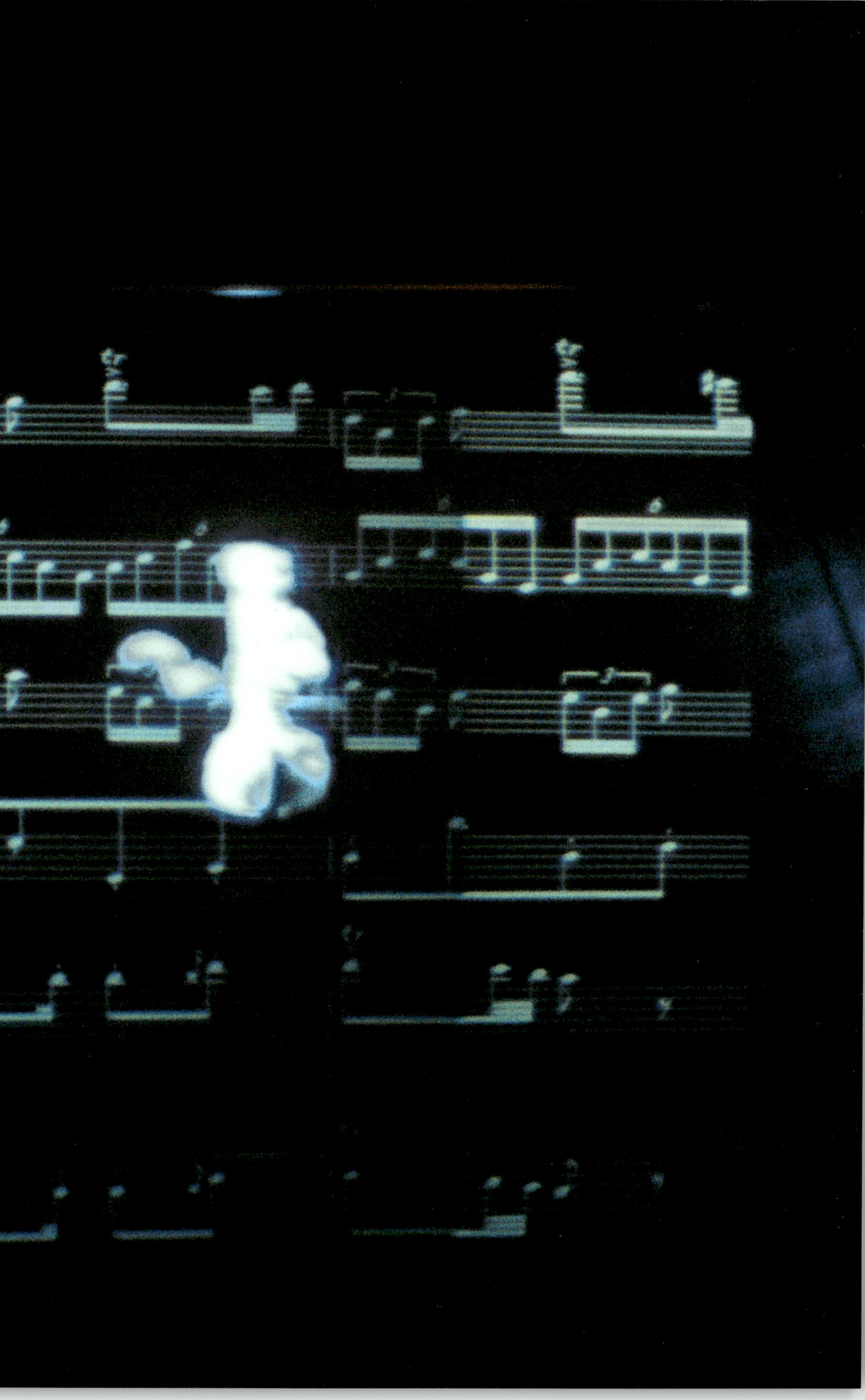

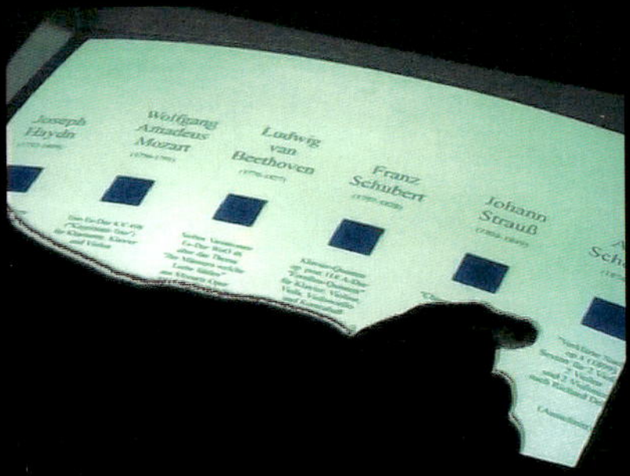

Touch screen selection panel with which to choose a musical piece.

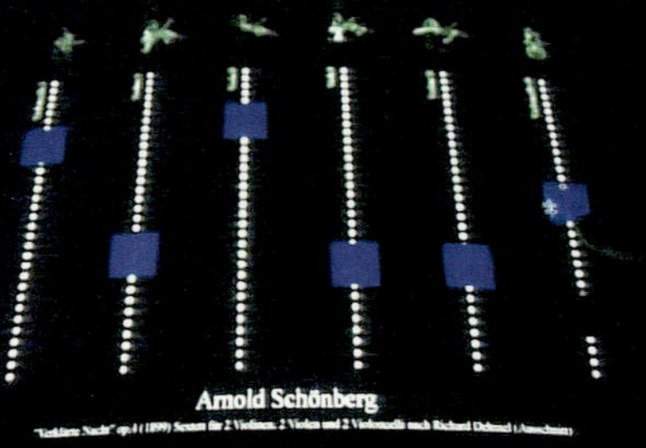

Touch screen mixer panel controlling the volume of an individual instrument.

www.christian-moeller.com/expanded_chamber_scoring_the_demix

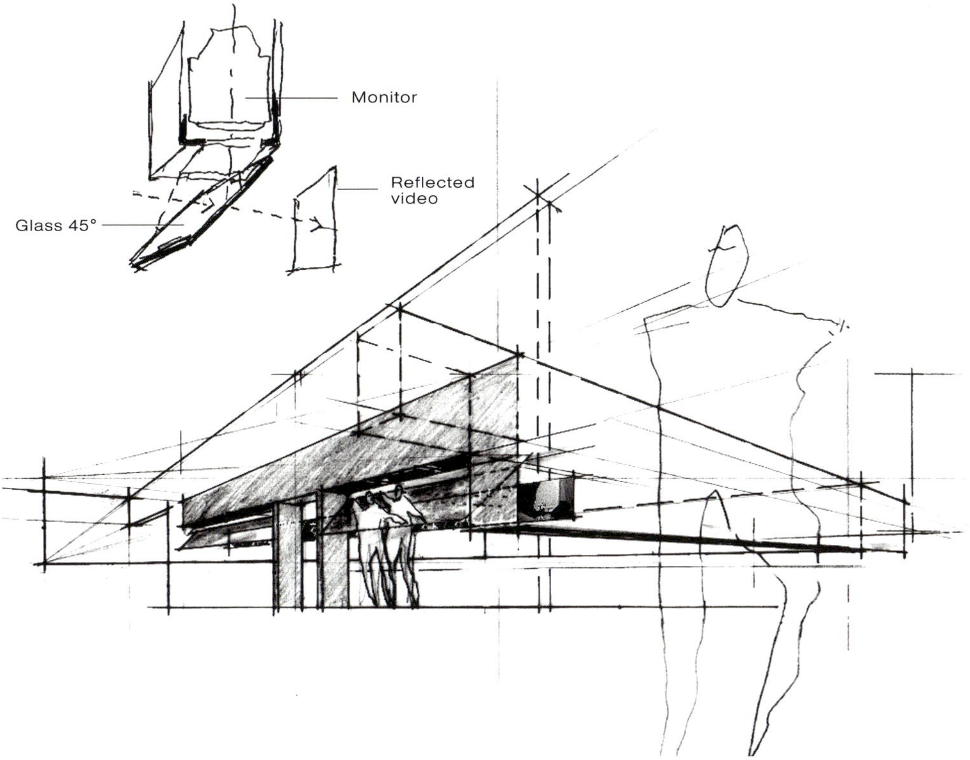
Monitor
Reflected video
Glass 45°

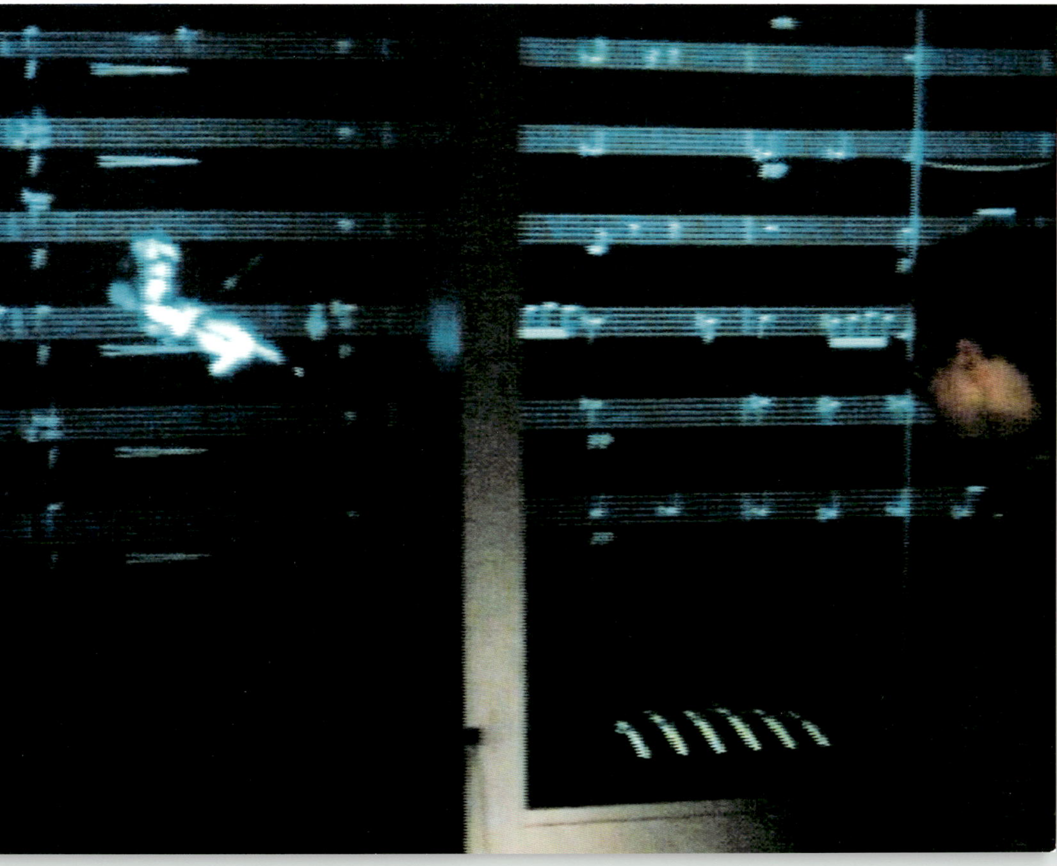

THE EXPANDED CHAMBER: ORCHESTRAL FLY

1996
www.christian-moeller.com/expanded_chamber_orchestral_fly
Botschaft der Musik, Kunsthistorisches Museum Vienna, Palais Harrach, Vienna
In collaboration with: Wilfried Seipel

Music: Mutare Ensemble
Conductor: Gerhard Müller-Hornbach
Recording: Willi Bopp
Programming: Daniel Schmitt
Exhibition design: Hans Hoffer

Music selection: Thomas Trabitsch
Die sieben letzten Worte unseres Erlösers am Kreuz (String quartet, Haydn)
Kegelstatt-Trio (for Clarinet, Viola and Piano, Mozart)
Bei Männern welche Liebe fühlen (Variations for Violoncello and Piano, Beethoven)
Chineser-Galopp (Quartet for 3 Violins and Contrabass, Strauss)
Forellen-Quintet (for Piano, Violin, Viola, Violoncello and Contrabass, Schubert)
Verklärte Nacht (Stringsextet, Schoenberg)

I get inspired in different ways. Often the ideas come from a particular exhibition context. Sometimes, as in the case of Orchestral Fly, inspiration comes from a fascination with a particular technology. In such a case, instead of developing a concept through aesthetics or content, I wait for just the right opportunity to employ the technology in the new, unexpected way.

The technical development of this piece, actually based on a very cleverly simulated 3D audio environment, has its roots in the defense industry. Engineers realized at one point that if combat machines are fully automated, certain perceptional abilities of the soldiers are augmented so as to make them more efficient. For example, when a missile is approaching the pilot, the virtual sound of its engine is simulated three-dimensionally in his cockpit, making it easier for the pilot to orient himself in space. By then this technology was available for civil applications at an affordable price. We used this acoustic simulation technology for this part of the chamber music installation.

The idea was to create an environment for music with which we are familiar, now heard from a perspective we can never have, namely, that of a fly. A real time computer graphics system draws a simulated space in which the instruments/musicians are represented as three-dimensional word sculptures. In this virtual concert hall the participant can move around in real time at the crazy speed of the fly and can hear music which is not altered, but imbued with a spectacular, varying dynamism.

On the monitor you see the word "violin" in the room. The music emanates so to speak from this word/instrument. The word "violin" represents the exact location of this musical sound in the virtual room, heard with the help of headphones. An appliance the size of a matchbox which on the following page my colleague, Sven Thöne, is holding in his hand, allows the listener to fly freely around the room. When the spectator approaches a virtual instrument in the spatial simulation, he hears its simulated presence clearly filtered from out of the overall ensemble. The sound can be louder or softer depending upon his distance from the virtual instrument.

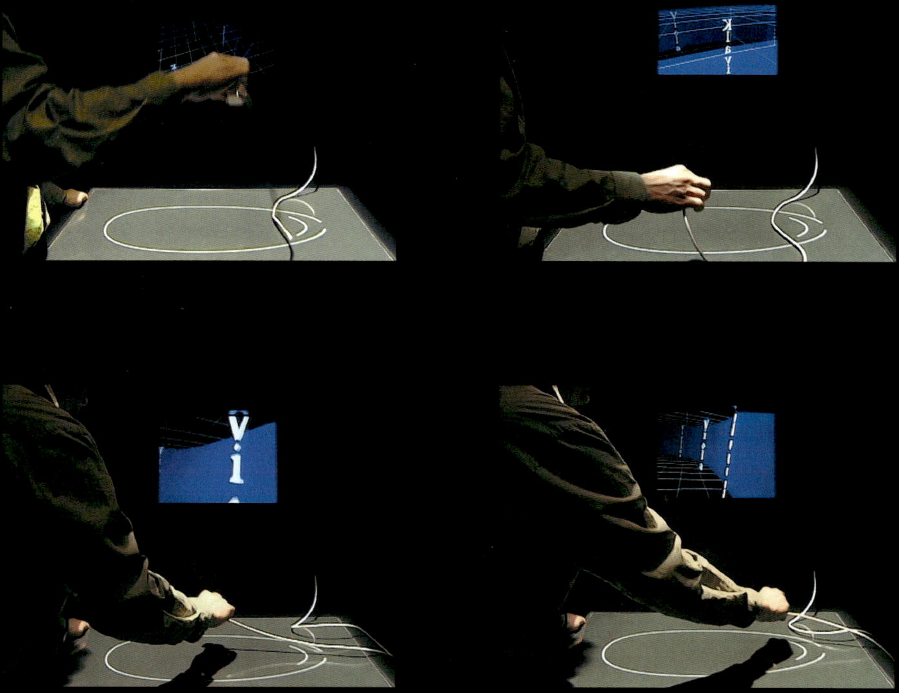

3D-Navigation around musical instruments represented by their names, using a Polhemus sensor.

www.christian-moeller.com/expanded_chamber_orchestral_fly

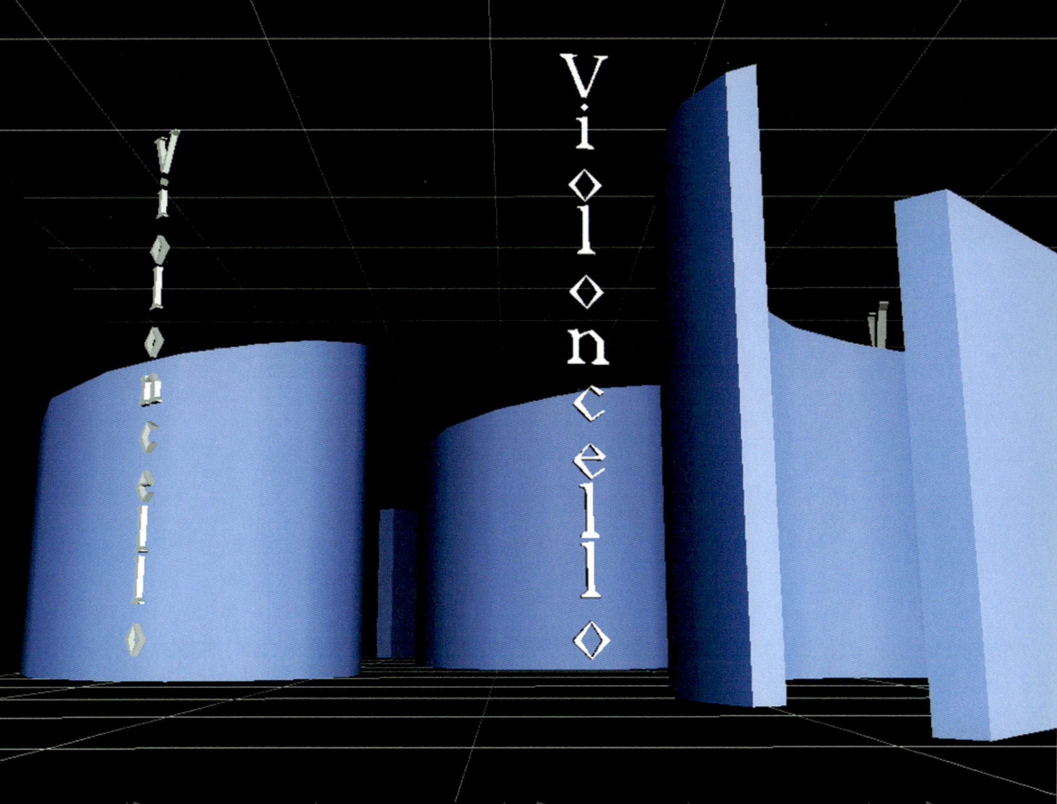
Violoncello
Violoncello

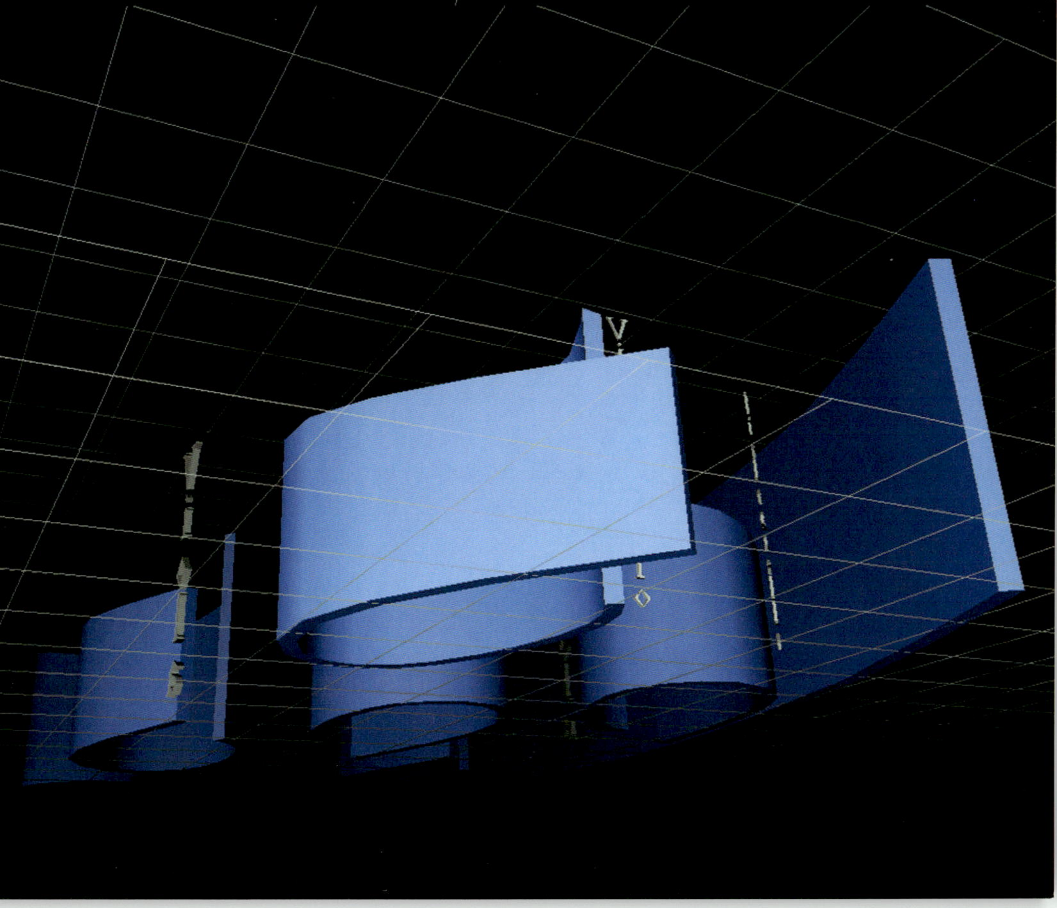

AUDIO PENDULUMS

1994
www.christian-moeller.com/audio_pendulums
ISEA 94, Helsinki and Galerie Aedes, Berlin

Curator: Susanna Koskinen and Minna Tarkka
Sounds: Peter Namlook
Programming: Daniel Schmitt

The installation was for the Lasipalatsi in Helsinki, a beautiful building from the 1930s, which since then had aged a lot and was in the course of being renovated and transformed into a media center.
Our proposal was to affix seven steel rods like pendulums along the main façade.These pendulums move in the wind, and a video camera on the roof follows their movements and transmits these to a computer system which in turn measures them and transposes them into musical sounds along the pentatonic scale.
In a straight vertical position, the pendulums are silent. The further they swing back and forth in the wind, the louder the peak in the modulating sounds generated by their continuous movement. The result, a mix of the tones generated by the pendulums and the noise of the traffic on the street, is a droning, ambient composition. When the sun sets in the evening, blinding the camera, the pendulums fall silent until dawn.
We built a large scale, fully functional model but the project itself was not realized.

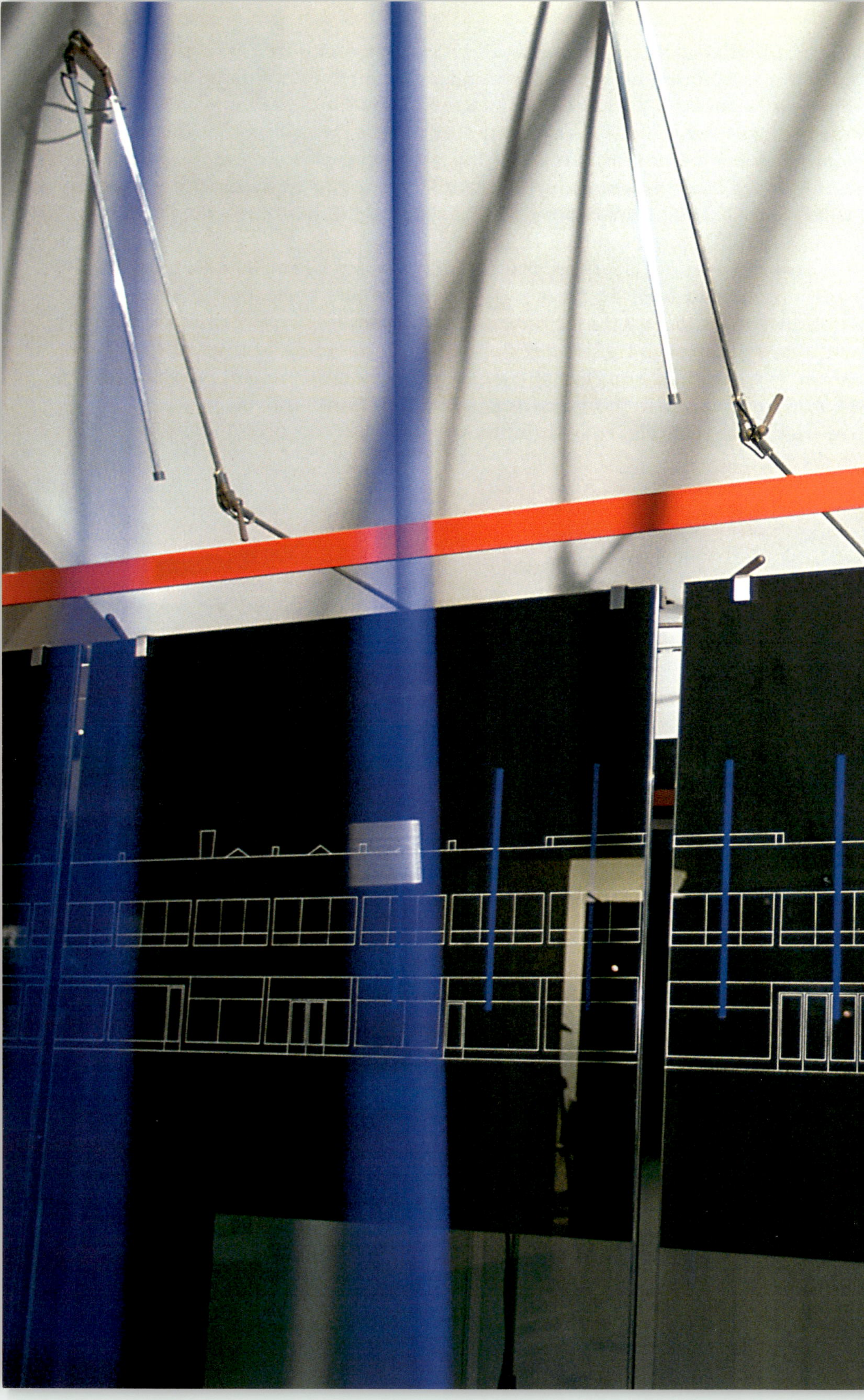

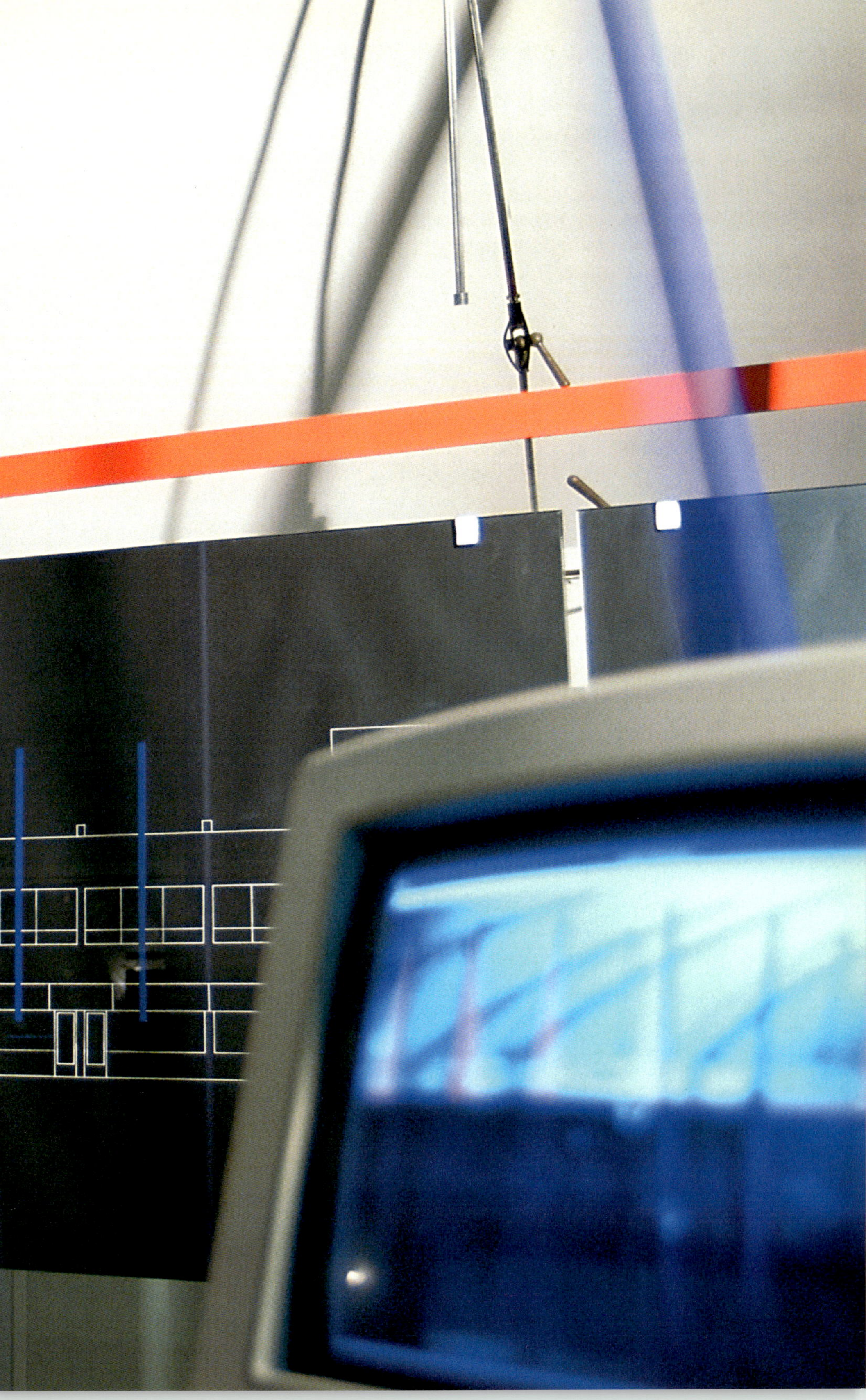

KALEIDOPHONE

1999
www.christian-moeller.com/cellphone_as_musical_interface
Installation proposal, ZKM (Center for Art and Media), Karlsruhe, Germany

Sound: Ludger Brümmer
Light design: Nathan Thompson
Programming: Sven Thöne
Hardware: Wolfgang Schemmert
Research and Design: Petra Trefzger
Supported by: Atelier Markgraph

Public space is valuable. It's harder to keep it clear than to completely cover it with street furnitures, art sculptures, flower beds and so forth. My approach for making an art intervention in the public realm develops more and more toward trying to do so in the most immaterial way possible. Compared to all these silly interactive kiosks I found the mobile phone to be an ideal interface. It's already there, people carry it in their pockets and they know how to use it. It enables interaction between citizens and the urban backdrop, a theme I began considering back in 1998. Funnily enough, athough I have been relatively successful in getting most projects realized, I seem to run up against brick walls everywhere I go with my mobile telephone theme. It's just the way it goes.

After a not altogether successful collaboration with Deutsche Telekom during Expo 2000 in Hanover, together with Joachim Sauter and Atelier Markgraph, I received a commission from Peter Weibel of the ZKM in Karlsruhe. The project was to take the form of a very large cube made up of a scaffold measuring 40x40x40 meters temporarily surrounding the dimensions of an existing building. Inside this structure were gauze-like textile screens, behind which loudspeaker and lighting systems were hidden. Telephone numbers were cut out from the base of the construct and back-lit. When a passer-by dialed one of the telephone numbers from his mobile phone he would be connected to the installation's control system and could use the keys of his phone to vary the lighting of the installation and evoke sounds. This concept came very close to realization. All the technology for the sound and interface system was fully developed but it died an unfortuate death when, due to a "global expenditure reduction" by the City of Karlsruhe, the funds made available to the ZKM were unexpectedly recalled.

The next opportunity was in collaboration with the Catholic Church. With the Church's public relations department I developed the idea of enabling the citizens of Frankfurt to ring the cathedral bells using their mobile phones. It was to be realized at the Saint Bartholomew Cathedral, the Imperial Cathedral of the City of Frankfurt. Frankfurt's Imperial Cathedral has chimes consisting of nine bells: 1. Gloriosa, 2. Barolus, 3. Bartholomäus, 4. Salve, 5. Mette, 6. Kleine Uhr, 7. Johannes, 8. Zei, 9. Kleinste.

At given times on Easter Sunday citizens would have been able to dial the cathedral to play the chimes using the nine numbers on the keypad of their phone. Everyone involved was very keen. I thought it would be really fantastic to get the Pope to press the keys of his telephone on his desk in Rome to ring the bells for the people of Frankfurt as an Easter Greeting. After a brief period of general enthusiam, the project was dropped. I don't know exactly why but all of a sudden communications went silent.

My fourth attempt to realize a cell phone project came at Mediatheque in Sendai, designed by architect Toyo Ito and probably the most interesting building, architecturally speaking, of the year 2000.

In traditional building design, floor slabs are held up by load bearing columns. Ito's innovation is to replace the conventional idea of the column as a solid element, and instead irregular latticed tubular steel structures, similar to a "Mikado" game, form the building's supports. They stand as expressive figures within the otherwise very basic geometry of this stunningly transparent building. My light designer, Nathan Thompson, and I were invited by the City of Sendai to develop a concept for the official opening of the Mediatheque. I saw this as an oportunity to make use of the mobile telephone interface technology we had previously developed. The idea consisted of treating the 13 support strctures in the building as urban musical instruments, which passers-by could conduct with their cell phones forming an orchestra of electronic sounds. A nice idea. But after a long silence from the city administration of Sendai, this project was also dropped. We received our fee, had a good time, and that was that.

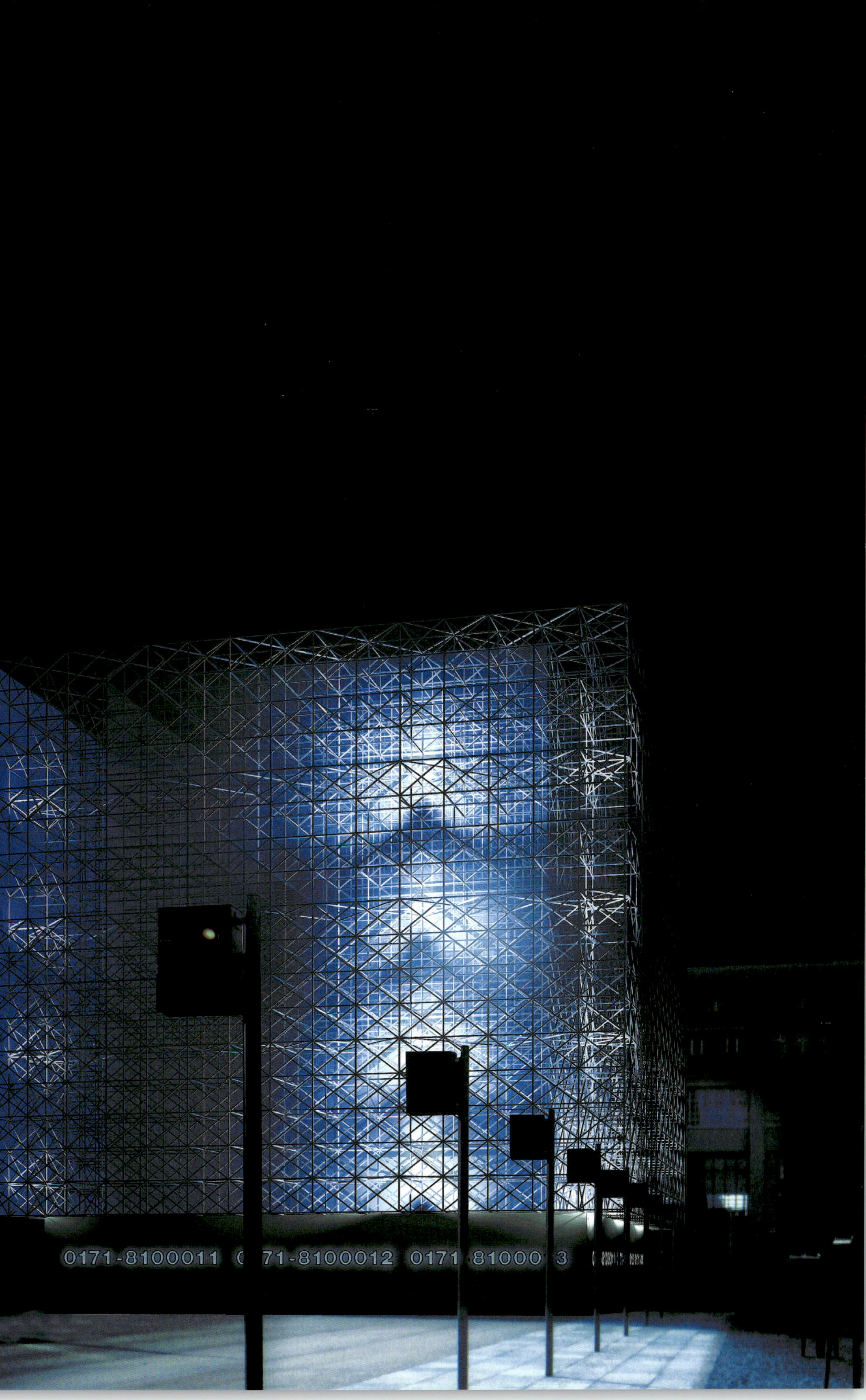
0171-8100011

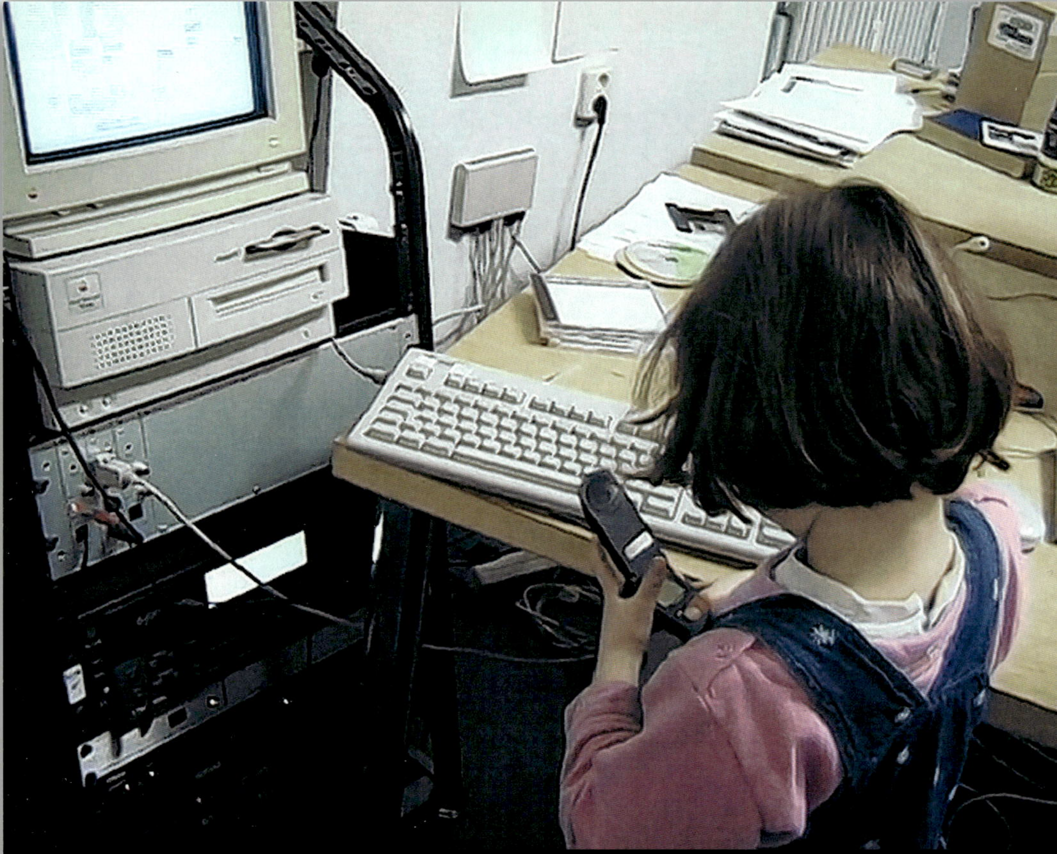

Maria Moeller turns a cell-phone keypad into an electronic music interface by dialing into the system.

Sketches from an installation proposal for the Mediatheque in Sendai, Japan that would turn the building's support columns into urban-scale musical instruments.

www.christian-moeller.com/cellphone_as_musical_interface

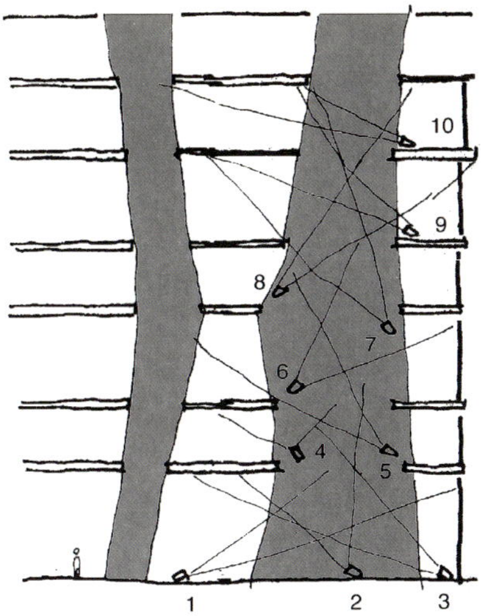
10
9
8
7
6
4
5
1
2
3

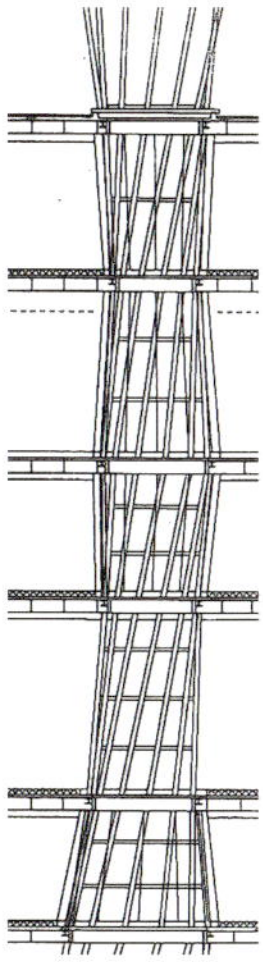

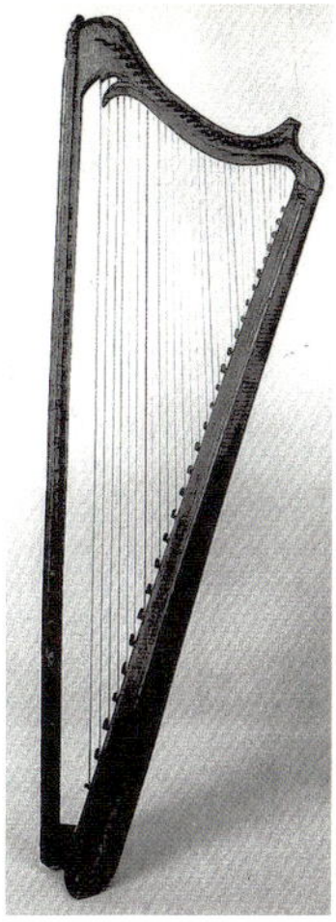

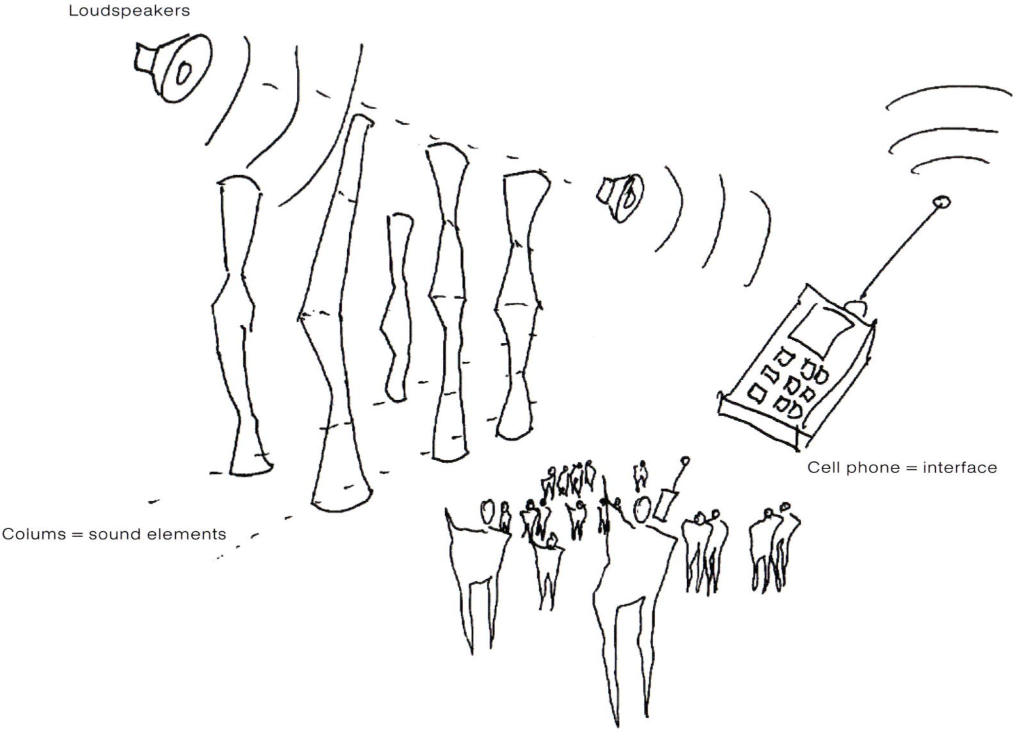
Loudspeakers
Cell phone = interface
Colums = sound elements

ELECTRO CLIPS

1994
www.christian-moeller.com/electro_clips
TAT, Theater am Turm, Frankfurt/Main and Ars Electronica 94, Linz, Austria

Artistic Director (TAT): Tom Stromberg
Dance and Choreography: Stephen Galloway
Music: Peter Namlook
Light: Louis Philippe Demers
Programming: Louis Philippe Demers and Sven Thöne

Electro Clips is a project I realized in 1994, in collaboration with the Theater am Turm in Frankfurt, and ARS Electronica in Linz. It was an experimental dance piece with sound elements by electronic music composer Pete Namlook. It was based on a really simple idea, but was technologically quite ambitious. At the time, Frankfurt's Theater am Turm was the top independent theater in Germany. Directed by Tom Stromberg, it became the hub of an international theater avant-garde. Personalities such as Rainer Werner Fassbinder made history at that theater, and in the early to mid-1990s, the Wooster Group, Jan Fabre, James Turrell, Saburo Teshigawara and Marina Abramovich were regulars. In a short period of time, this theater with an outstanding international reputation was closed, reopened, relocated, and unfortunately artistically neutralized under a conservative, not-so-intelligent mayor. It is a sad chapter in the city's recent history.
In 1994, when things were still going strong there, I started work on Electro Clips. The idea was to have the dancer produce all the sounds, his movement creating the entire musical event. The dancer would become the conductor of a virtual orchestra whose instruments he activated by his movements in and through light projections. Tom Stromberg proposed Stephen Galloway, at the time the lead dancer in William Forsythe's ballet company.
An interactive performance by itself is not neccessarily more interesting to watch than a conventional dance performance. Technology, by itself or how it's made, is not interesting at all for an audience, and so the demands on the performer are considerable. He needs to be able to respond to a set of possiblities rather than a composed score with a fixed choreography.
Together with Lighting Director, Louis Philippe Demers, we designed the interactivity by measuring the changes of light and shade on the floor of the stage whenever Stephen Galloway moved in the spotlights. Phototransistors, small thumb-nail sized light sensors, were distributed around the stage floor. In order to create a third dimension for the "interface", at the back of the stage where a row of upright metal rods with more light sensors at the top. The dancer is then literally inside a musical instrument, moving in a kind of ambient piano, as the beams of the stage spotlights become "strings" which produce sounds when touched.
We did not expect repeat performances but as we staged them, tickets always completely sold out on the first day of sales. A small, poorly financed experiment turned into a surprisingly big success. This installation was shown repeatedly on MTV, and the CD, "Music for Ballet," sold out in record time. This project, which had a huge audience, was the source of an important insight for me: the success of a project does not always depend on the artist's talent or even the project's quality. What can also be very important is to do a project at just the right time in the right place.

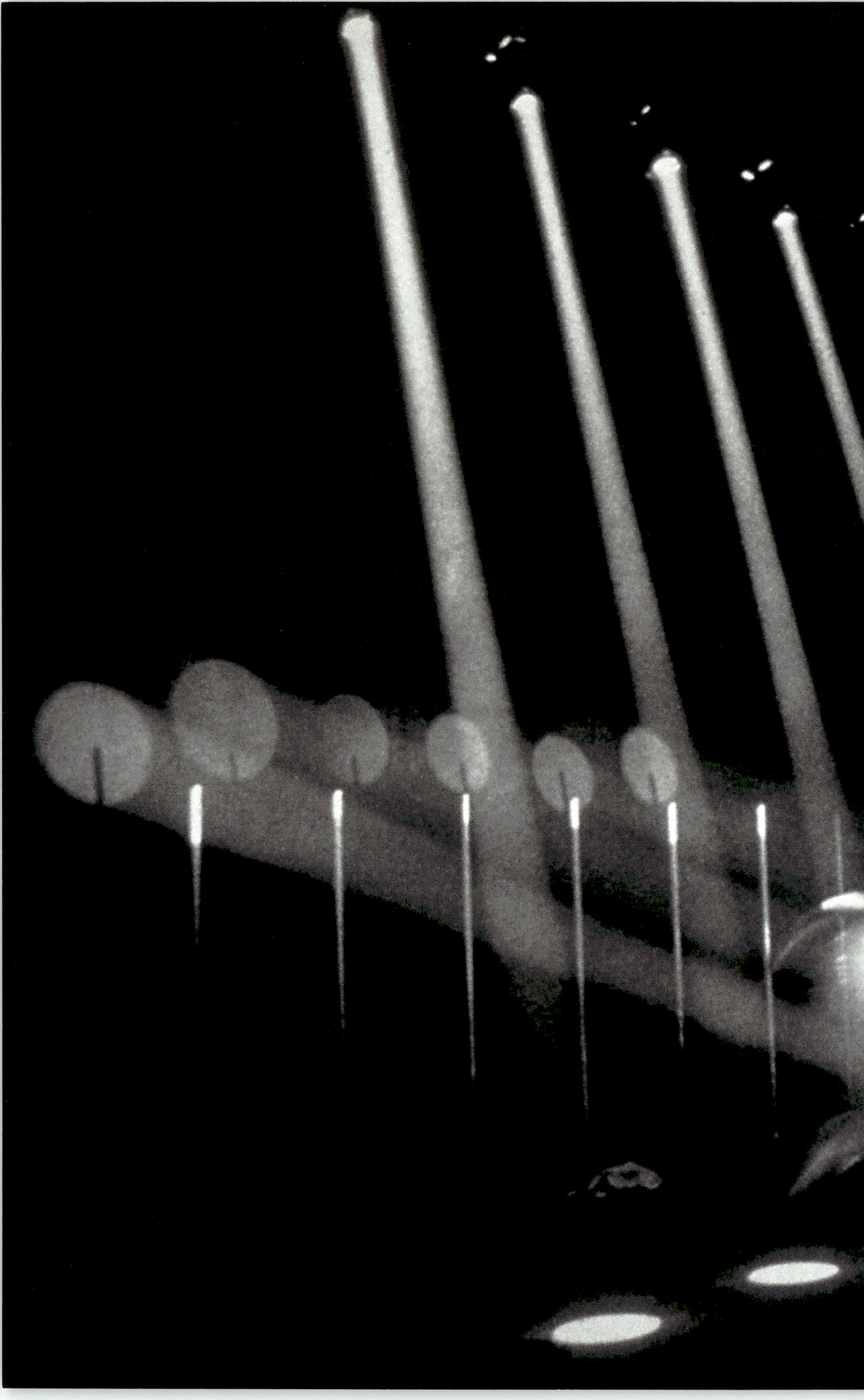

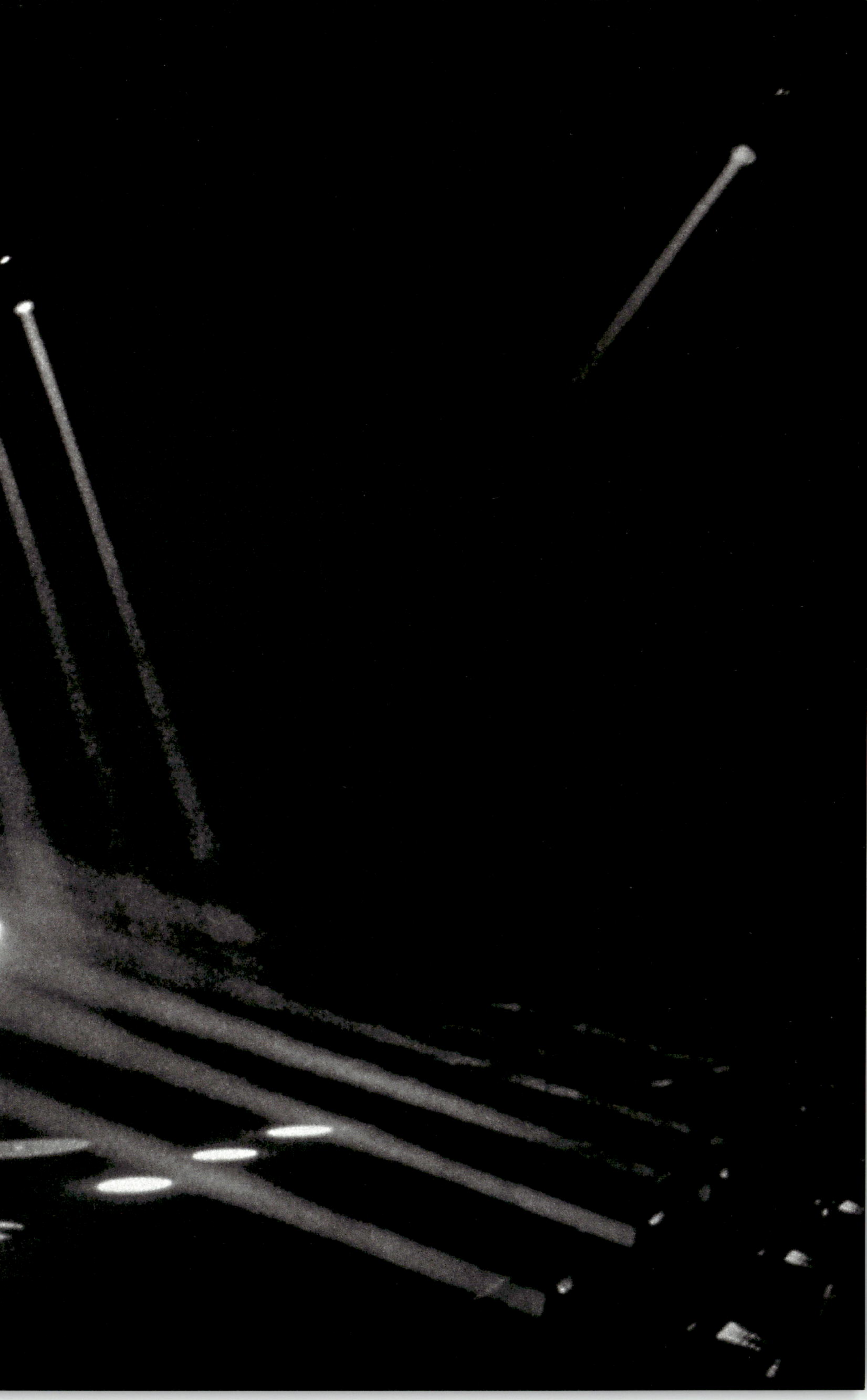

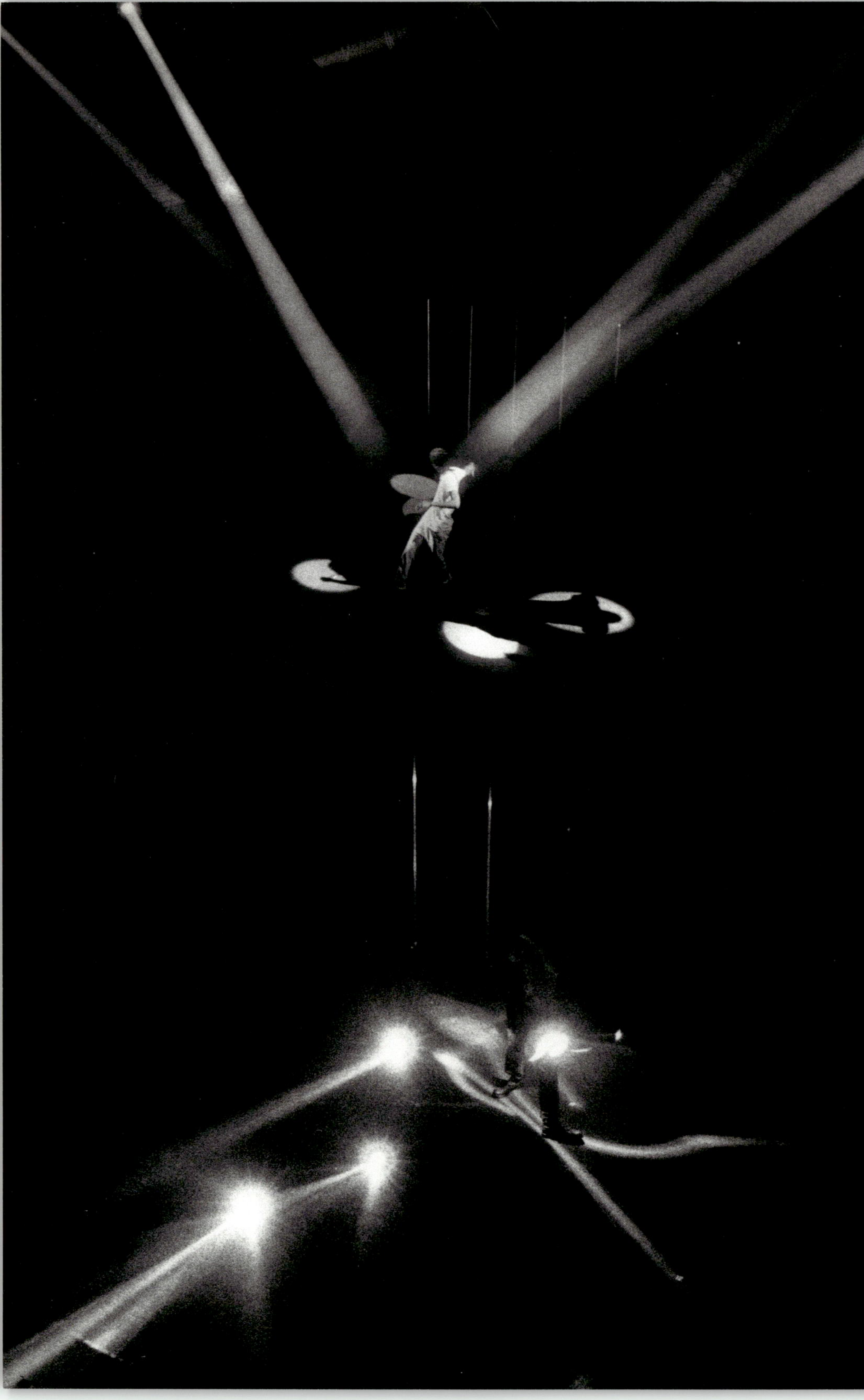

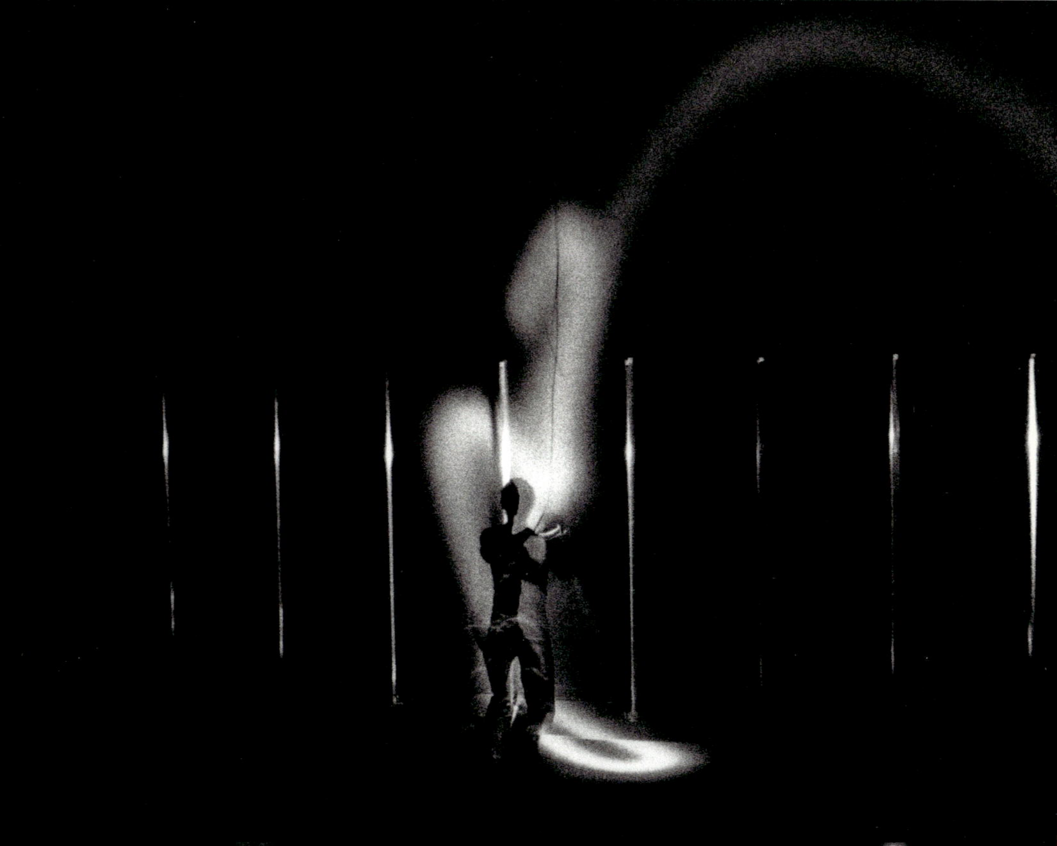

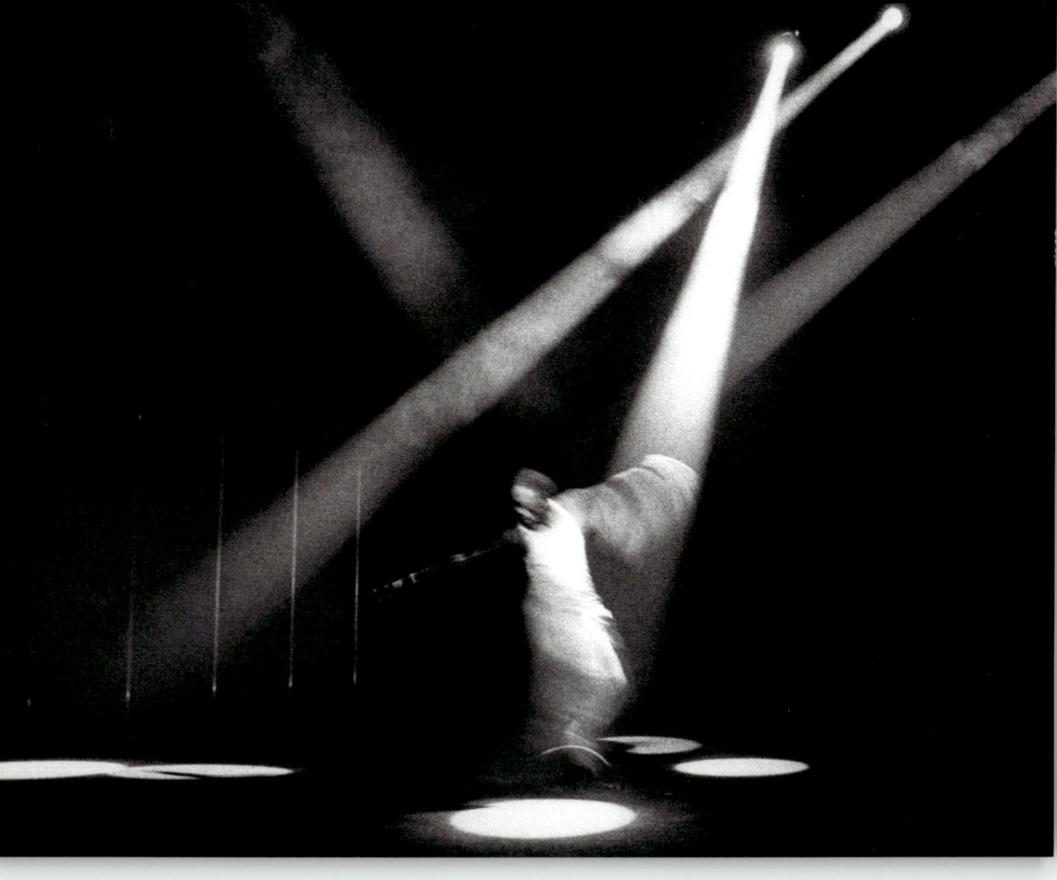

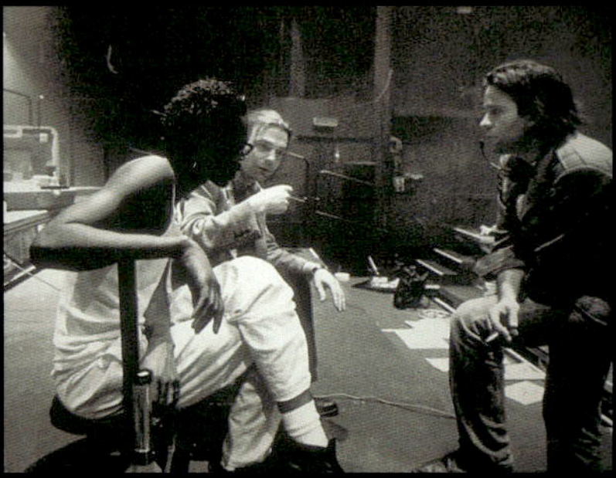

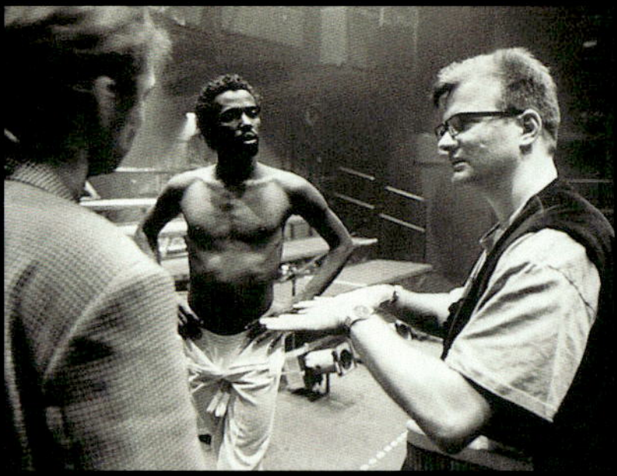

From left to right: Galloway, Moeller, and Demers

From left to right: Moeller, Galloway, and Namlook

Stephen Galloway conducts the electronic orchestra by his movement through the lights.

www.christian-moeller.com/electro_clips

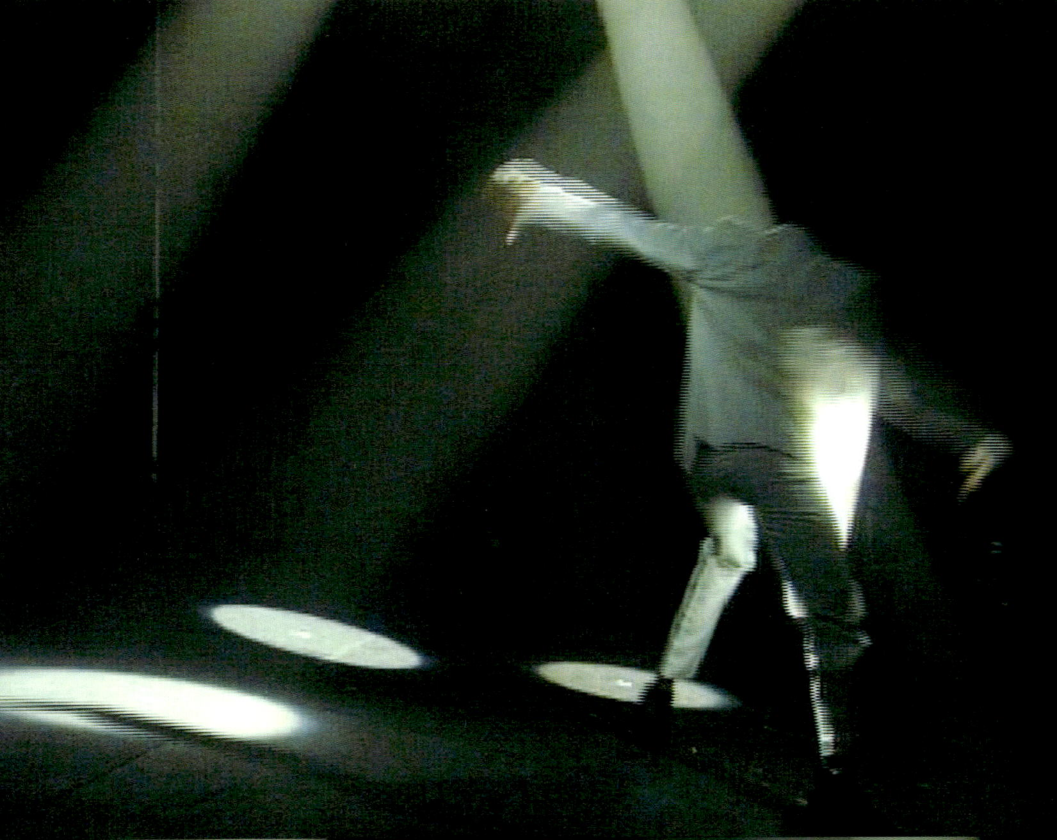

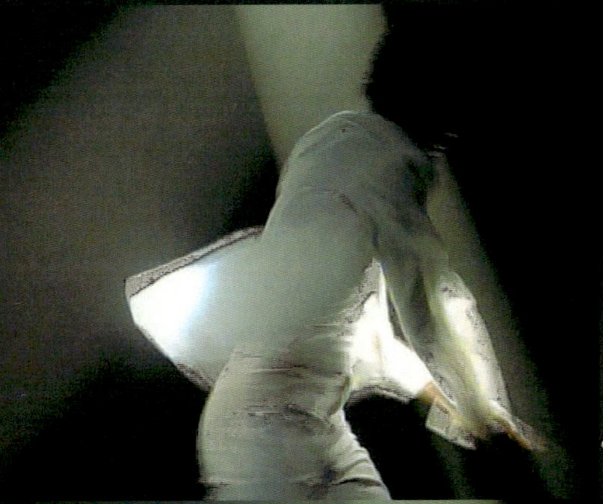

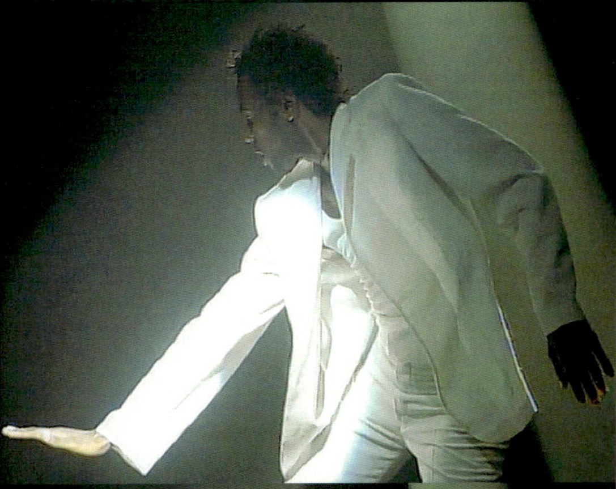

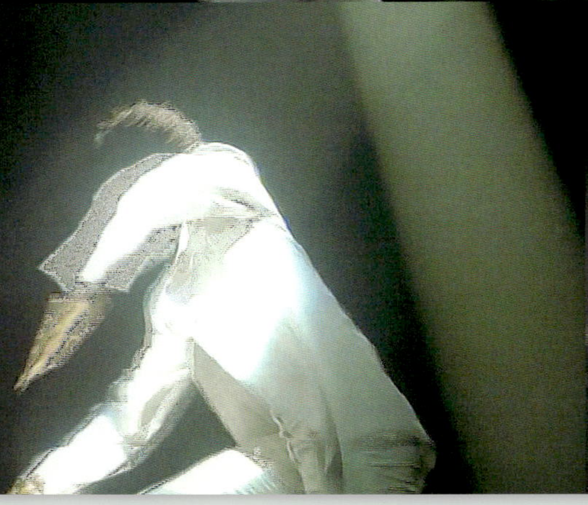

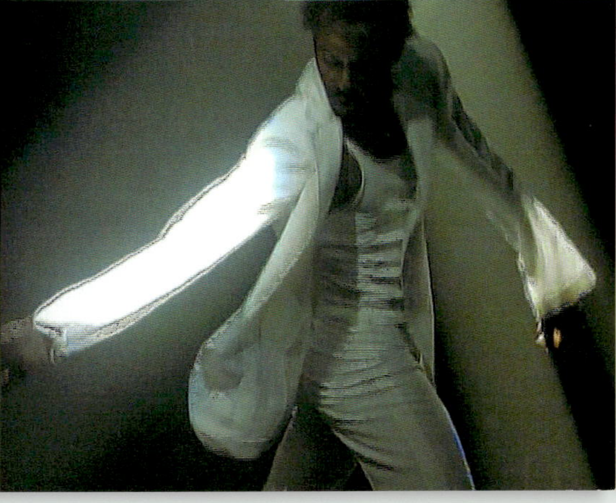

AUDIO PARK

1995
www.christian-moeller.com/audio_park
Museumpark, Rotterdam

Curator: Alex Adriaansen and Andreas Broeckmann
Sound: Pete Namlook
Light design: Louis Philippe Demers
Hardware: Hermann Gruber
Programming: Louis Philippe Demers, Philippe Jean, Daniel Schmitt
Production: V2_Organisation, Institute for the Unstable Media, Rotterdam and Archimedia, Institute for Arts and Technology, University for Art and Industrial Design, Linz, Austria

A group from Rotterdam announced that they were coming to one of the Electro Clips performances. They were called V2, Institute for Unstable Media, and were very interested in the work. Months later, Alex Adriaansen approached me, asking if I could imagine doing a variation on Electro Clips on a much larger scale for a public space. The location in question was the Museum Park in Rotterdam, a quite unusual park designed by Rem Koolhaas. Like many parks in other big cities, Museum Park also had the problem that due to poverty, drug-related crime and the bleaker elements of modern urban life, the citizens of Rotterdam no longer felt secure in this park at night and subsequently avoided it. So an important aspect of the experiment was to attract people to the park at night with an installation, and in doing so to make it a functioning urban site once again.

We installed a huge roofless wooden deck in the park and surrounded it with eight sound and light towers, and like the stage floor for Electro Clips, this wooden floor had photo transistors built into it. During the day the sun shone on them, at night they were lit by more than 100 aircraft landing lights. Park visitors produced dense ambient sounds, less rhythmical than in Electro Clips. Another idea was to move sounds around three-dimensionally inside the installation, so that they could be experienced spatially.

The installation had its fans, although "musically", it was rather unsuccessful. I had become obsessed with the idea of designing a huge, outdoor three-dimensional sound space, but there was no opportunity to carry out a realistic prototype on this scale. The evening before the opening I realised that the outdoor 3D soundscape simply didn't work, and over night, we had to invent a new sound concept, something which might not be particularly interesting musically, but was instead loud.

Despite these shortcomings, the resulting installation was not all that bad. It became a meeting point for the young people of Rotterdam. Usually, when we do a work, visitors come, whether they like it or not, just once. But here they came every evening, again and again. The piece had regulars; hundreds of people, every evening, literally occupying the place and making it their own. I still do not know why it worked so well, but I have a suspicion. I believe that the wooden deck, lit by the bright lights created a color temperature similar to familiar ambience of our family living rooms in the evening. Weather permitting, a wooden floor without a roof in the late evening, invites people to linger.

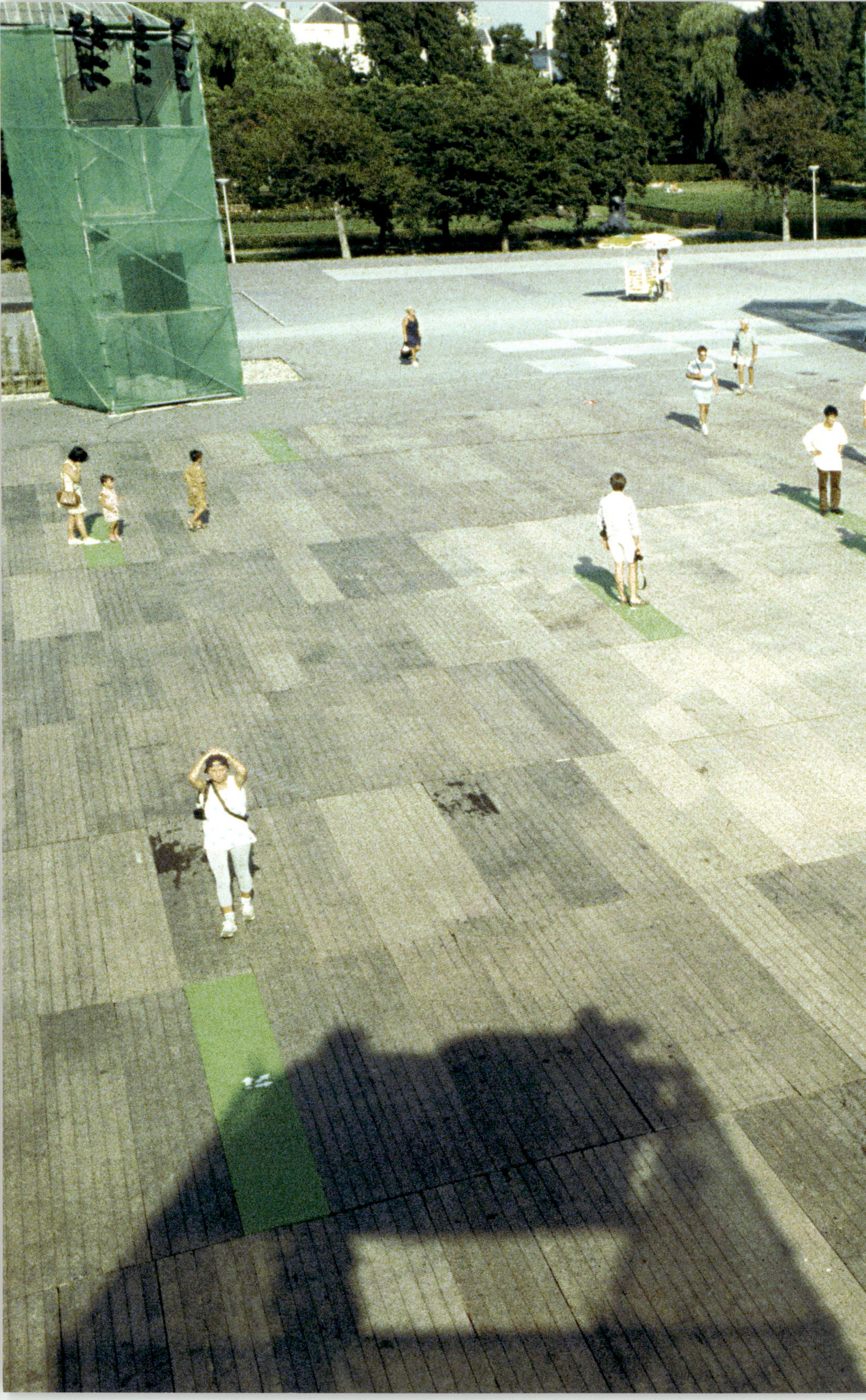

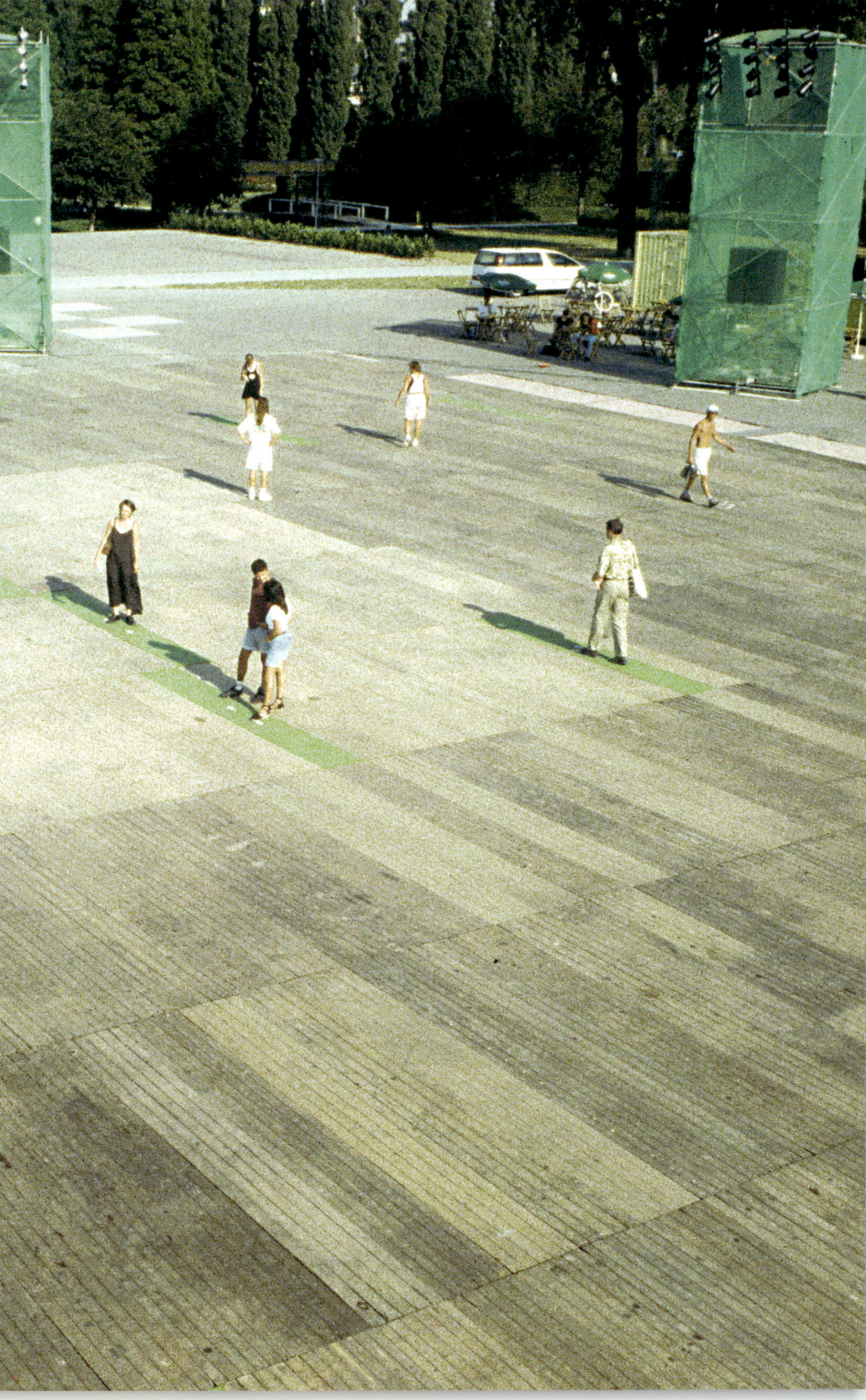

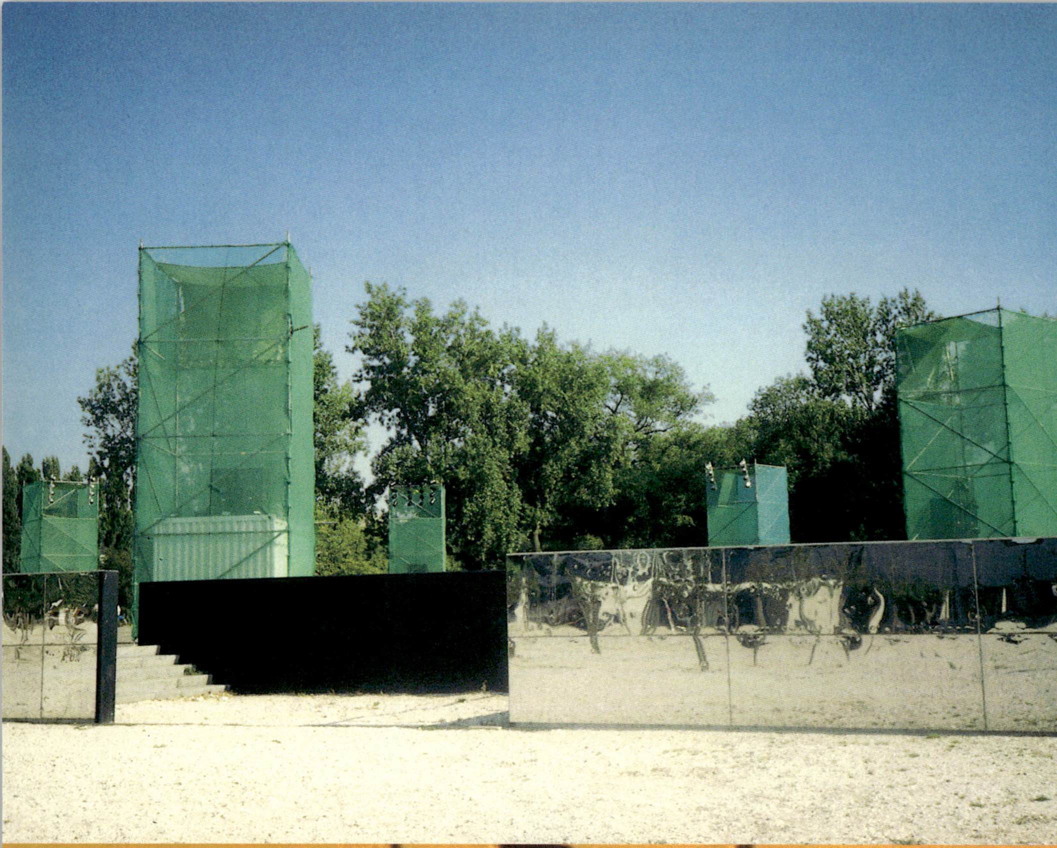
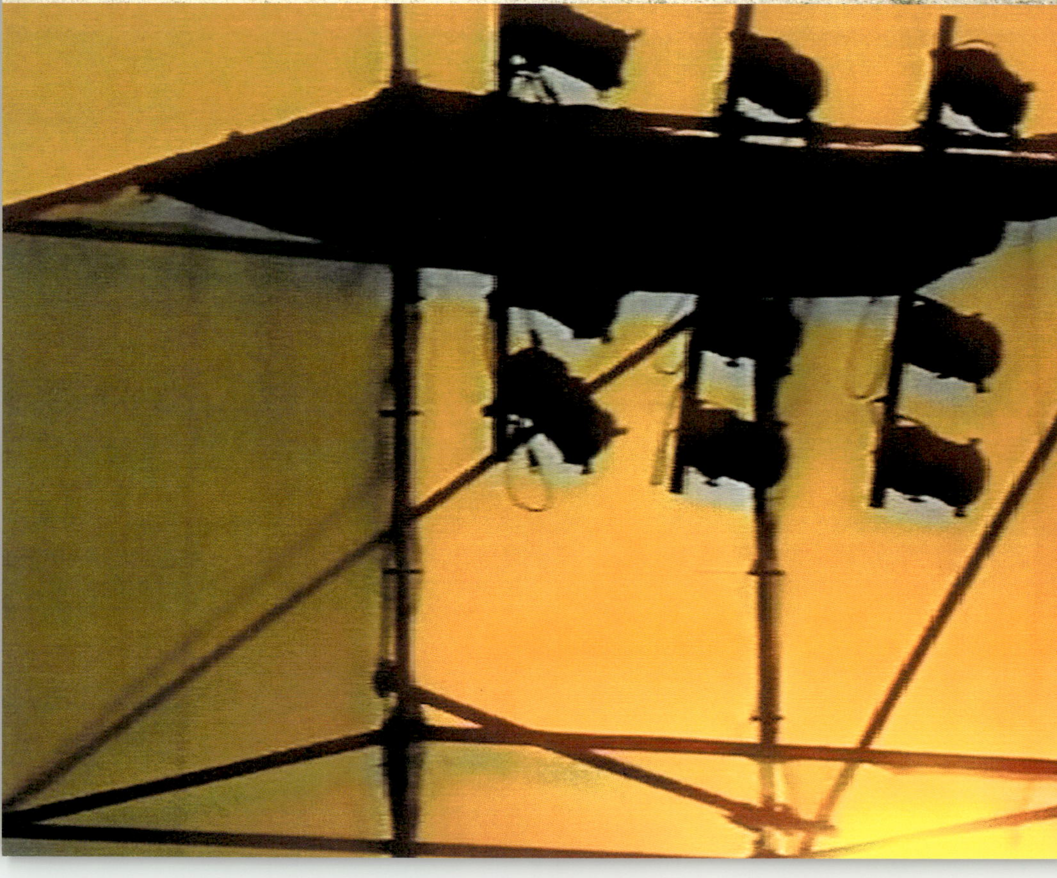

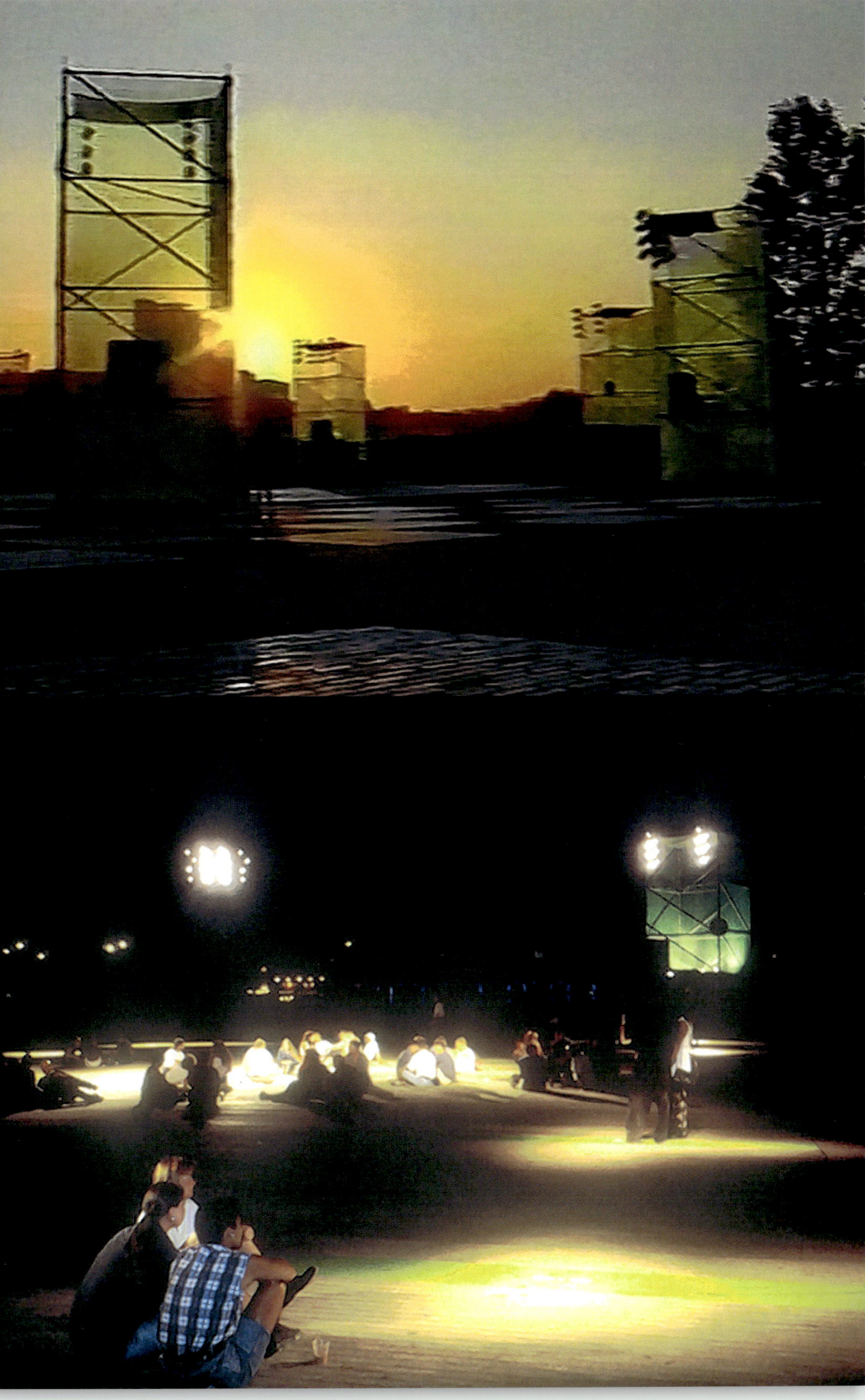

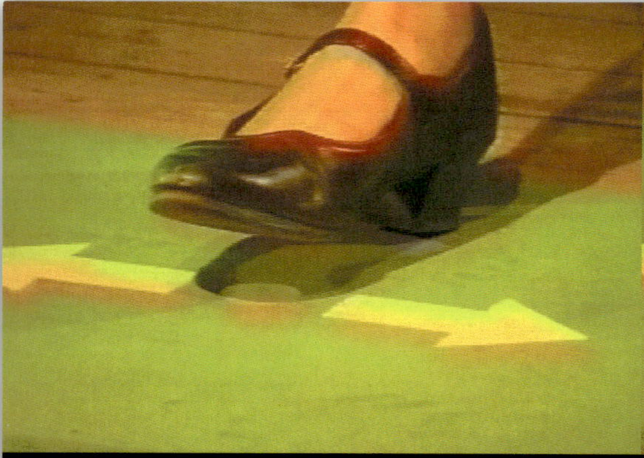
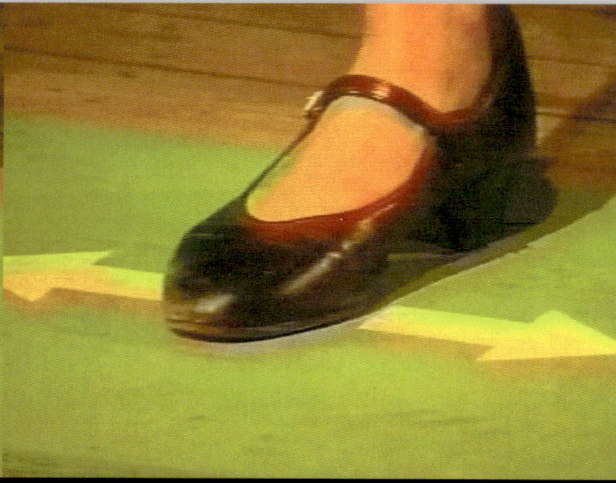

Light sensors in the floor enable visitors to control the ambient sound.

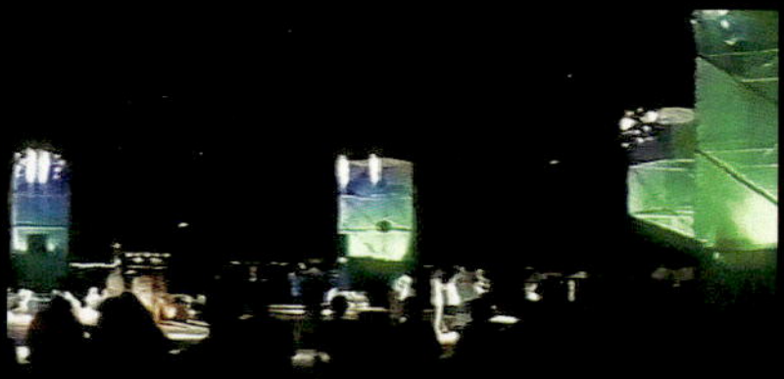
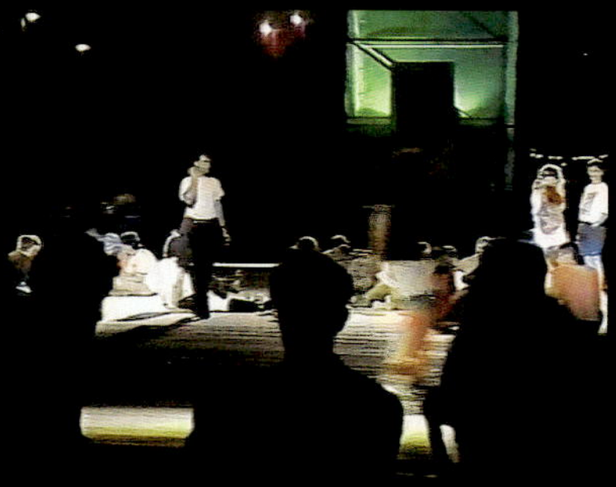
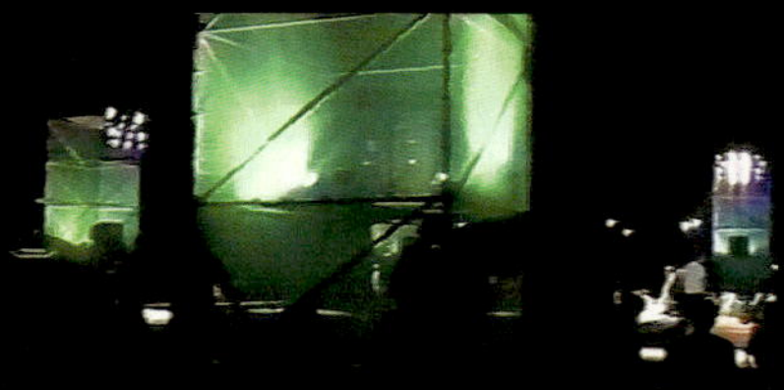

www.christian-moeller.com/audio_park

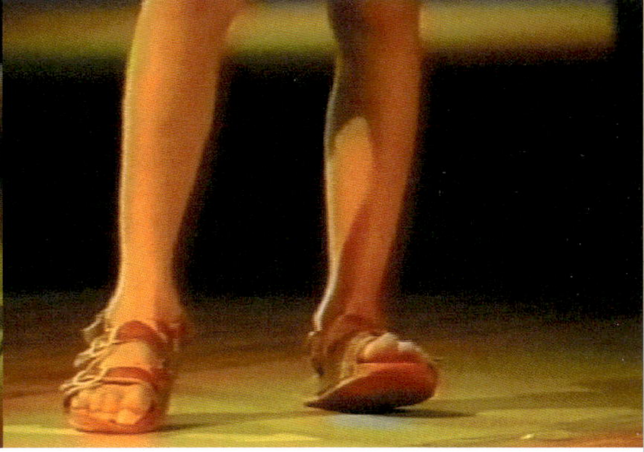
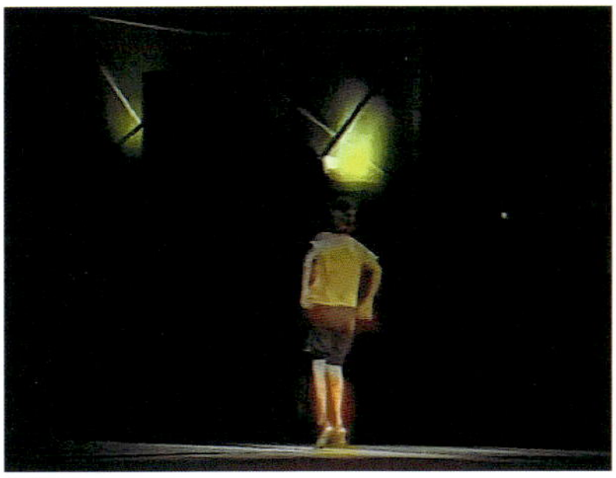
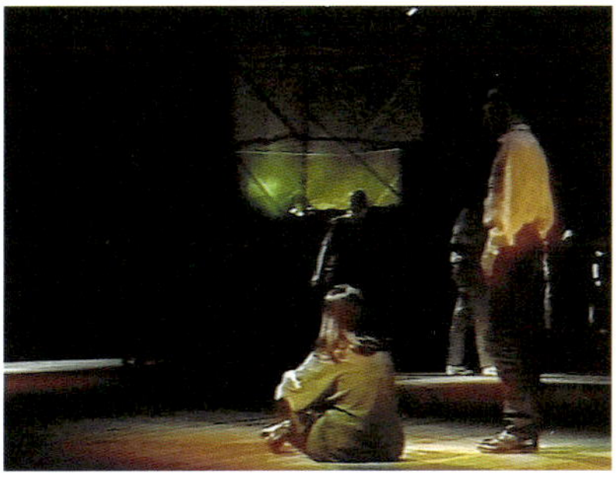
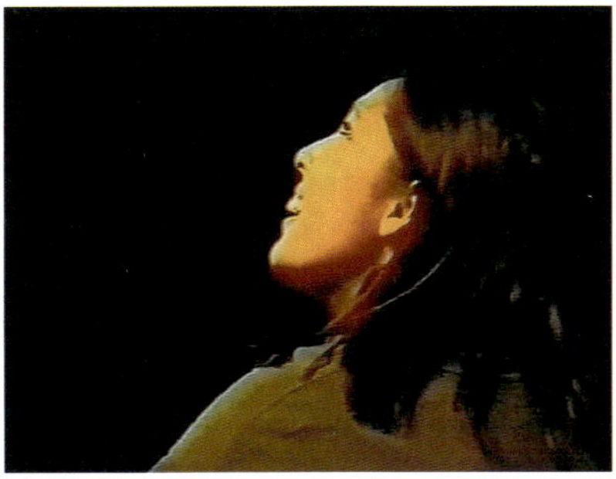
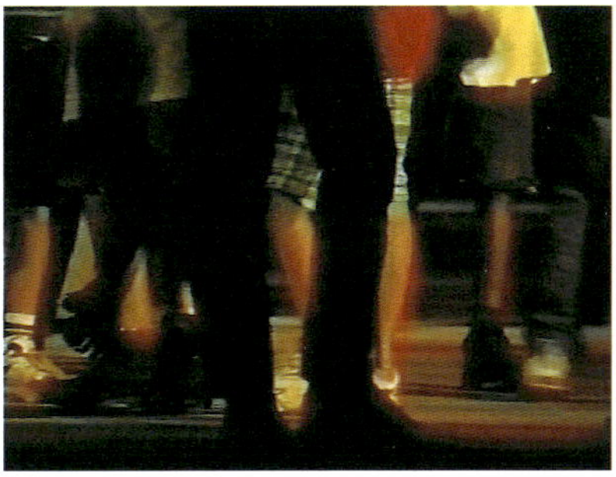

LIGHT BLASTER

1993
www.christian-moeller.com/light_blaster
Lichtfest, Design Horizonte 93, Naxoshalle, Frankfurt/Main

Programming: Daniel Schmitt and Sven Thöne
Laser technology: Bison Lasertechnik
Mechanical engineering/construction: MBM, Metallbau Möckmühl
Supported by: Peter Müller and Hartmut Florin

For the Design Horizonte **in Frankfurt, I was invited to do an installation for an exhibition on the theme of "Architecture and Light". This is a theme which, in Germany, is unfortunately dominated by engineering companies. In their solutions to serious questions like how is natural light to be brought to the exhibits in a museum, or how can I get enough daylight on the desks of people working in offices half their lives, they have certainly contributed quite a lot for daylight systems and that must be acknowledged. The problem is that far too much emphasis on the mere utility of light has robbed designers of their feeling for the sensuousness of environments. The result, too often, is just boredom packaged as high-tech.**
The installation was set up in a darkened room and consisted of an approximately 5x5 meter membrane of light which the visitor would move and control with the pulse frequency of his heartbeat. The clip on the visitor's finger is the infrared end of a pulsoximeter, which transferred his heartrate and blood oxygen level to the system controls.
We built a machine on which a belt-driven guidance system moved a laser light scanner back and forth in the room. The idea of producing an immaterial wall of light, a curtain made out of nothing, required extensive mechanical effort. Conceived as a small experiment, it resulted however in a highly complicated apparatus, and quite literally a big waste of energy. In a way, this most expensive technical monster turned out to be an even more idiotic sort of thing than the packaged boredom I criticized above.
A scanning mechanism at the end of the drive faces the visitor. On its electrical engine is a mirror surface, at an angle of 45 degrees, onto which the ray of light is projected. This mirror rotates at great speed like the rotors of a helicopter and scans the ray of light vertically into the room, 360 degrees around the horizontal axis. If the light aggregate is operating at its maximum, it makes all the vapor and dust particles in the air visible, forming an almost solid wall of light.
Though this was not complex, it was a stunning audio-visual event nevertheless, and a frighteningly effective feedback system. So effective, in fact, that the visitor synchronized himself to the installation almost immediately through his own autonomic system and thus unintentionally transcended himself. Fortunately, all the visitors survived this experience, but I sometimes became weak at the knees, for fear that sooner or later someone would faint.

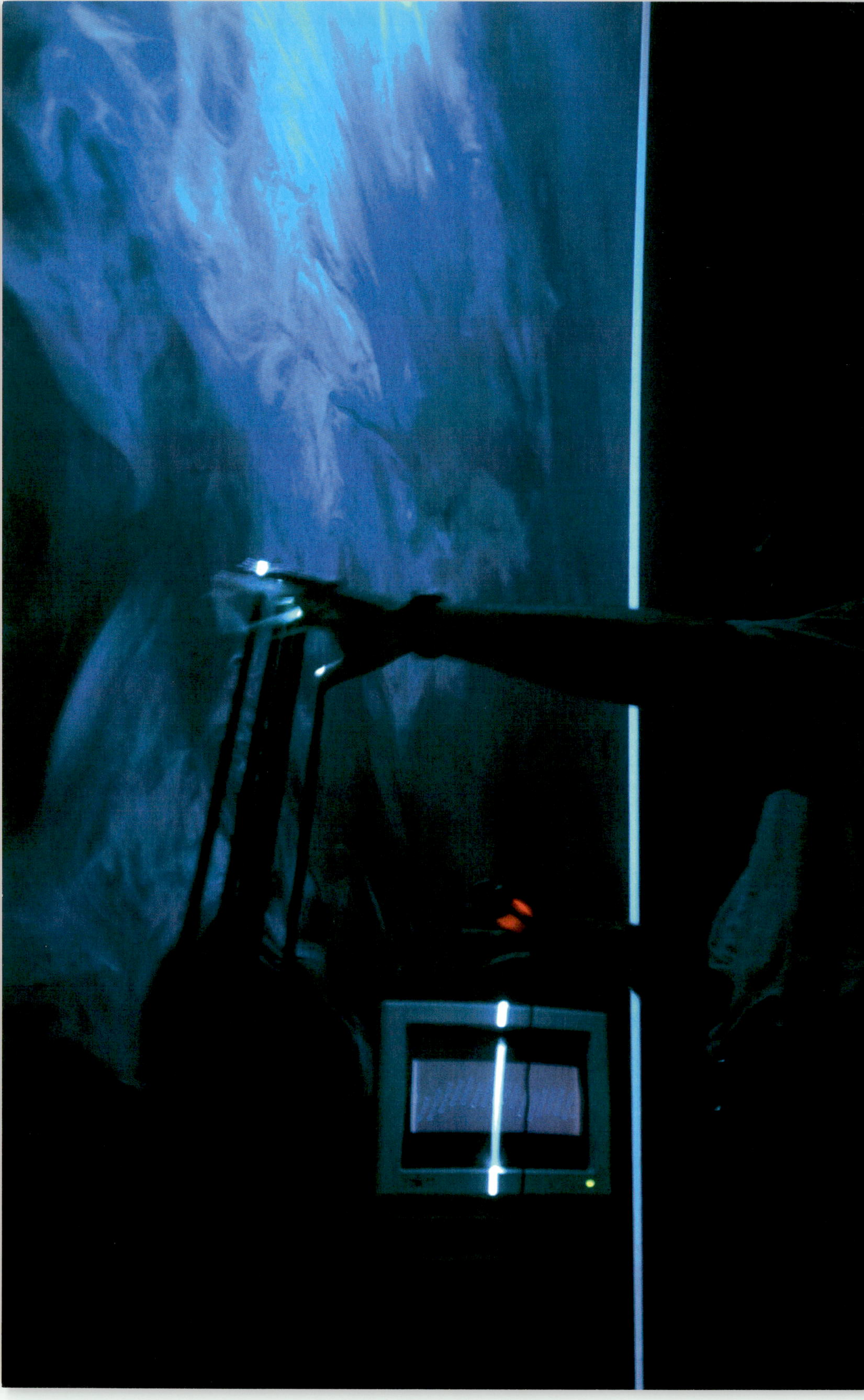

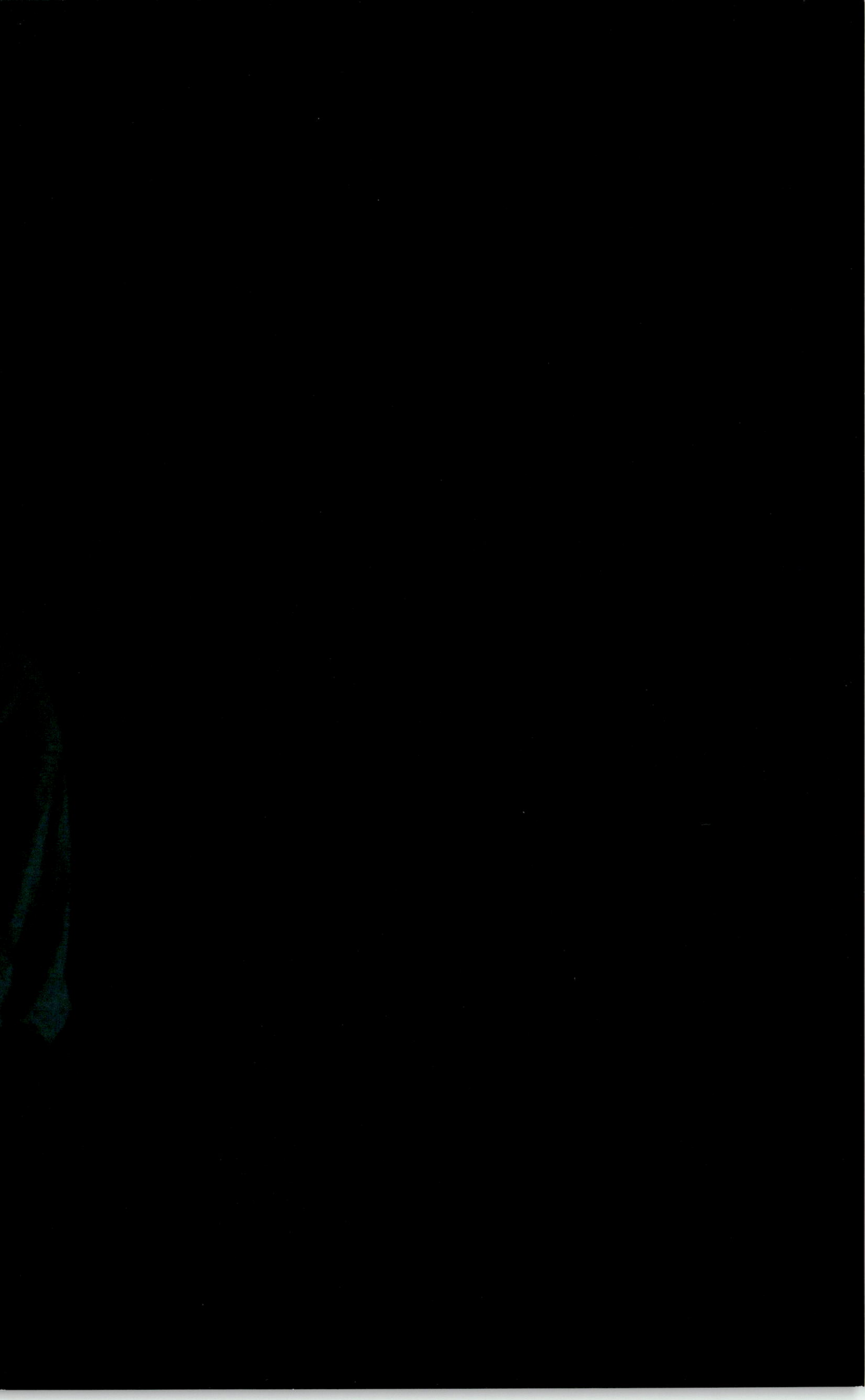

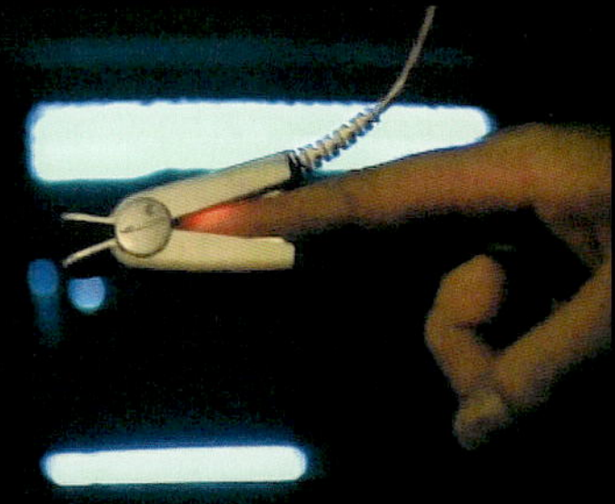

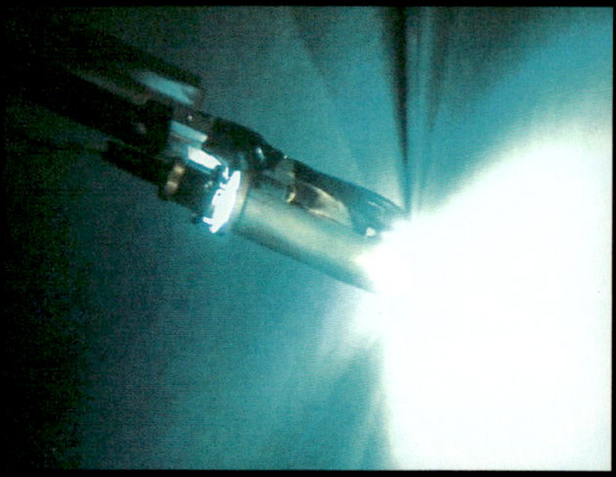

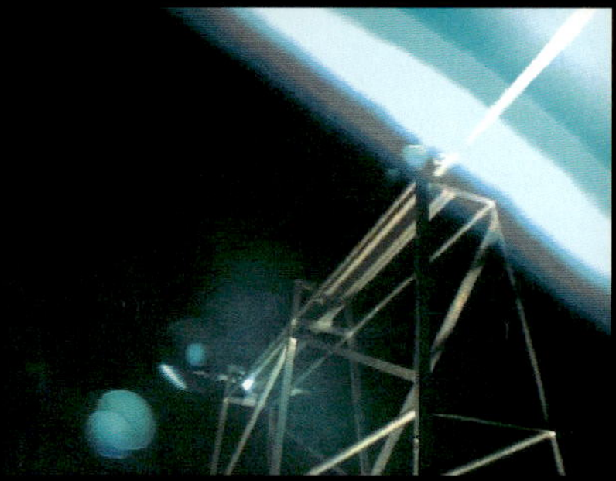

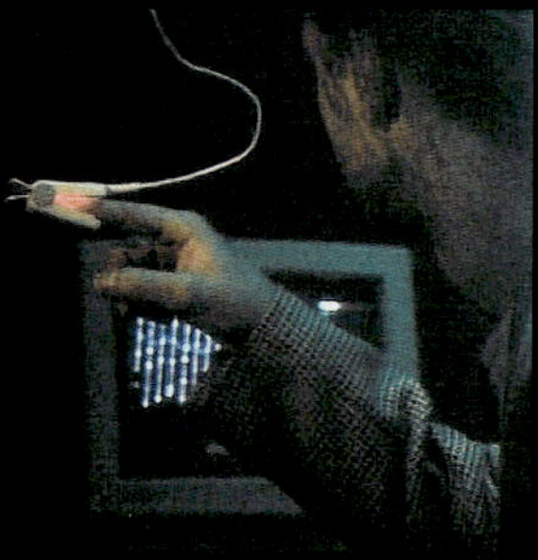

A pulsoximeter measures visitors' heartbeats and translates them into the movement of the light membrane.

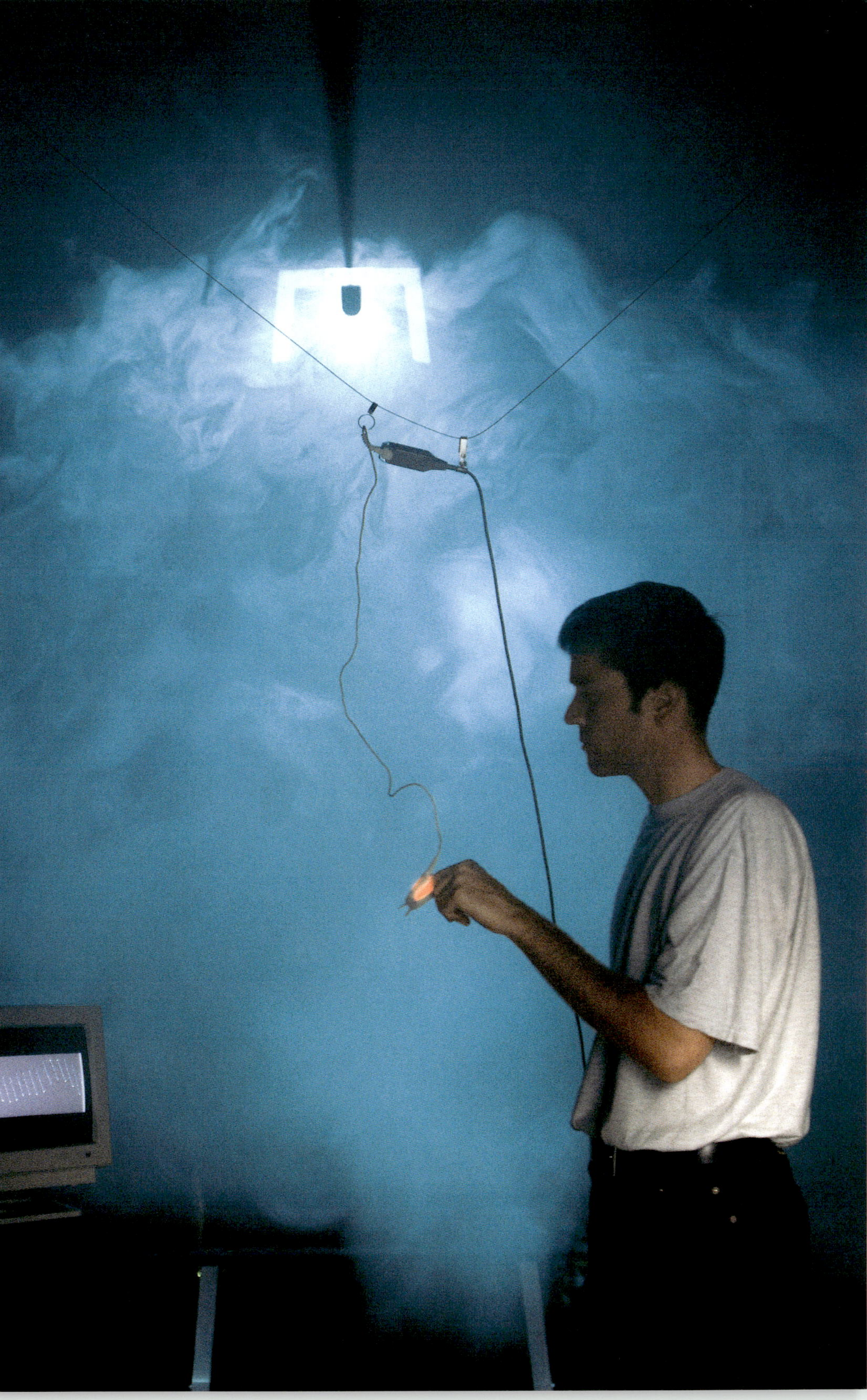

ELECTRONIC MIRROR

1993

www.christian-moeller.com/electronic_mirror

Eigenwelt der Apparatewelt, Institut für Neue Medien, Städelschule (1993), Frankfurt/Main; Intelligente Ambiente, Ars Electronica, (1994), Linz; Press Enter, Gallery Power Plant, (1995), Toronto

Curator (Frankfurt, Linz): Peter Weibel
Curators (Toronto): Louise Dompierre and Derrick de Kerckhove
Programming: Daniel Schmitt
Sensor electronics: Siemens AG, ASI/Gerätewerk Amberg

Peter Weibel approached me at short notice requesting a contribution to an exhibition in Frankfurt, and I had only a week to develop and realize a concept. Using materials from other works lying about in my studio, we built a rather strange mirror that, when you approached it, made your image disappear. In other words, a mirror in which you could only see yourself from a distance. This small ironic work caused quite a sensation and was cited in many international publications. It has not yet become a successful design product.

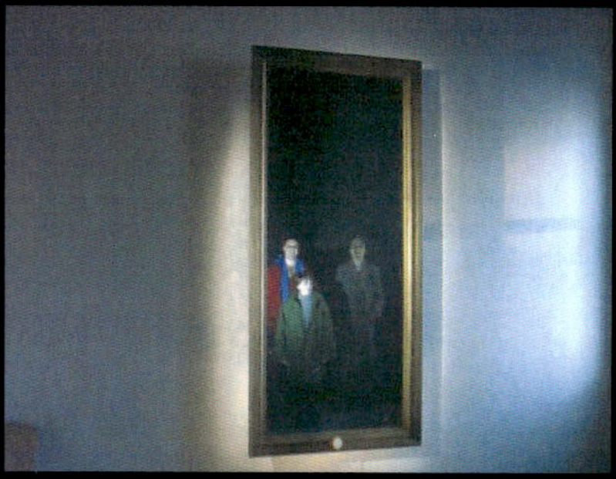

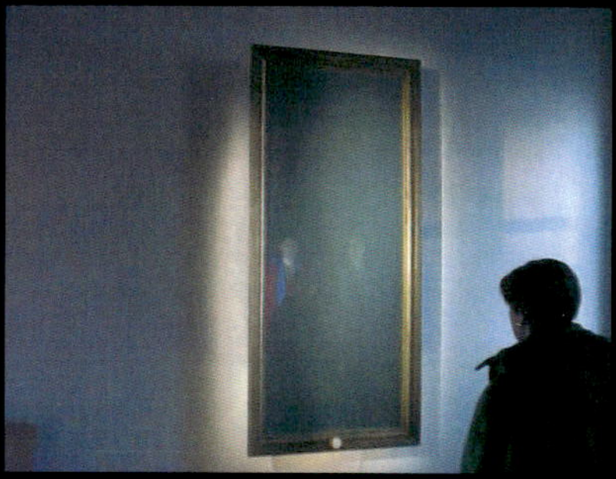

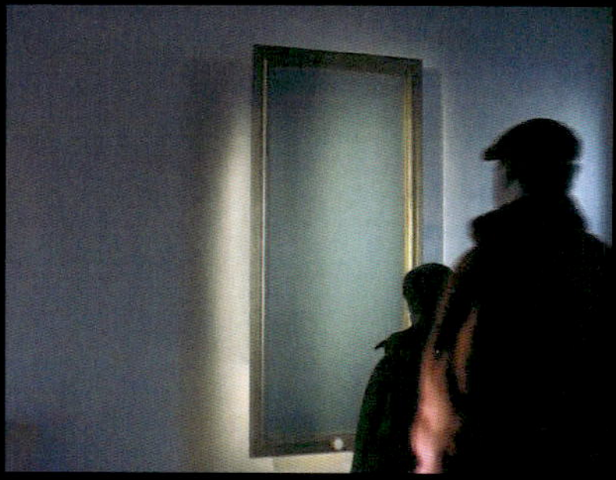

An ultrasound distance sensor causes the viewer's reflection to disappear as he moves closer to the mirror.

www.christian-moeller.com/electronic_mirror

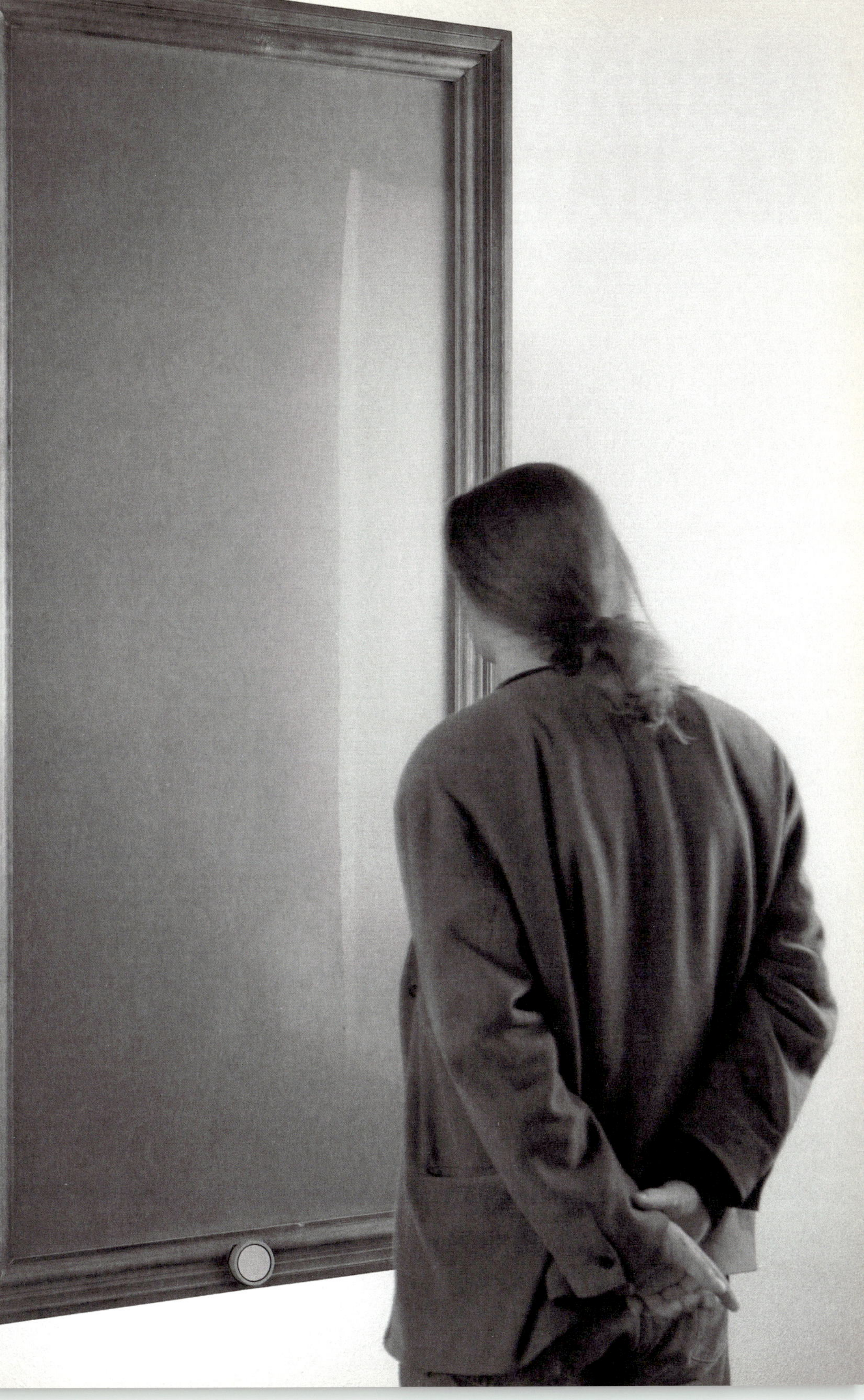

ALGORITHMIC HABITAT

1991
www.christian-moeller.com/algorithmic_habitat
Peter Weibel's "On Justifying the Hypothetical Nature of Art and its Non-Identity with the Object World", Tanja Grunert Gallery, Cologne

Programming: Dieter Beck and Gideon May
Hardware: Bob O'Kane and Dieter Selin
Construction management: Ulrich Schaaf
Production: Institut für Neue Medien, Städelschule, Frankfurt/Main

For Peter Weibel's exhibition "On Justifying the Hypothetical Nature of Art and its Non-Identity within the Object World" at the Gallery Tanja Grunert in Cologne in 1991, I designed both the exhibition architecture and a piece of virtual architecture projected inside it. This quite early example of algrithmic architecture used what were at the time, the most powerful computer graphics available.
You enter the room through a light trap. On the floor are circular metal pressure sensitive plates on which the visitors can walk. The visitors, according to the sequence in which they step on the sensors, produce algorithms which in turn transform the cubic volumes defining that virtual space. These "architectonic break-downs", transformations of this virtual interior space, were viewed on a back-projection screen.
I got the idea for this after seeing a photo in a daily newspaper, a special disposal site for refrigerators close to Frankfurt. Similar-sized cuboid elements produce interesting geometric surfaces, landscapes in a topography made up of quadratic segments.

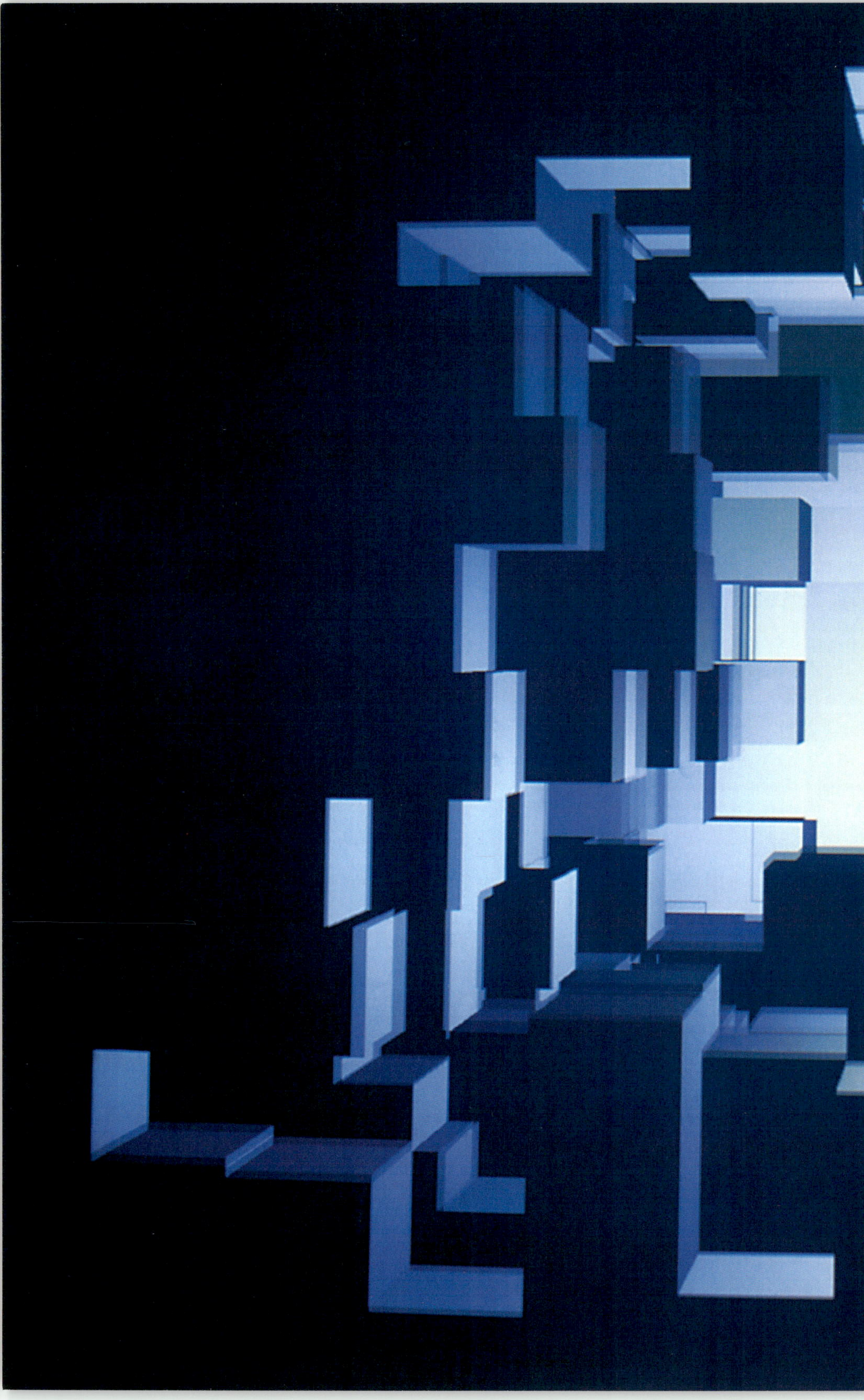

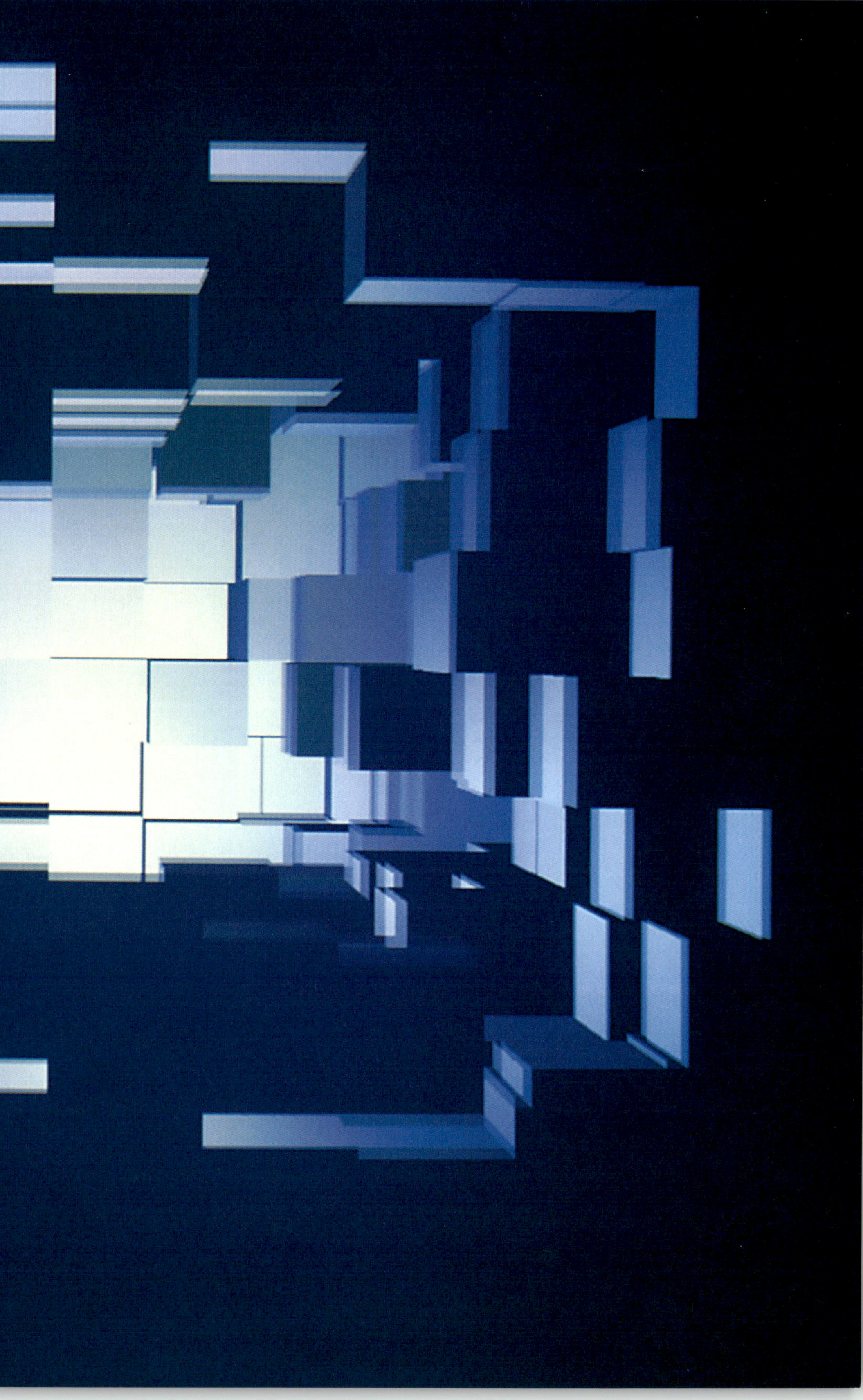

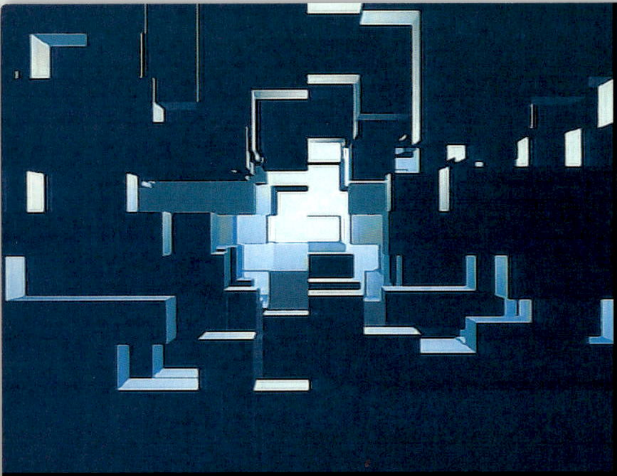

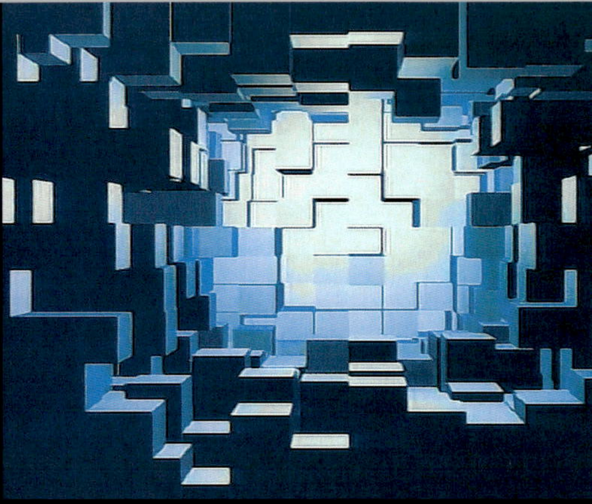

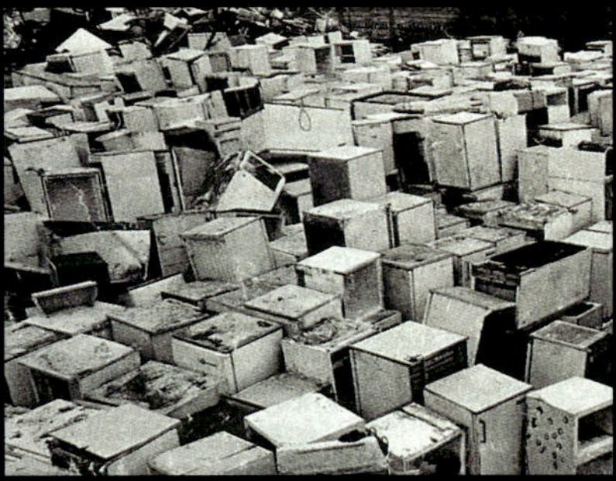

Special disposal site for refrigerators.

www.christian-moeller.com/algorithmic_habitat

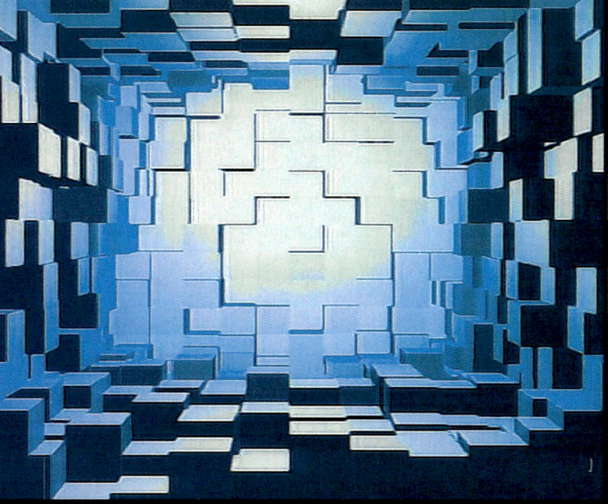

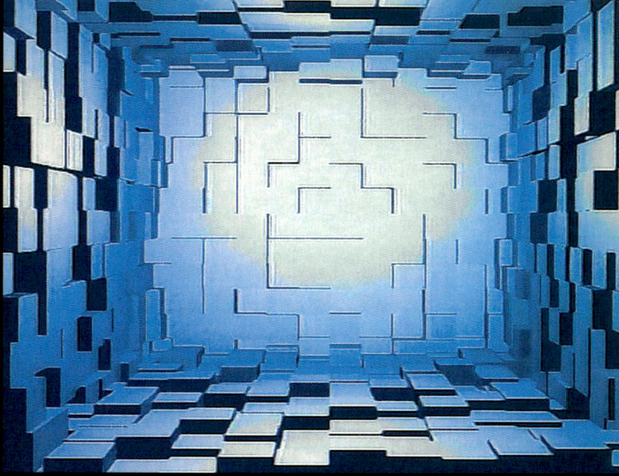

By stepping on pressure sensors
embedded in the floor a visitor
transforms this virtual interior.

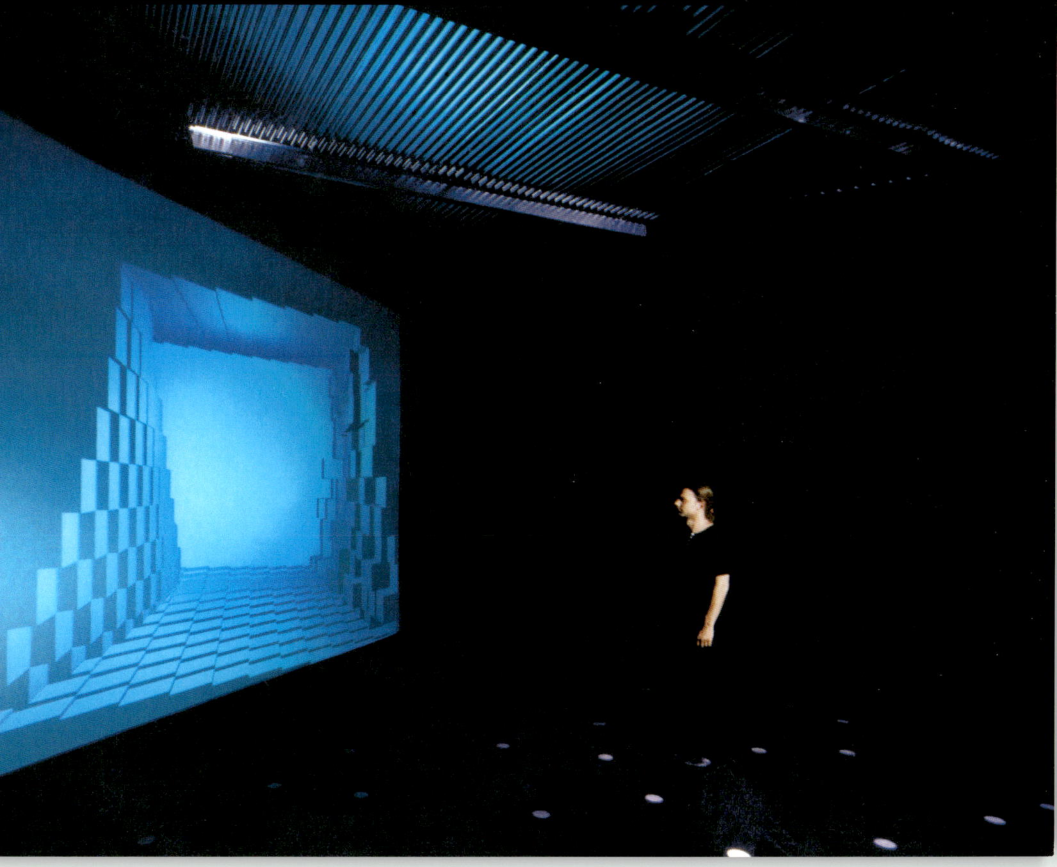

SPACE [IM]BALANCE

1992
www.christian-moeller.com/space_balance
Endo und Nano, Ars Electronica 1992, Danube Park, Linz, Austria

Curators: Peter Weibel and Katharina Gsöllpointner
Programming: Dieter Beck
Mechanical engineering and construction: MBM Metallbau Möckmühl
Video projection: SVV, Hans Walchhofer
Production: Institut für Neue Medien, Städelschule, Frankfurt/Main
Supported by: Peter Müller

Space (Im)Balance is a VR installation in the Danube Park in Linz. It is a real building which can be in two different states of equilibrium at the same time. The exterior space is in stable equilibrium, and the interior space is in what we call “indifferent” equilibrium, which in this case more or less corresponds to the condition experienced below deck on a sailing boat.

Again you enter the room through a light trap. The floor of the installation moves on its horizontal axis and slopes under the weight of the visitor. In front of and behind the visitor the interior space is simulated in 3D on back projection walls in real time. The idea was to create a building in which the orthogonality between walls, ceiling and a sloping floor is maintained and would thus upset our sense of balance.

The mechanical floor revolves around a vertical pin and its motion is cushioned by hydraulic springs. Two optical potentiometers transmit the respective slope in the floor to the computer system.

Computer graphics, which by today’s standards seem elementary, were produced by two Silicon Graphics workstations, madly expensive in 1992. Spherical elements clatter around the room according to a gravitational algorithm. To heighten the illusion, whenever these virtual spheres touch one another or hit the wall elements, this event is carefully balanced and acoustically transmitted into the real space.

The installation was an architectonic critique of “Head-Mounted Displays” which were all the rage at the time among the broader public, and were the icon for access to virtual reality. Homo Virtual, the man with the idiotic-looking data mask by companies like VPL, was very much in fashion. Very few people had the opportunity to try out such complicated systems, and the interest of people waiting in line at demonstrations was as enormous as the disappointment of those returning from the supposedly so fascinating data trip. From the very beginning, I thought it was quite meaningless to confront visitors with technology so closely that you had to screw an apparatus onto their faces. With my swinging room I wanted to show that there were architectonic entries into the virtual world which could expand the scope of sensory perception, without sticking helmets over people’s heads like putting blinders onto horses.

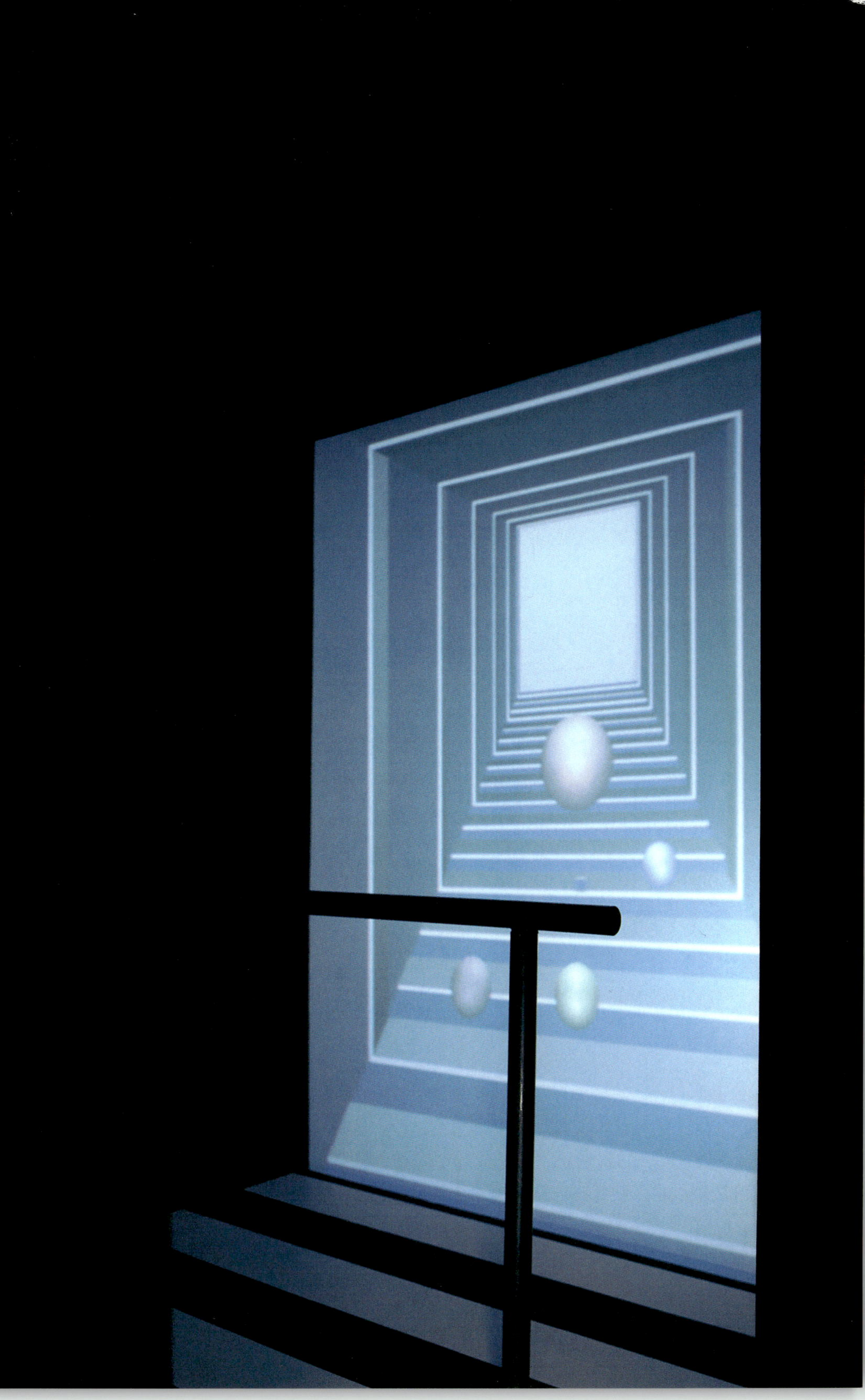

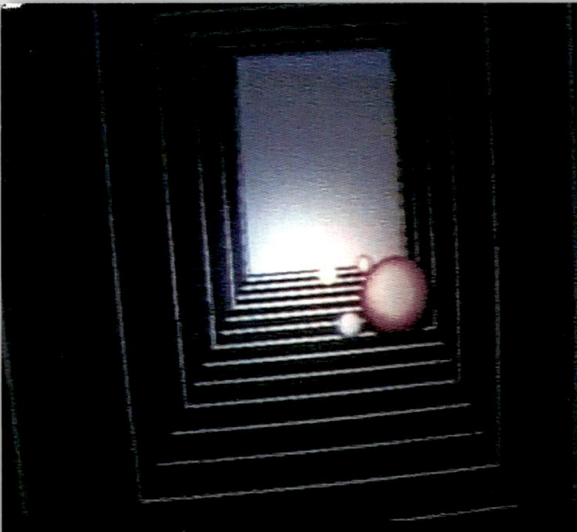

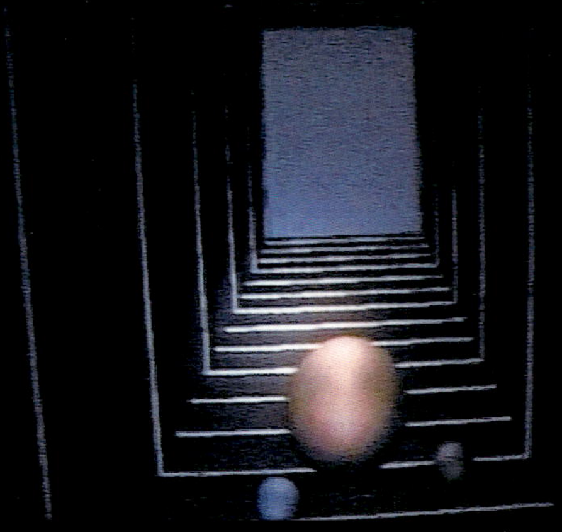

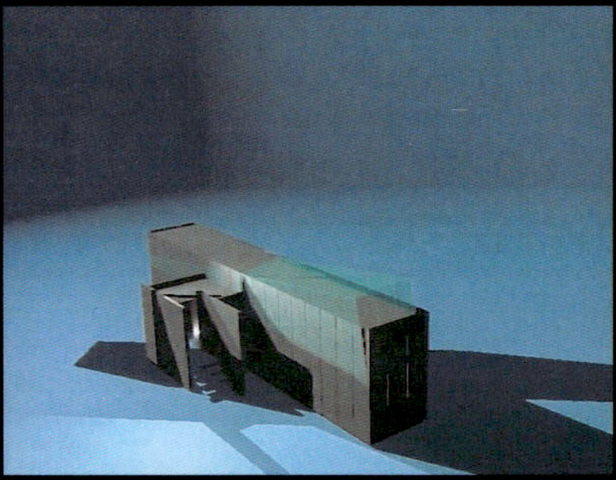

Digital model of the installation exterior.

www.christian-moeller.com/space_balance

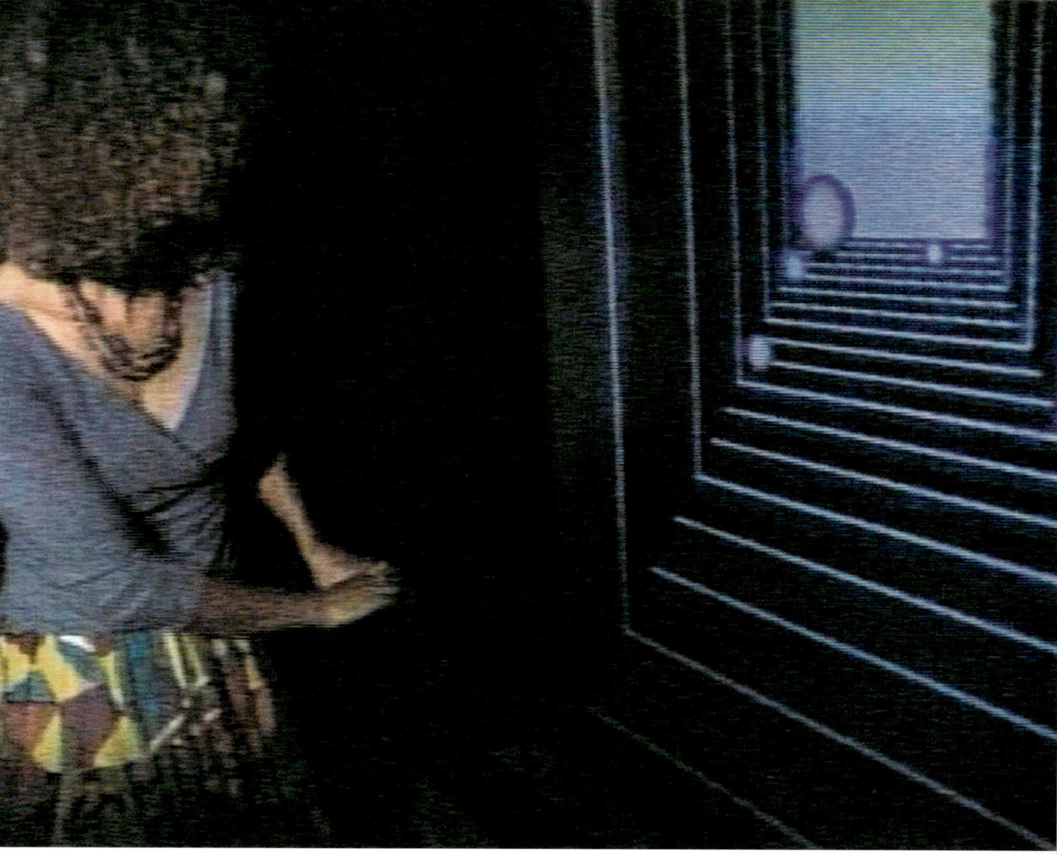

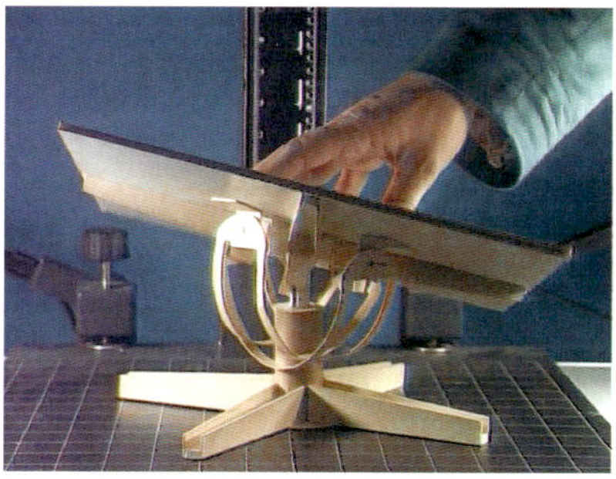

Mechanical model of the balance platform.

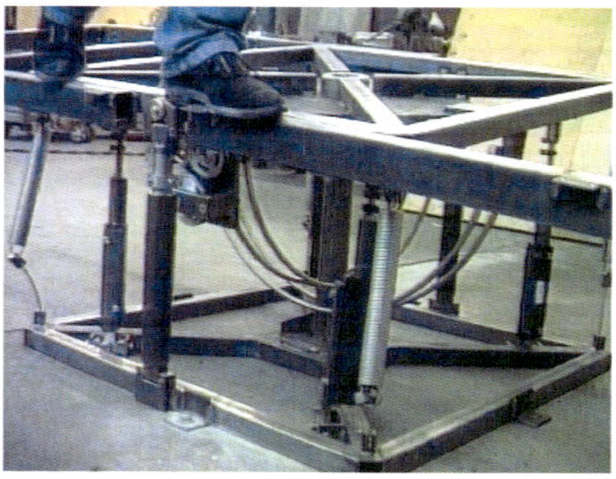

Technical adjustments to the balance platform at MBM.

VIRTUAL CAGE

1993
www.christian-moeller.com/virtual_cage
TAT (Theater am Turm) Frankfurt/Main (1993)
and at ARTLAB-Prospect2, P3 Art & Environment at Tochoji Auditorium, Tokyo (1997)

Artistic Director (TAT): Tom Stromberg
Curators (ARTLAB): Yukiko Shikata and Kazunao Abe
Producer (P3): Shinobu Ito
1st voice (Nature sounds): David Dunn
2nd voice (Trautonium): Oskar Sala
Sound: Peter Namlook
Programming: Gideon May
Mechanical engineering and construction: MBM Metallbau Möckmühl
Laser technology: Bison Lasertechnik
Supported by: Peter Müller and Hartmut Florin

The balance platform for Space (Im)Balance was a relatively expensive apparatus, and after the exhibition in Linz, it was standing around in my studio. I got the opportunity to recycle the system at the Theater am Turm within the context of a performance festival. We constructed an unusual theatrical space in which the visitors were left to their own devices. We called this theater-beyond-theater "Virtual Cage".

To the platform used in Linz we attached laser scanners, the same principle employed later for the Light Blaster installation. These scanners projected a virtual floor onto the stage space—appearing like an artificial lake of light.

The visitor would walk across a ramp to the movable platform. The interior was controlled by this light floor, which set the whole space in motion as soon as a visitor stepped onto the platform. A particle system invisible to the visitor moved three-dimensionally through the room like a swarm of insects, a creature which you cannot see but can hear and follow acoustically as it moves around the room. This complex virtual creature was represented within the stage space by means of a 5-channel audio system. Like the spherical elements in the Light Blaster installation, this swarm moved by a gravitational algorithm. In an interplay with the sloping positions of the virtual floor, the swarm of particles moved with an incredible din. The closer the swarm came to the visitor on the platform, the more aggressive the nature of its resounding movements.

The sounds used where recordings of microscopic insects under water, collected by David Dunn. He discovered these sound worlds quite by chance one afternoon somewhere in New Mexico while recording ambient noises for a film. His curiosity was aroused by an almost dried-up puddle. Using an underwater microphone and headphones, he "dived" into a cosmos of chirping insect noises which, appropriately reprocessed and amplified, were to produce an impressive concert of insects later released on CD.

Virtual Cage is one more of the few installations which I have presented several times. I received an invitation to Tokyo from the curator Yukiko Shikata, who asked if this installation could be presented in the Tochoji Temple.The monastic temple in Shinjuko has a cemetery in the inner courtyard which consists of an artificial pond. A very meditative place. In the pond are stone cubes arranged 8x8 in squares. Like an urn, each cube of black granite, contains the ashes of a dead person whose name is engraved on the surface. Miniaturized "gravestones" are arranged in squares and float on the surface of the water like lilies. While I always take a lot of care to design my installations for a specific context and its spatial surroundings, in this case, the Japanese context suited the existing work so much better than the theater for which I had originally designed it. From this I learned that "site-specific art" cannot finally exist for me as an autonomous pursuit.

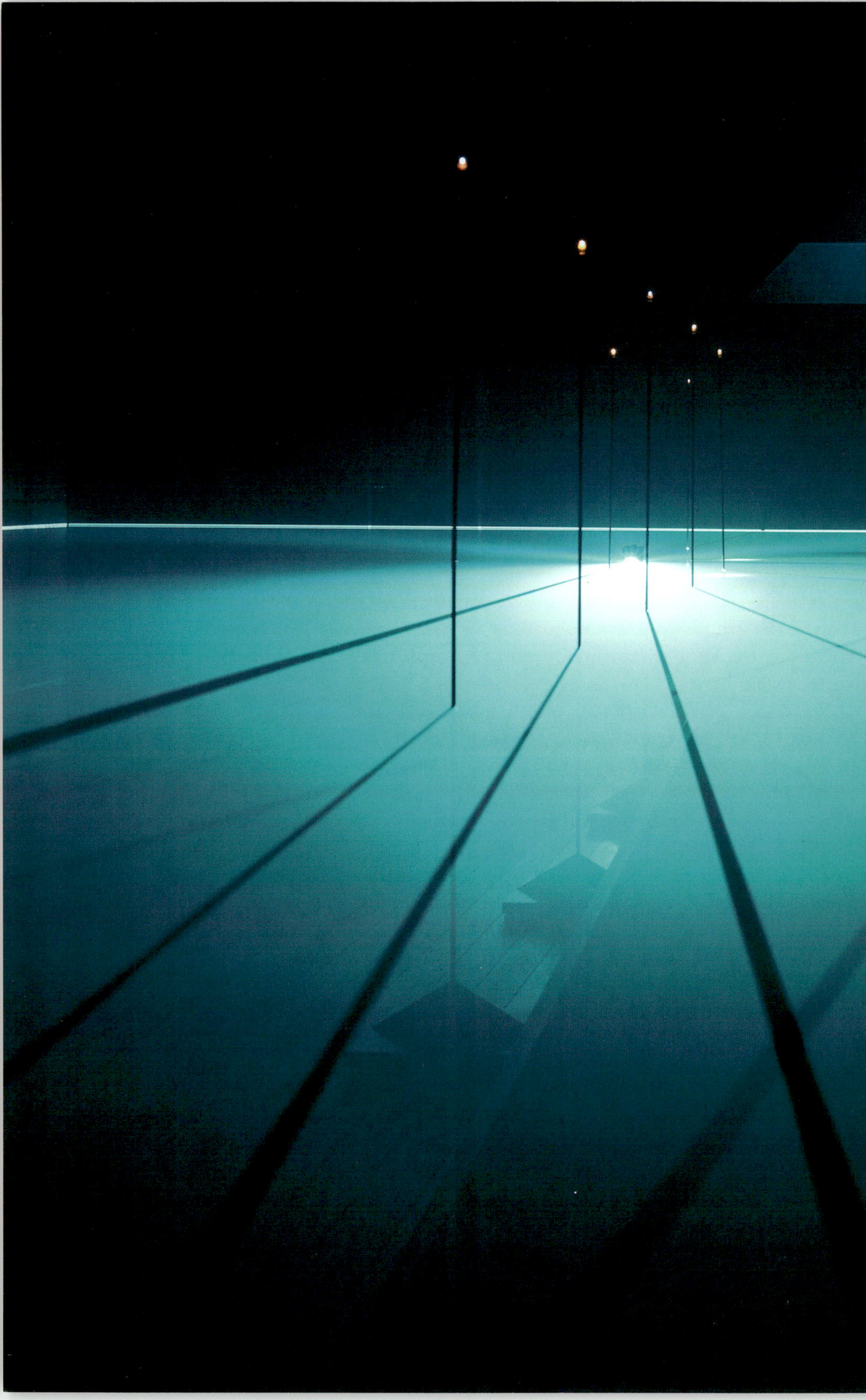

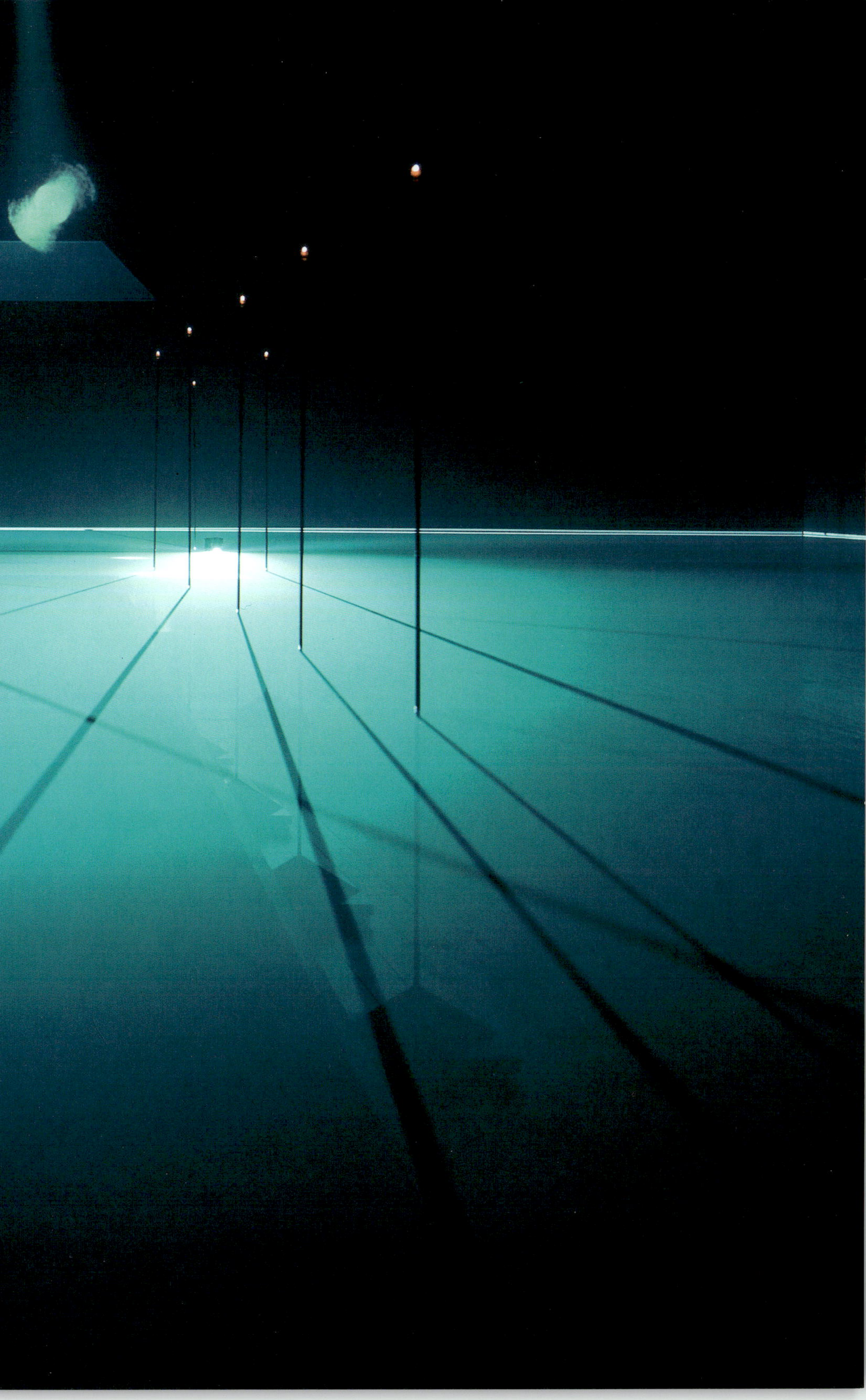

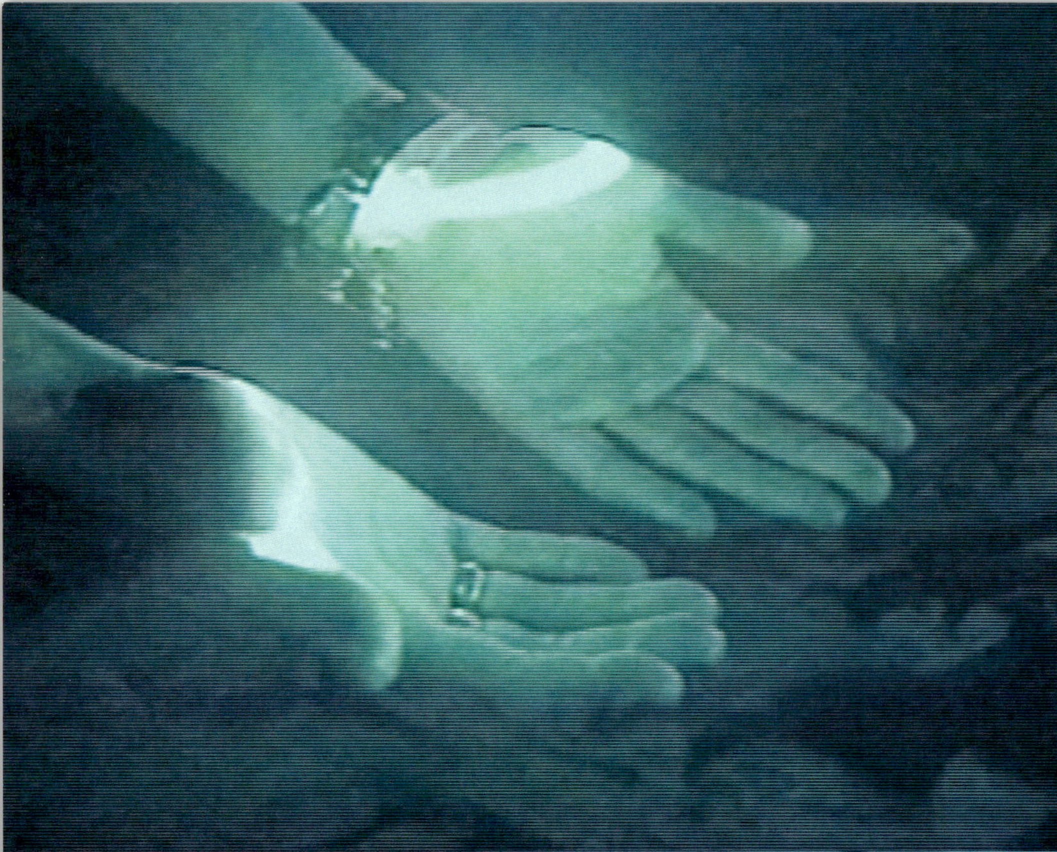
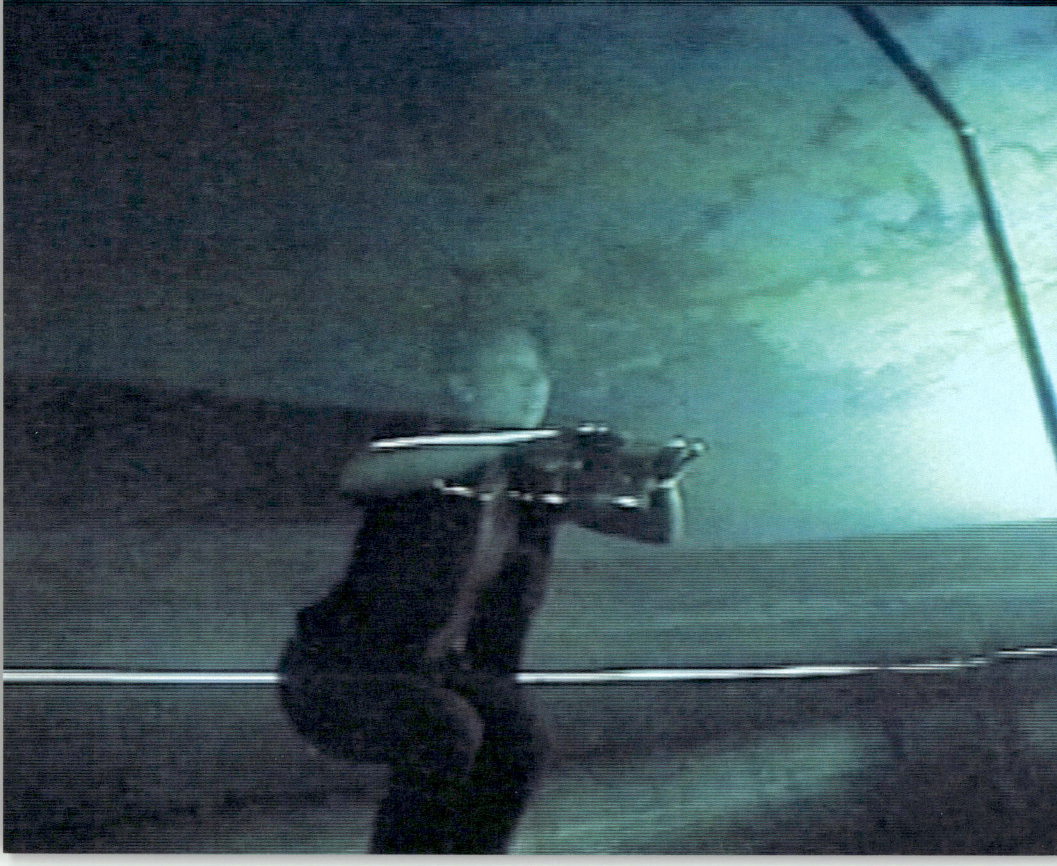

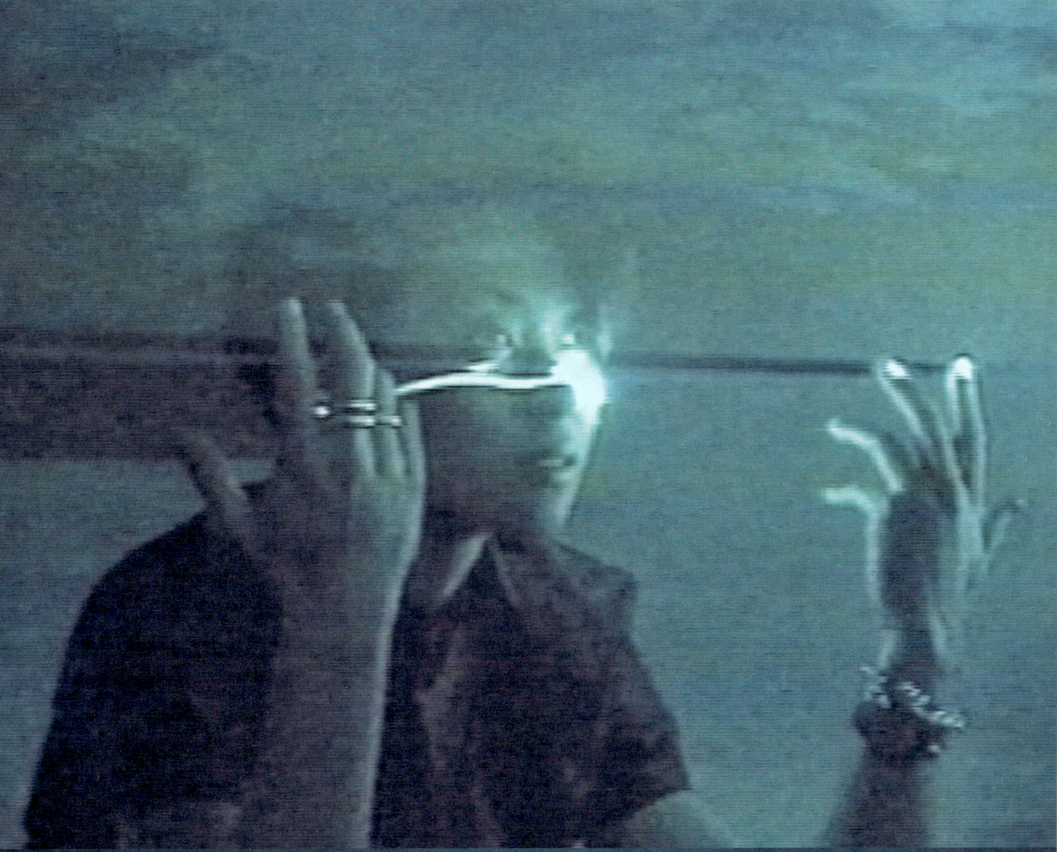
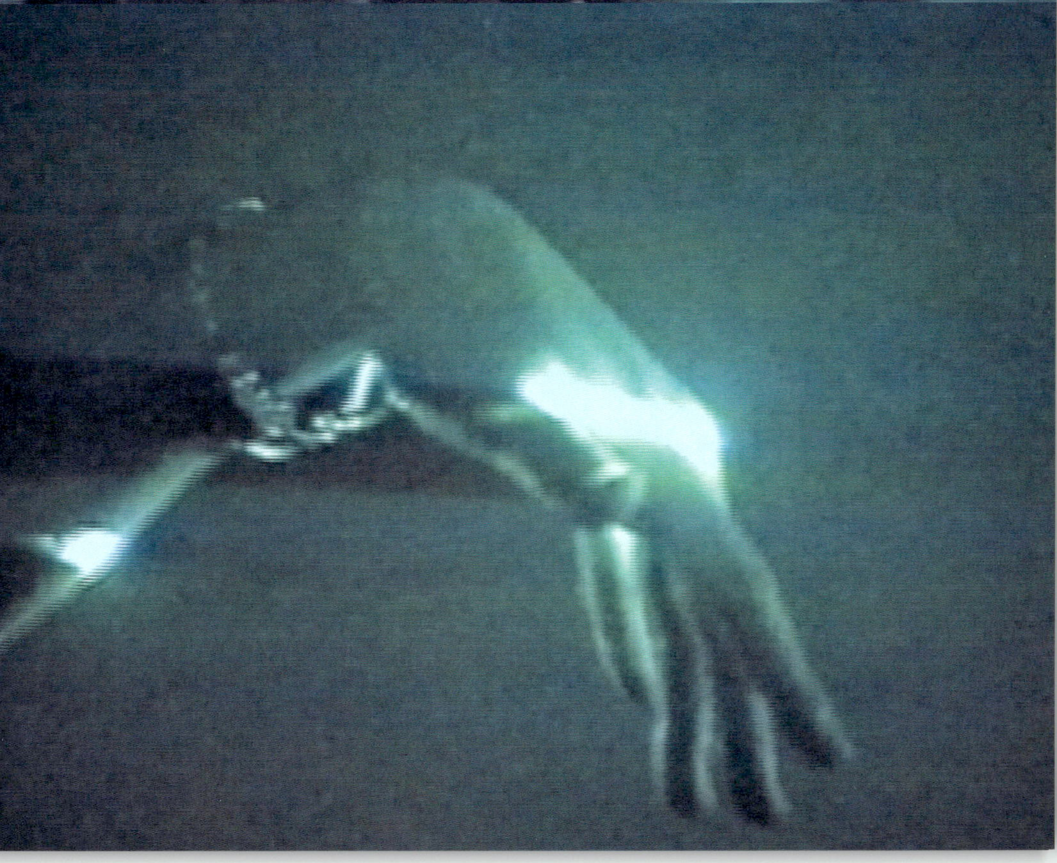

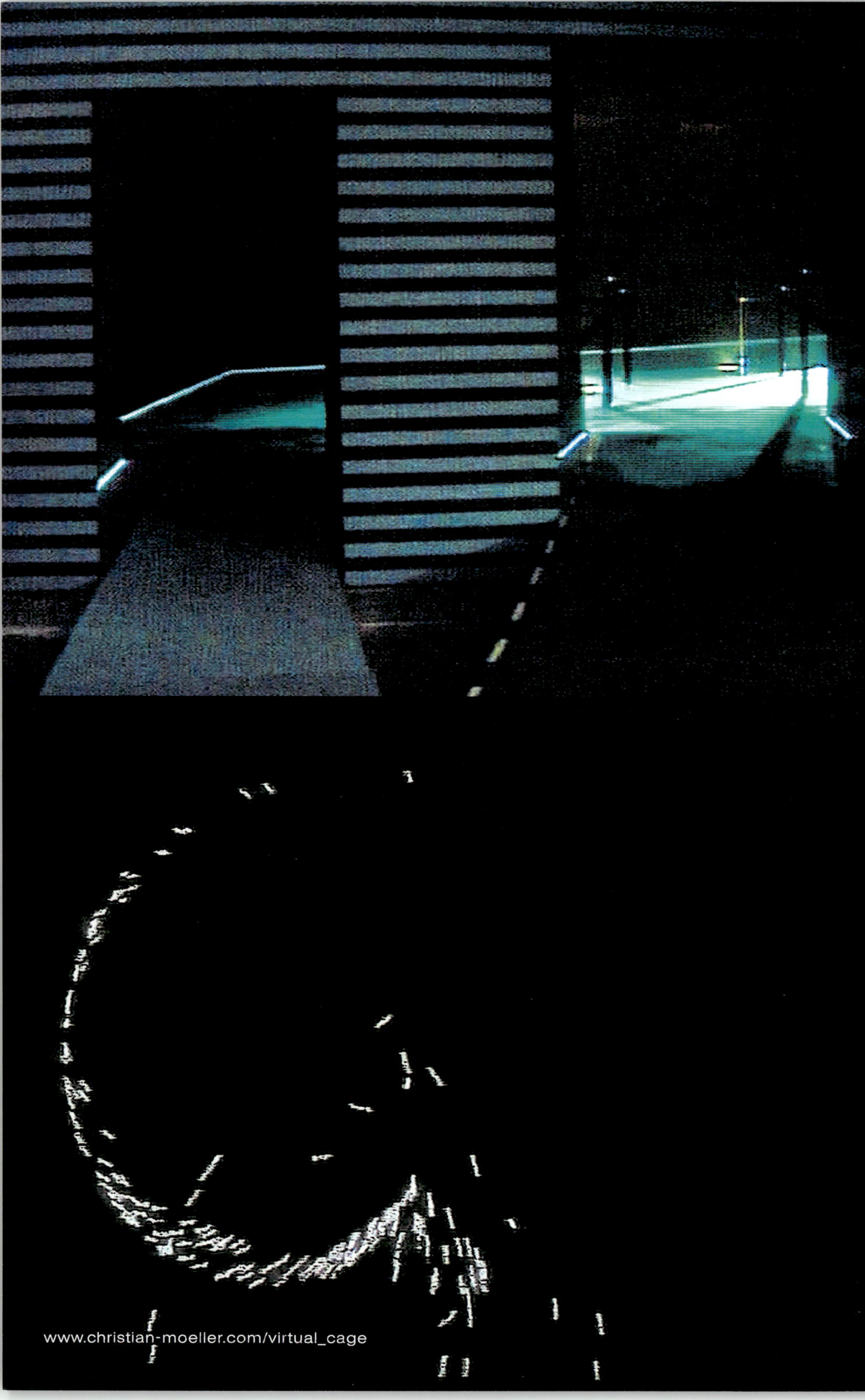
www.christian-moeller.com/virtual_cage

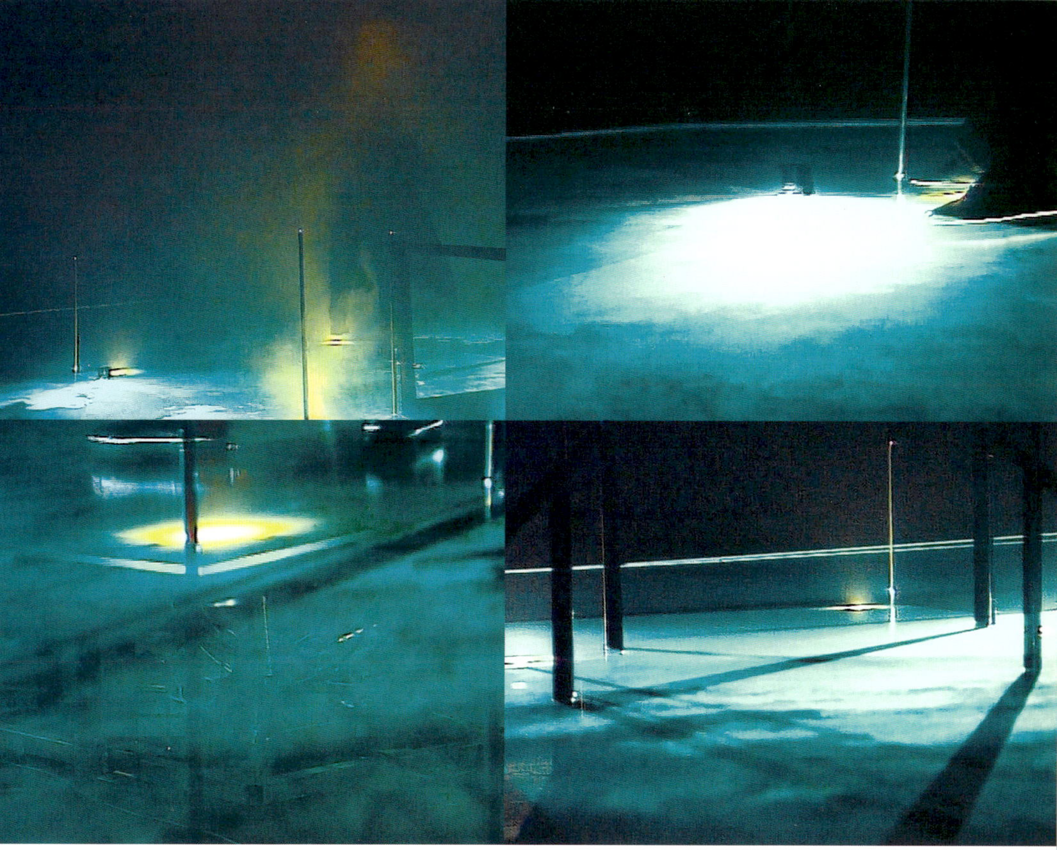

A “lake of light” generated by two Argon lasers shifting with the visitor’s position on a balance platform.

This page:
TAT, Theater am Turm, Frankfurt
Previous pages:
Tochoji Auditorium, Tokyo

DOWNLIGHTS

1999
www.christian-moeller.com/down_lights
Petrobras Exhibition of Virtual Reality, Centro Cultural Candido Mendes, Rio de Janeiro, Brasil
In collaboration with: Jytte Basler

Curator: Rejanne Spitz
Producer: Raquel Francois
Costume design: Monika Heinisch

In 1999 an invitation arrived from Rio de Janeiro to participate in an event focusing on "artificial spaces". At this point I had grown a bit tired of realtime computer graphics, and so together with Jytte Basler I designed a quite minimalist performance for costumes with interior lighting. The core idea was to bring a light source unnaturally close to the performers, one emanating from them and illuminating the entire space. This would produce a strange artificiality and the transformation of an otherwise completely unstructured space into an "alien world". For this exhibition we created a window-display and then placed 6 actresses, separated from the spectators by a pane of glass, and choreographed a sequence of repetitious movements.

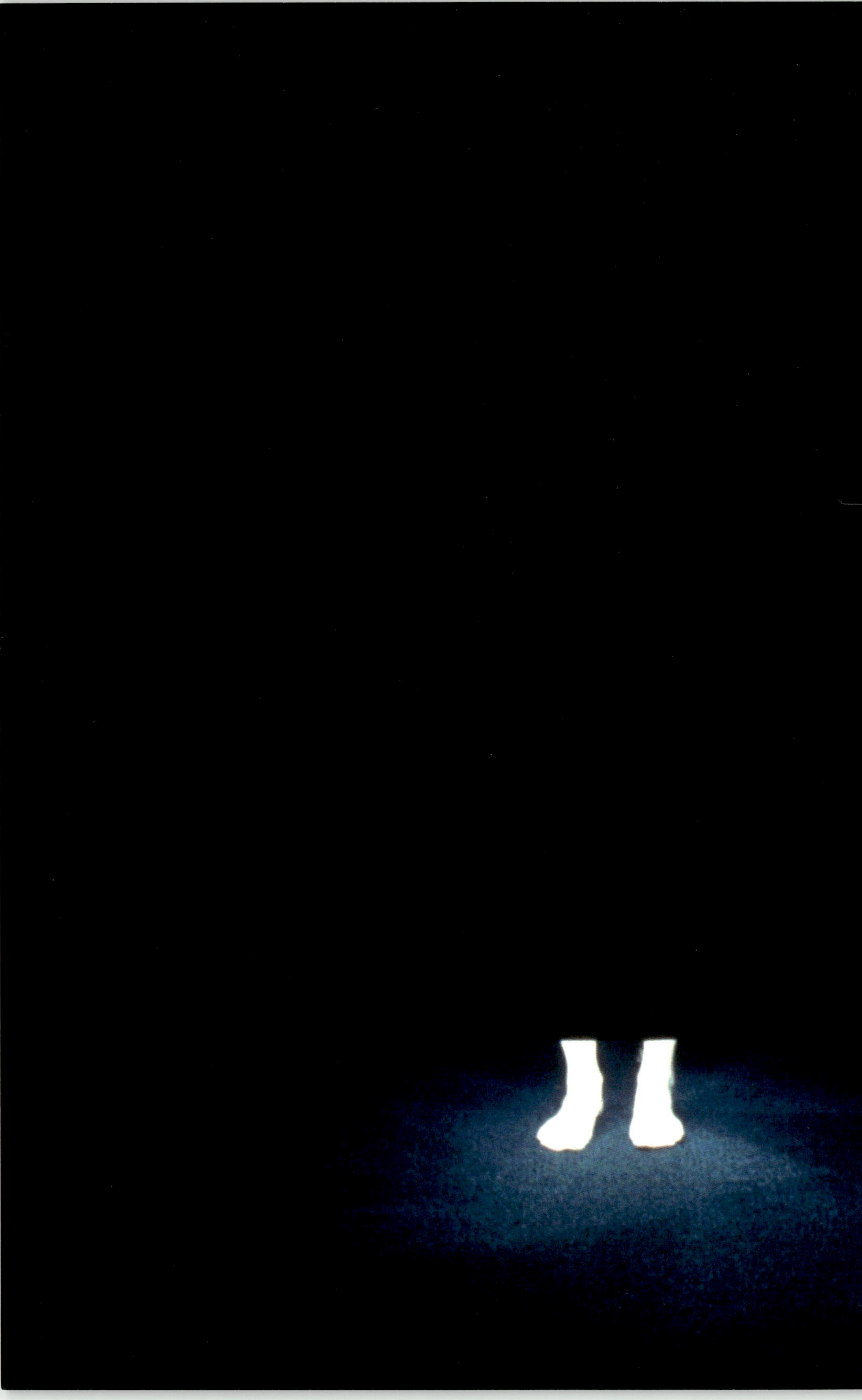

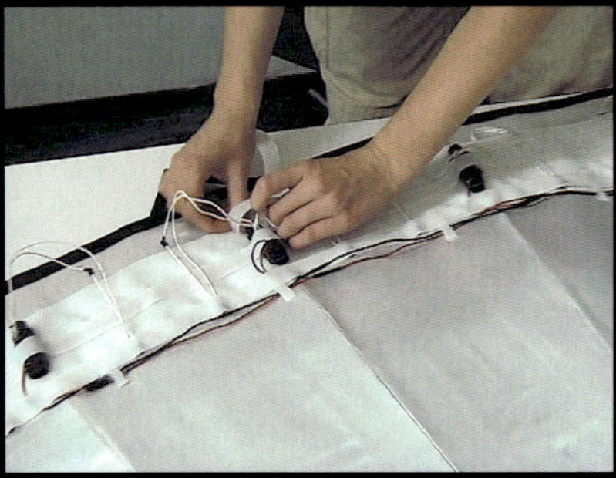

Costumes illuminated from inside by fluorescent lights.

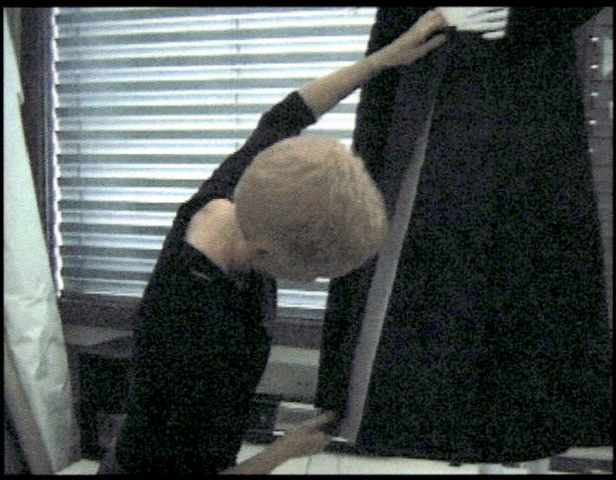

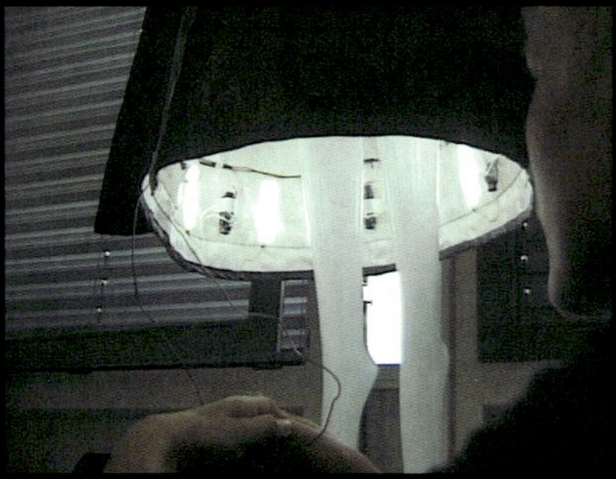

www.christian-moeller.com/down_lights

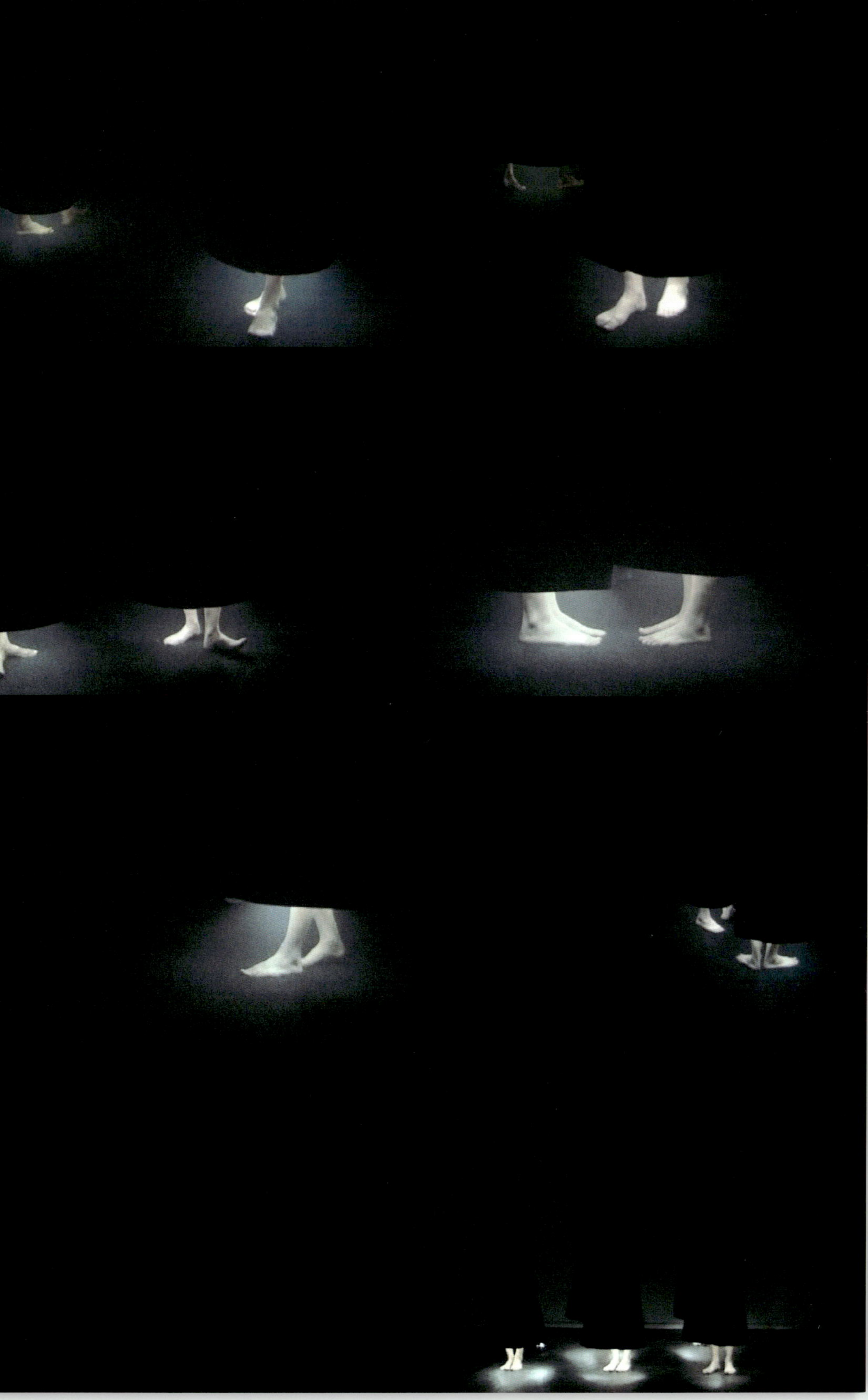

STATIONS OF THE IMAGE

1993
www.christian-moeller.com/stations_of_the_image
Kapitel III, Karmeliter Kloster, Frankfurt
In collaboration with: Stephan Morgenstern

Curator: Klaus Klemp
Programming: Daniel Schmitt

Stations of the Image took place in the Carmelite Monastery in Frankfurt, surely one of the most historically important buildings in the city. The precious frescoes in the cloister of that monastery prevented the walls themselves from being used for exhibition purposes. My intention nevertheless was to mount a photography exhibition in the cloister and to design an appropriate display system.

Starting from the perspective of a helicopter above the city from which you see the high-rise skyline, Stephan Morgenstern photographed the city of Frankfurt for me. From this perspective on high, the photographs zoomed down into the city's social hot spots.

The display was such that the images followed one another in linear sequence. As the viewer moves back and forth in front of this display, he walks through a sequence of points to which particular images have been assigned and these correspondingly appear on the monitor the moment he passes those stations.

With the use of ultrasound, these points are measured as the distance between the viewer and the monitor. The viewer travels through the city from the skyscrapers of the banking center of Frankfurt into the abyss of the impoverished peripheral groups of drug addicts and homeless people, a theme that preoccupied Morgenstern at the time.

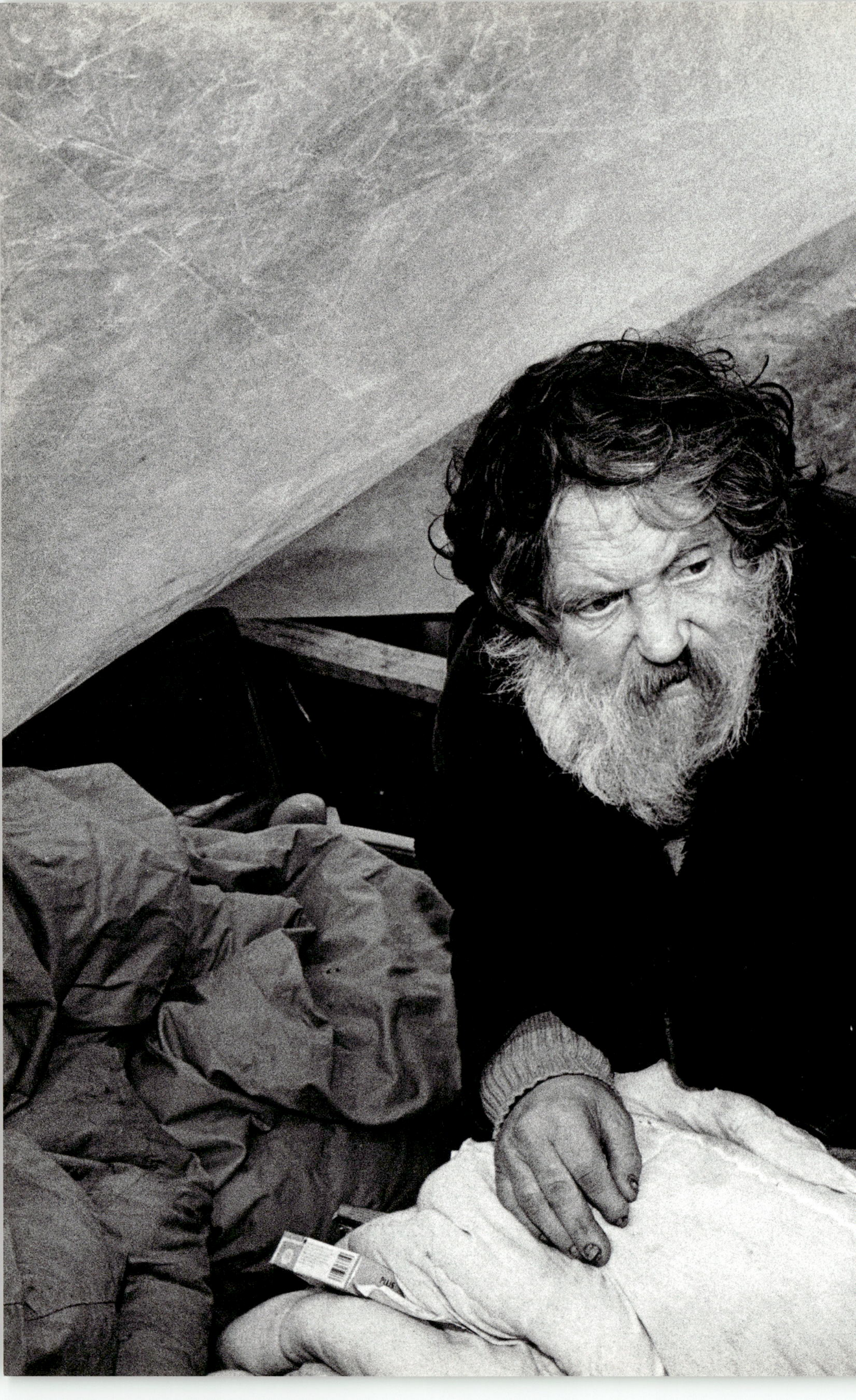

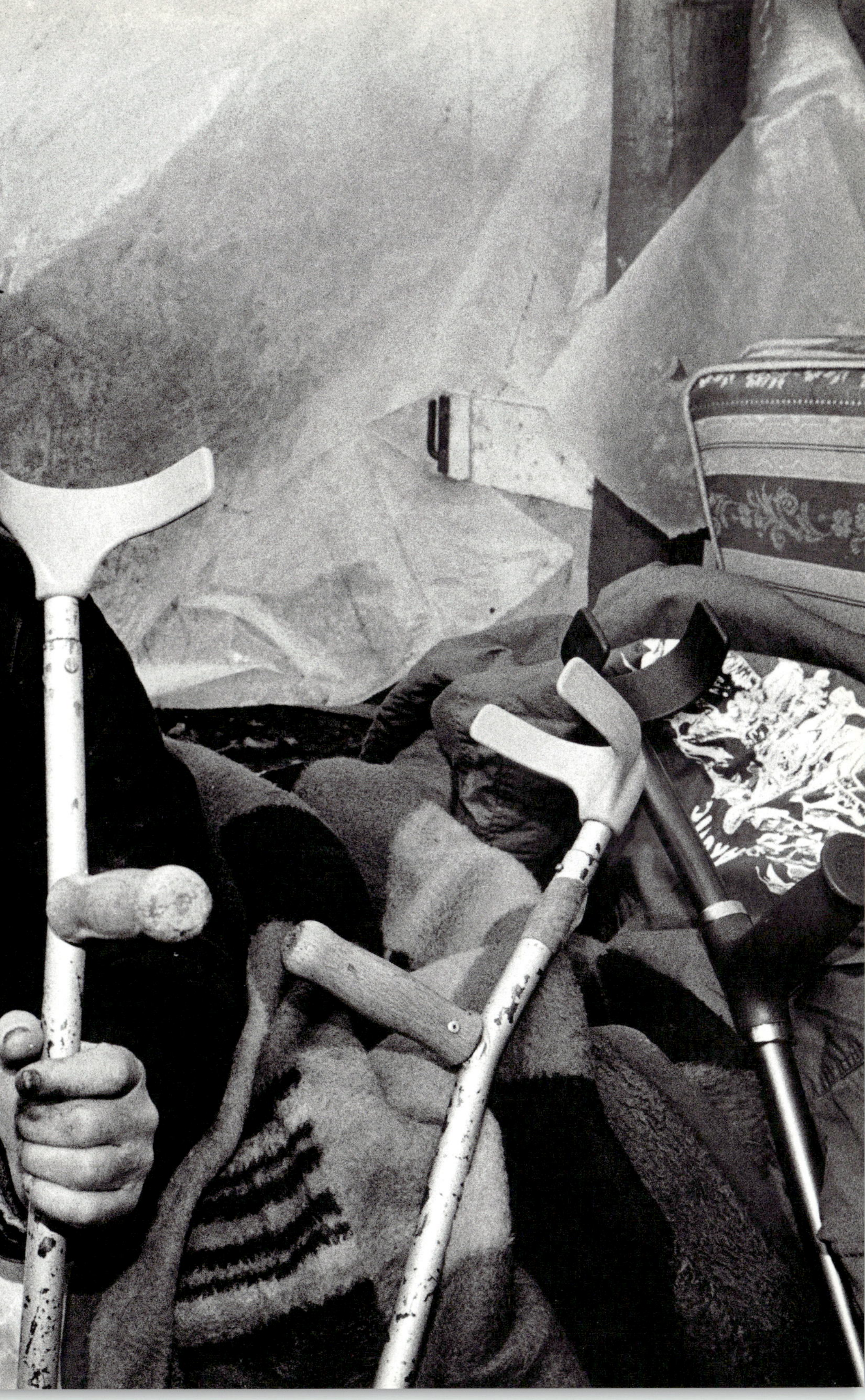

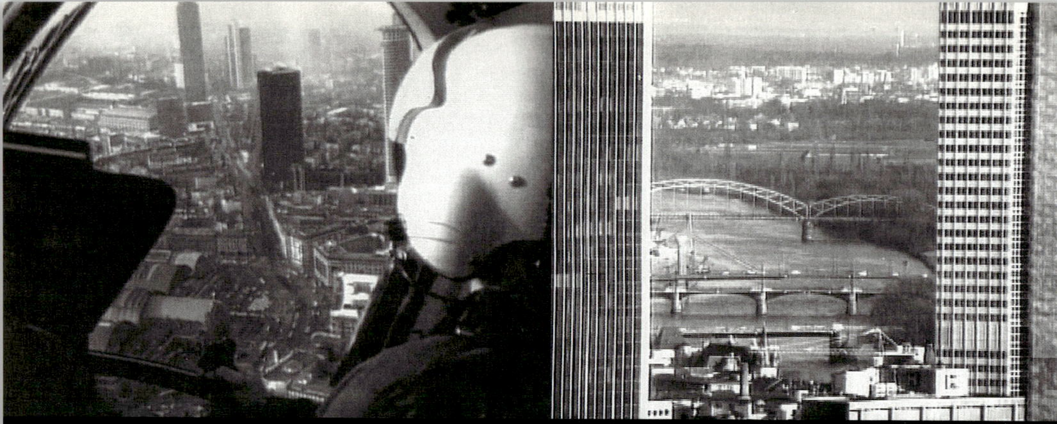

www.christian-moeller.com/stations_of_the_image

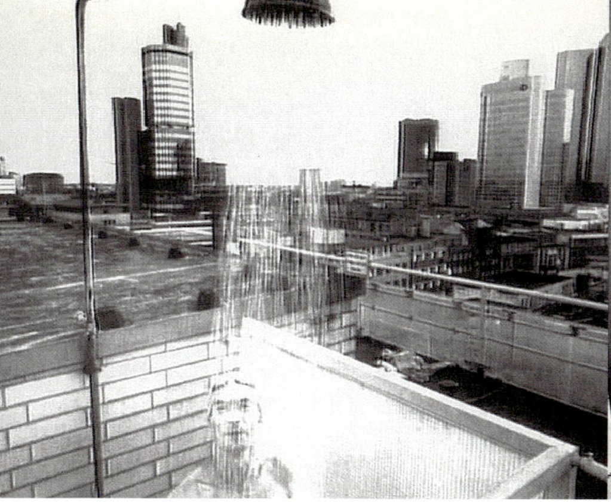

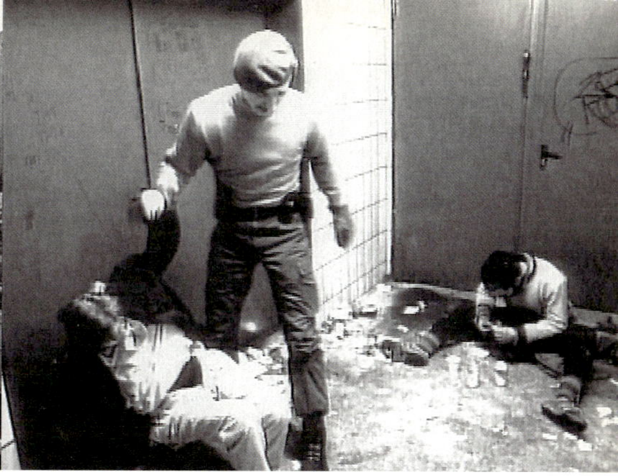

An ultrasound sensor controls
the video images according to the
viewer's distance.

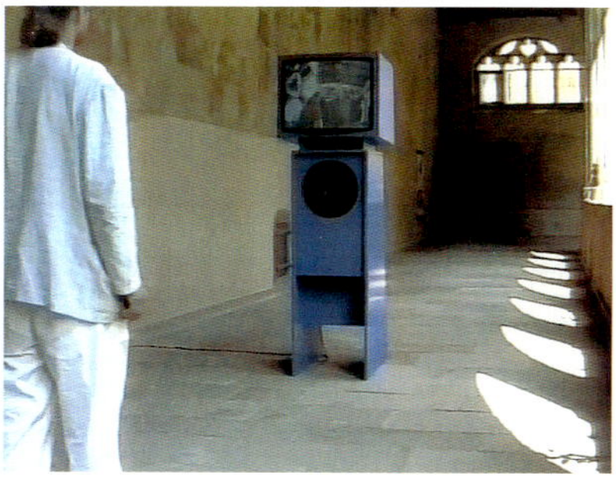

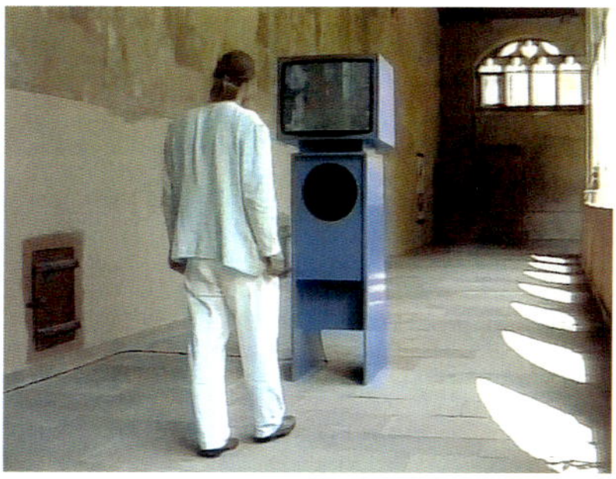

CHRONOLYZE

1993
www.christian-moeller.com/chronolyze
Intermedienschauplatz Lindentunnel, Berlin

Curator: Wolfgang Watzlaw
Video projection: SVV, Hans Walchhofer
Programming: Daniel Schmitt and Sven Thöne
Sensor electronics: Siemens AG, ASI/Gerätewerk Amberg

The project was made possible with the kind support of the Preussischer Kulturbesitz Image Archive, the Berlin Municipal Archives, the Berlin Aerial Photograph Archives.

Chronolyze is a similar photography exhibition concept realized in the Lindentunnel a few years after the fall of the Berlin Wall. This subway tunnel has an interesting history. It was built in 1914 under Kaiser Wilhelm II, not so much for technical purposes, for the simple reason that at the time no one could envisage a mechanical construction like a streetcar clattering across the urban landscape. The tunnel was built primarily for aesthetic reasons, to avoid the sight of tracks and streetcars in this highly symbolic part of the city known as "Unter den Linden."

The streetcar track system above the ground was destroyed during the war, but the tunnel remained and, largely unnoticed, served many and various other purposes. The Stasi (GDR secret service) is said to have had a surveillance operations here for years, and later the tunnel was used by the Maxim Gorki Theater for storing stage-sets. After the fall of the Berlin Wall, it was rediscovered and attempts were made to establish an exhibition venue there for Electronic Art. I was one of the first artists to have an opportunity to mount an exhibition in this unusual place.

What might come immediately to the mind of any designer involved in an installation project in a tunnel is the theme of a "time tunnel". Inspired by this idea, we tracked down very interesting black-and-white photographs of the destruction of the city during the war. These photographs were taken without permission during the last years of the war by local citizens. Private persons were prohibited from documenting the ruins of their homes and the destruction of their own cities. These photographs, confiscated by the authorities, were kept in an East German archive, which gave us permission to use them for this exhibition.

Chronolyze consisted of two projection areas, opposite one another and a portal, the "time gate", which served as an interface at the center of the installation. Written on the floor of the portal were the years "1933" through "1946." Visitors would walk through the year of their choosing, and thereby call up the associated images on the projection areas in front of and behind them, walking through the decline of a city step by step. We all know what Berlin looked like before the war. We have all seen film footage and photographs of the traffic on Friedrichstrasse in the 1920s and 30s. And everyone knows what Berlin looked like at the end of the Nazi regime in 1945: a heap of rubble. We all have those images in our minds, and of course we know what Berlin looks like today. But in between there were other images of the banality of everyday life in wartime. These images surprise us, the generation who did not have to experience those times. For example, in a picture of one of the first bomb sites in the city center we see a charred roof on an otherwise undamaged house built around the turn of the century. All the windows in the neighbouring buildings are broken, shattered by a bomb's huge blast wave. This picture shows a scene of a crowd gathered in the early hours; some are looking on and talking, others selling hot sausages, and there are craftsmen repairing the broken windows. In these touching images from a city center that, three years later, would no longer exist, the atmosphere seems almost festive.

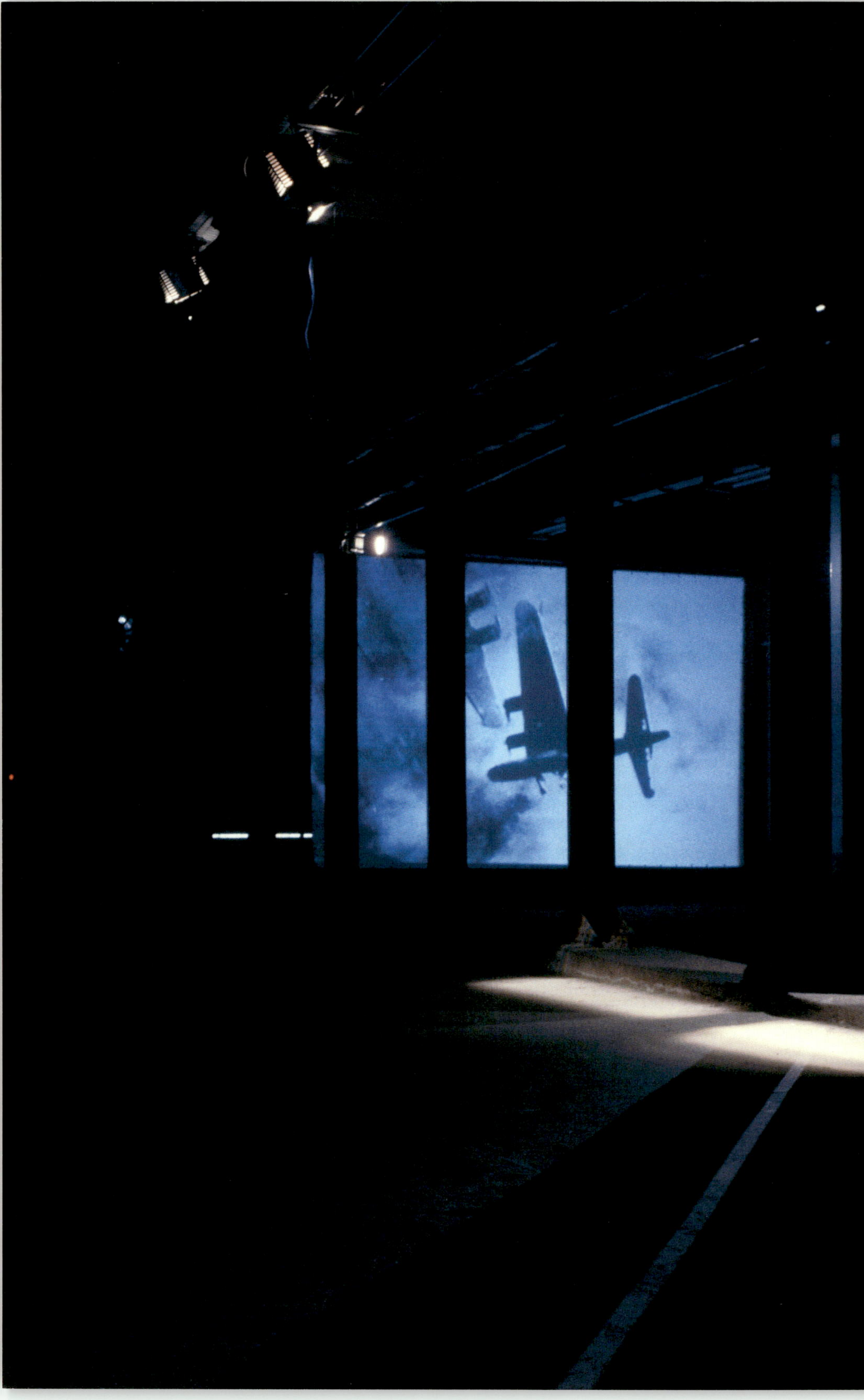

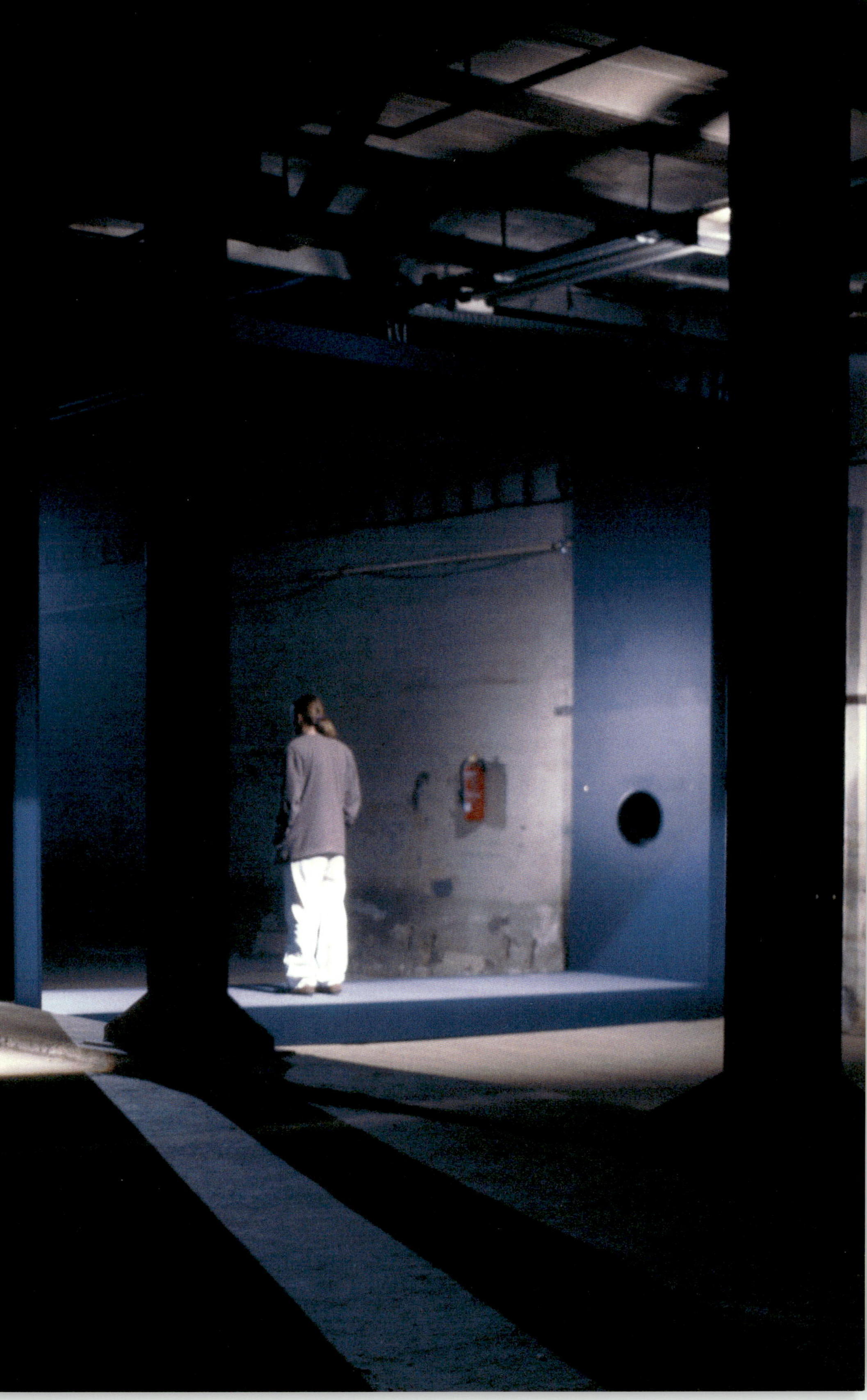

BACKBONE

1996
www.christian-moeller.com/backbone
Wunschmaschine Welterfindung, Kunsthalle Vienna, Object Video,
Landesmuseum Oberösterreich, Linz
In collaboration with: Herbert Lachmayer

Curator (Vienna): Brigitte Felderer
Curator (Linz): Gottfried Hattinger
Programming: Sven Thöne
Hardware: Hermann Gruber
Mechanical engineering and construction: Werner Raczkövi
Production: Archimedia Institute for Arts and Technology,
University for Art and Industrial Design, Linz, Austria

Another installation of images in stacked sequence was “Backbone”.
It was about man’s inventions, but instead of focusing on how “great” the invented thing is in itself, the interest was in how the inventor imagined the world that was supposed to need his invention in the first place. When Bell invented the telephone, he did not envisage it as a world-embracing communications medium, but rather as an instrument with which one could comfortably “attend” an opera remotely from home.

One section of the exhibition dealt with inventions based on human anatomy: exoskeletons, ancient prostheses, robots, and mechanical dolls.

At the time of this exhibition the “Visible Man” project was the talk of the town. As you will recall, this was a remarkable and controversial series of images of a dead body, frozen in a blue gelatine block at 70 degrees Celsius, from which 1820 one millimeter thick slices were cut. The aim of the Visible Man project was to produce the ultimate anatomical atlas of the human body.

Each of the sections of the body was photographed and digitized at a high resolution. Into the sequence of the real pictorial layers the third dimension was then added electronically as the respective intermediate space, so as to produce a three-dimensional model of the human body. This project could only be worthwhile if the corpse in question was of ideal average size and free of obvious ailments. For example, a person whose skull was shattered in a traffic accident or someone who died of a kidney ailment would not have been suitable. The subject was to be no less than six feet tall, not too skinny, but also not over-weight; an average citizen who would die for no other reason than a “good cause”. In Huntsville, Texas, a candidate was found on death row. In August 1993, Joseph Paul Jernigan was executed. On the same day his remains were flown to the Health and Science Center of the University of Colorado, Denver, where he was cut into slices and photographed, starting at his feet. The ethical premise raised by such a project still seems questionable enough to me for a work to be based on its consideration.

For my installation, I projected a linear sequence of large format images of the anatomic sections onto a movable screen mounted on the ceiling of the Kunsthalle. A machine slowly moves across the gallery space, and reveals one by one the sections visible according to their relative position in the body over an expanse of 15 meters. What emerged, traced in air, was the virtual figure of the corpse of Paul Jernigan, hovering above the exhibition.

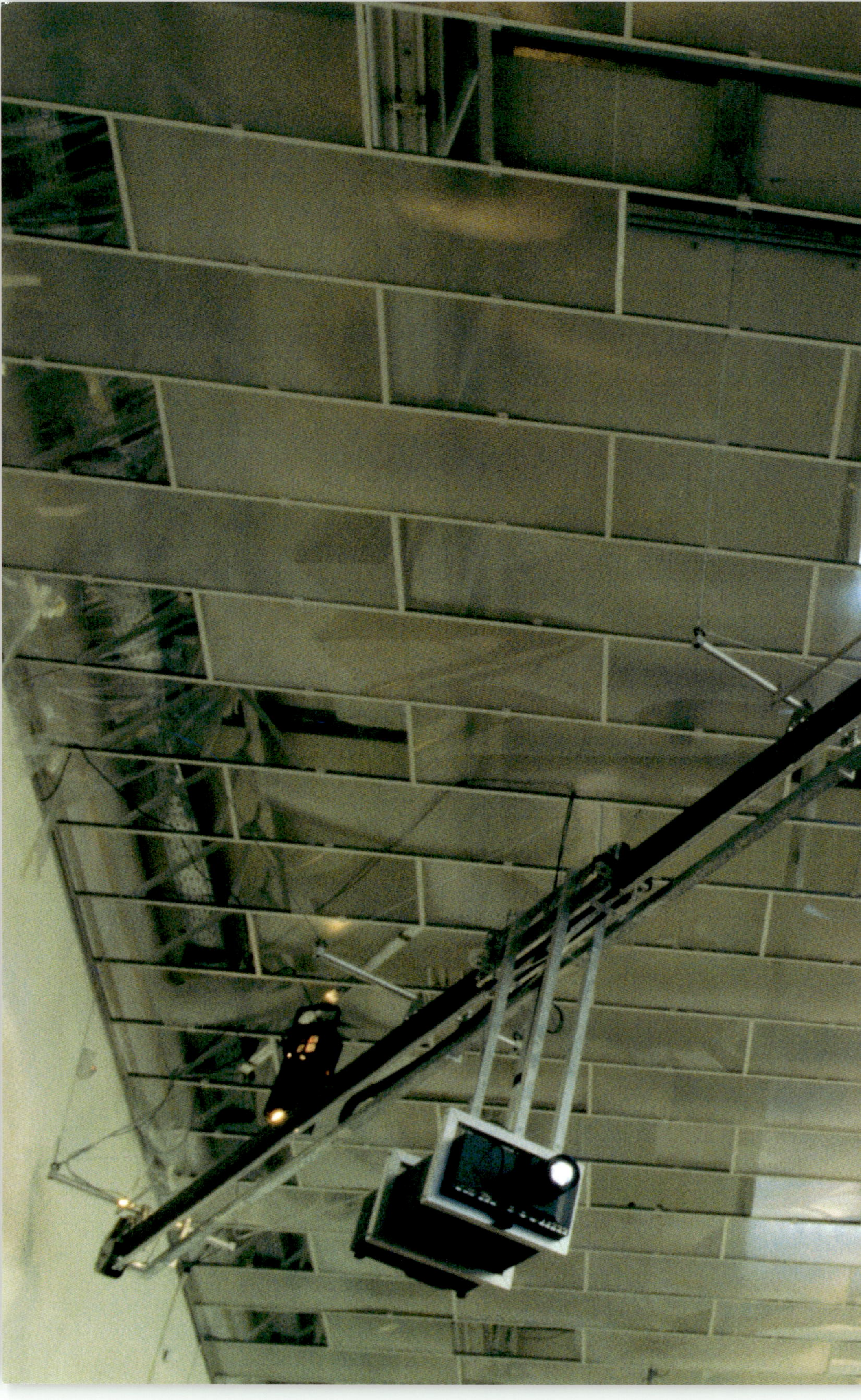

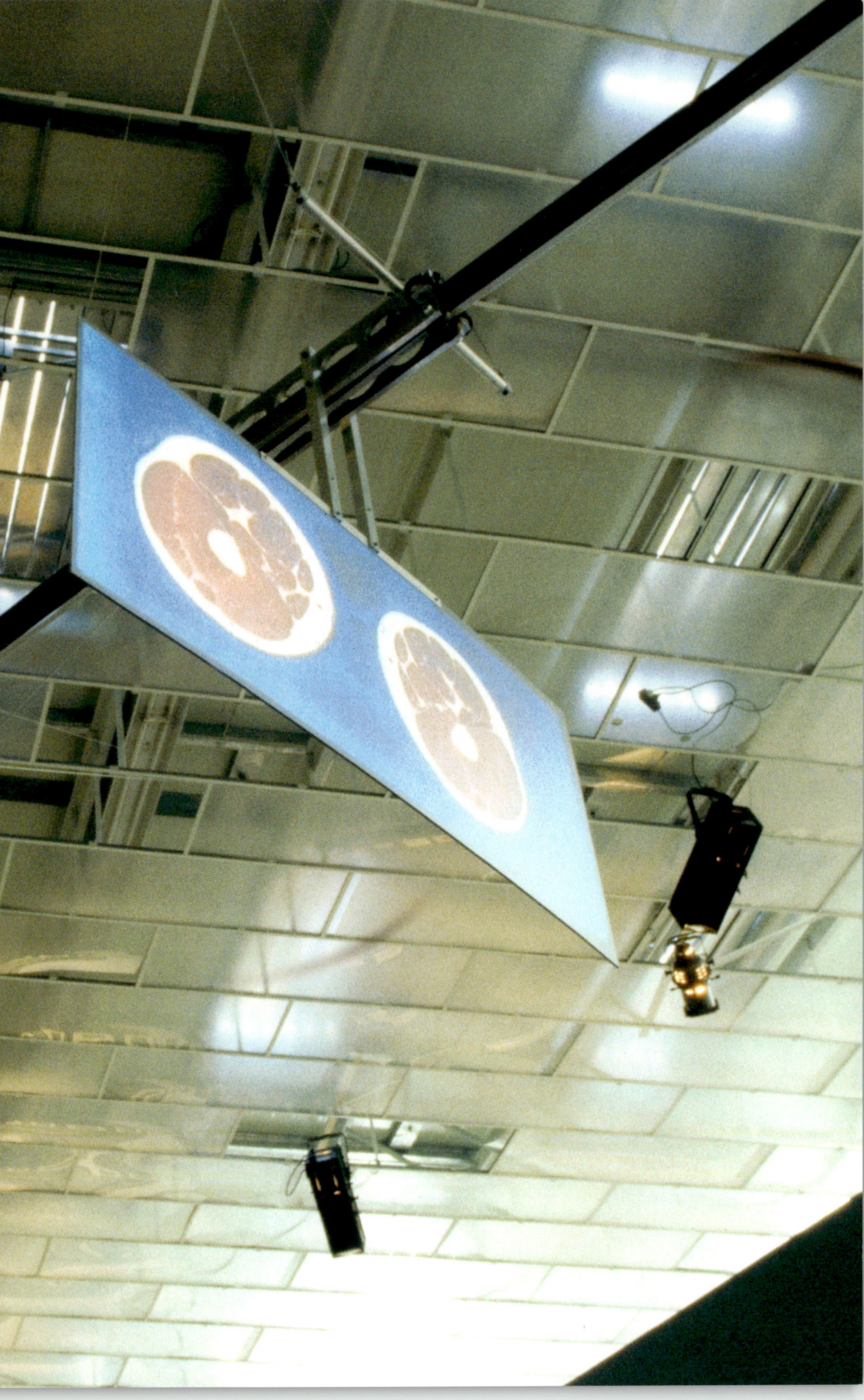

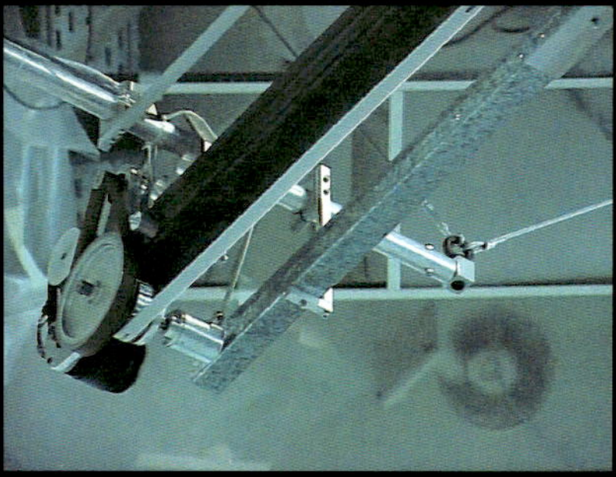

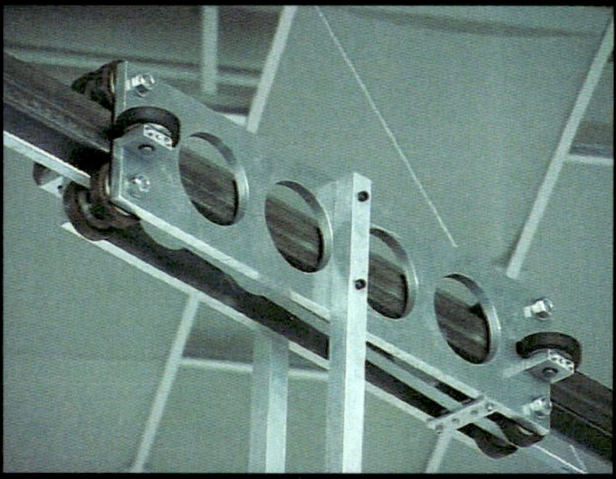

Mechanical details of the mobile screen's guiding system.

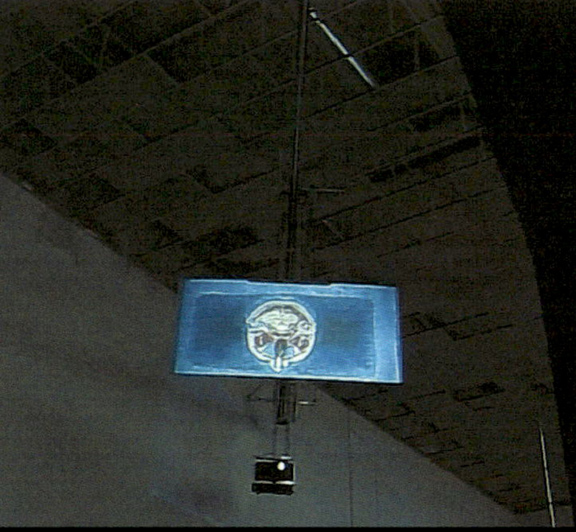

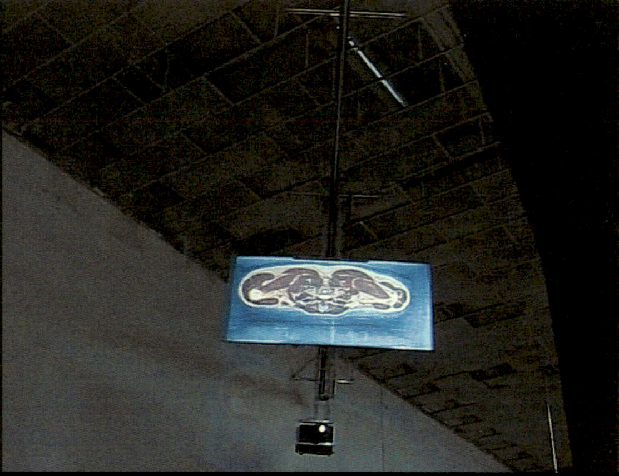

The screen moves through the exhibition space, tracing the anatomical slices according their positions in the virtual body.

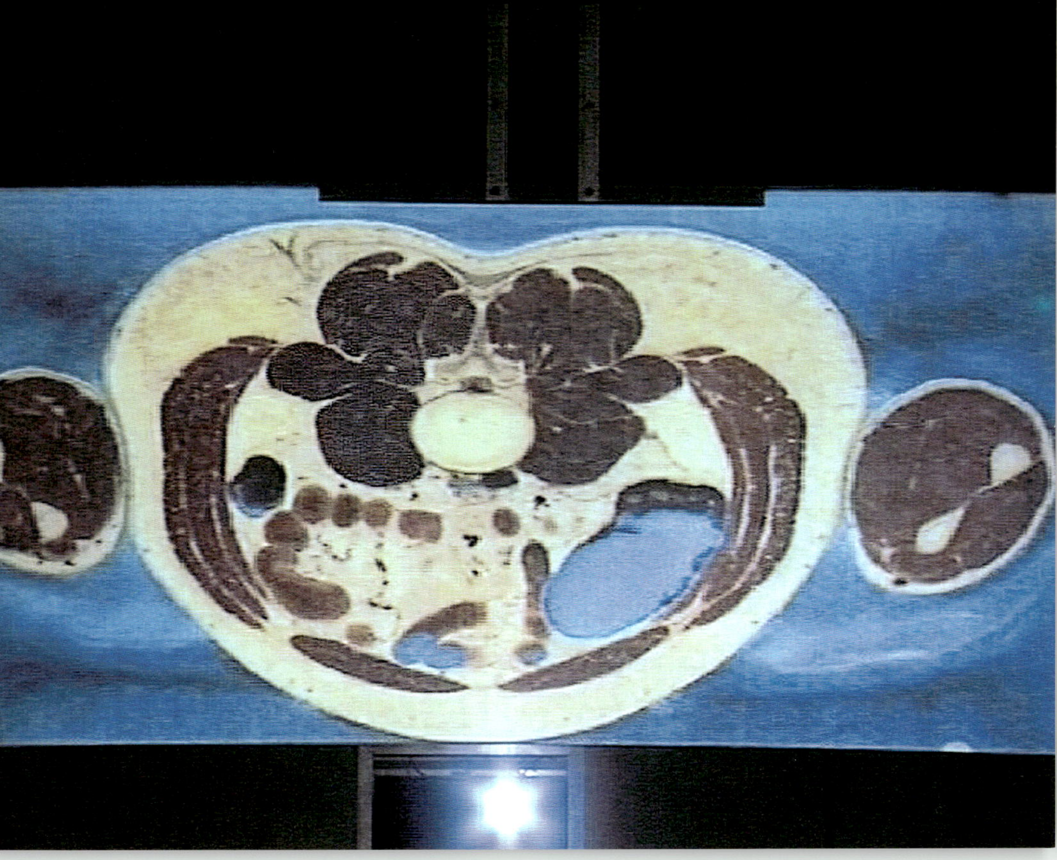

TINTORETTO

1996

www.christian-moeller.com/tintoretto

Archimedia Institute for Arts and Technology, University for Art and Industrial Design, Linz, Austria
In collaboration with: Maurizo Seracini, Herbert Lachmayer and J. E. Weidinger

Programming: Edith Spiegl
Hardware: Hermann Gruber

One more project exploring the dynamics of layering was "Tintoretto, The Third Dimension of Ritratto di Gentiloumo". This work was commissioned by the art historian and collector, J. E. Weidinger as a contribution to an exhibition about restoration techniques at the Kunsthistorisches Museum Vienna.
This work was based on the visual results of research by Florentine scientist Maurizio Seracini. On display there were very important paintings with pictorial layers exposed from beneath the top surface with the aid of X-ray and infrared technology. For example, in taking a look behind Leonardo da Vinci's Virgin and Child with St. Anne**, one could see the lines of the initial drawing in which the artist outlined his figures.**
Seracini performed these examinations with the aim of determining the degree of originality of certain artworks. We know that the successful artists of this time had large studios and employed many people who surely must have contributed to the works. Whether this is really an important insight is an open question, but these "backgrounds," revealed by this "archaeology of the pictorial layers" are in any case very interesting.
For my project, in addition to the original painting by Tinoretto, a virtual replica was made, the same size as the original. The surface of the picture was sensitive to touch and the visitors to the exhibition were able to "erase" their way through to the layers "behind" the painting by hand.

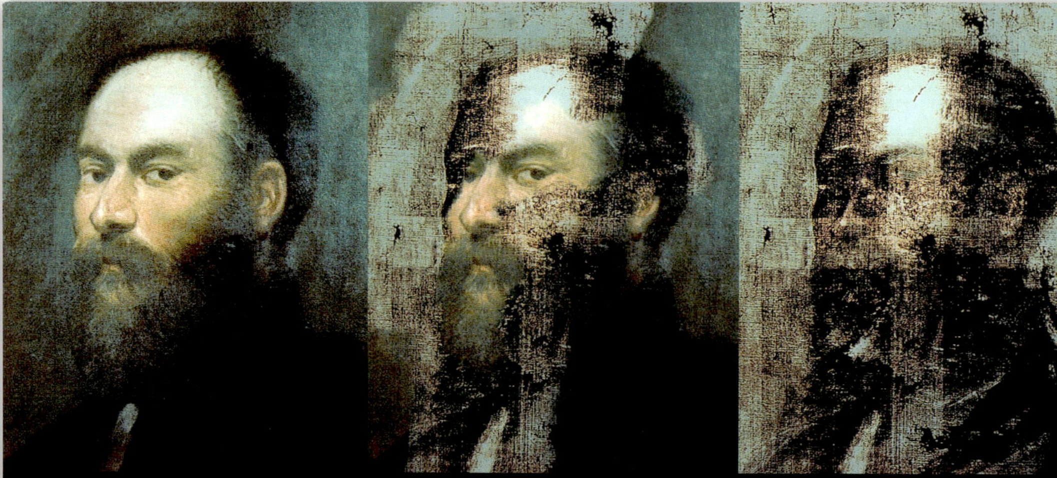

Touching the image exposes hidden layers beneath the surface of the painting.

www.christian-moeller.com/tintoretto

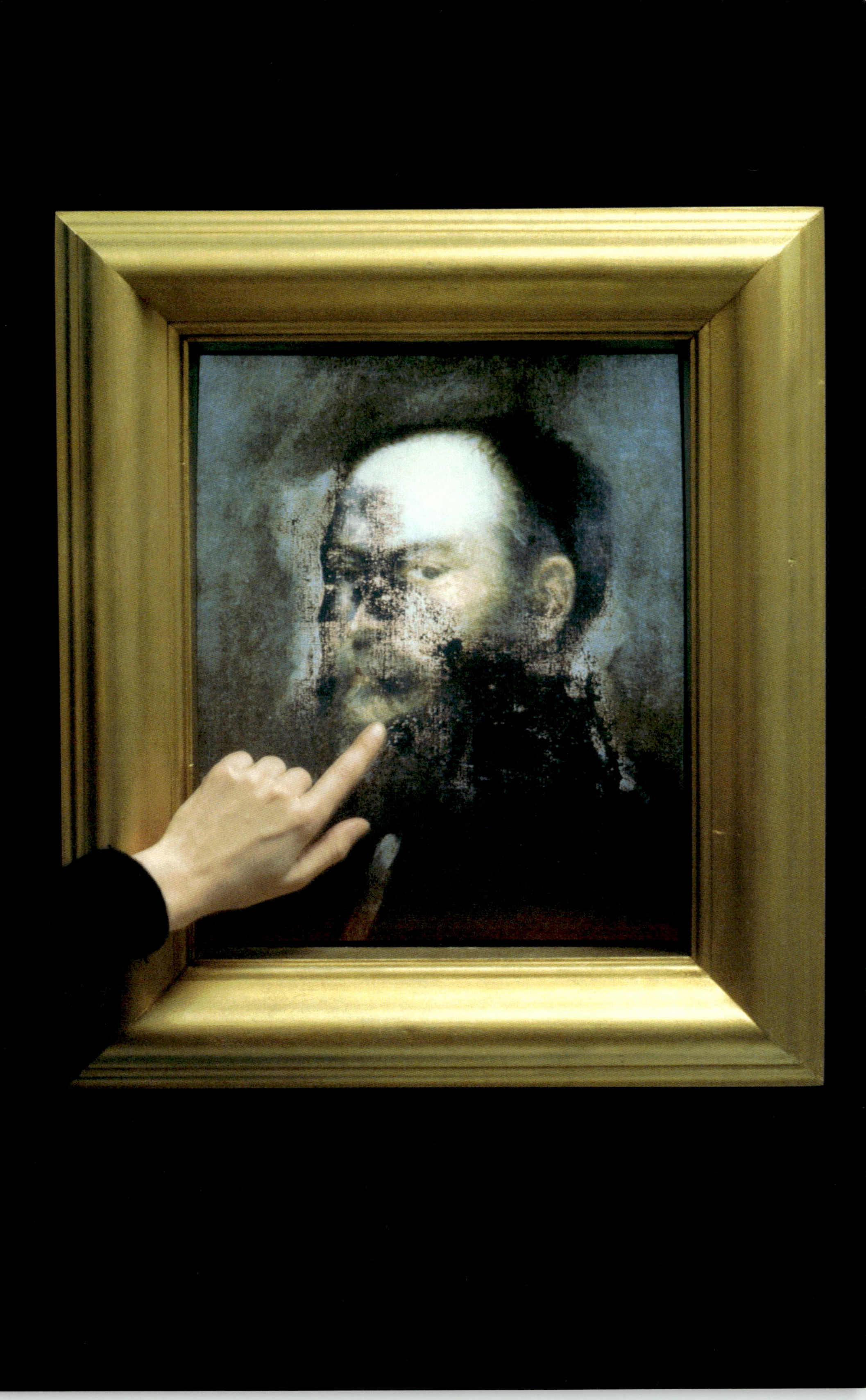

A-LINE

1991
www.christian-moeller.com/a_line
Off TAT (Theater am Turm) Event, subway tunnel, Hauptwache/Eschenheimer Tor, Frankfurt/Main
In collaboration with: Tom Stromberg

Technical consultant: Klaus Bollinger

"A-Line: Linear Cinematoscope" is an early work dating from 1990, which I started together with my colleague Falk Petry when we were both employed at the Behnisch and Partners Architects office. This project used a sequence of images, but in this case their presentation was completely analog. The proposal was to set up individual images along the walls of a subway tunnel, which would amount to a kind of flipbook cinema for the passengers as they pass looking out the train track window.
Together with Tom Stromberg, the director of the Theater am Turm in Frankfurt, we attempted an installation in a particularly suitable section of the underground tunnel between Eschenheimer Tor and Hauptwache. Instead of the usual single tube, two trains travel past one another in the same tunnel, separated only by a row of supports. The plan was to hang "shutter panels" in the openings between these supports. Each of these panels would have two narrow vertical slit openings which would allow the passing viewer a kind of stroboscopic view of each individual image on the tunnel wall opposite. At a speed of about 60 km per hour, the individual images would appear to be set in cinematic motion.
During the planning phase we used rotating image drums with the help of an endoscope, with which we could simulate the view from the perspective of the passengers. We needed these preliminary tests in order to be able to optimize the relationship between the width of the slits in the shutter panels and the quantity of light we had to project onto the images.
Unfortunately the installation could not be realized. The financing had been secured with the TAT and the city officials were enthusiastic. We got the project off to a very good start when the decisive opposition came from the director of the underground railway authority. His reservations were that by upgrading the underground tunnels in this way, young people might be inspired to spray graffiti on the pictures, and the possible danger of an accident was a responsibility they could not accept. This argument was difficult to refute. I'm quite sure today that young people would have gone in and done exactly that, but whether or not they would have been run over is another question.

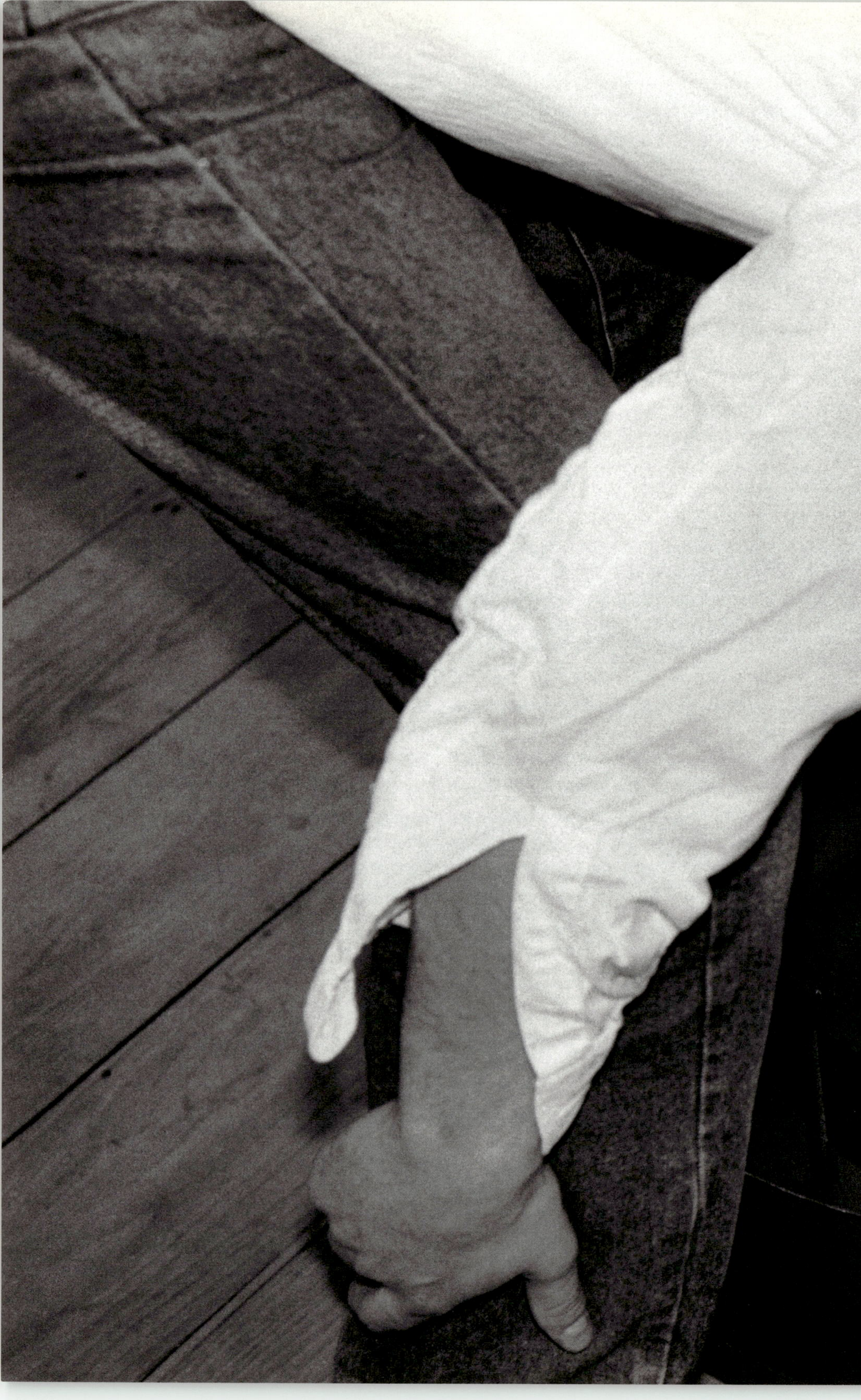

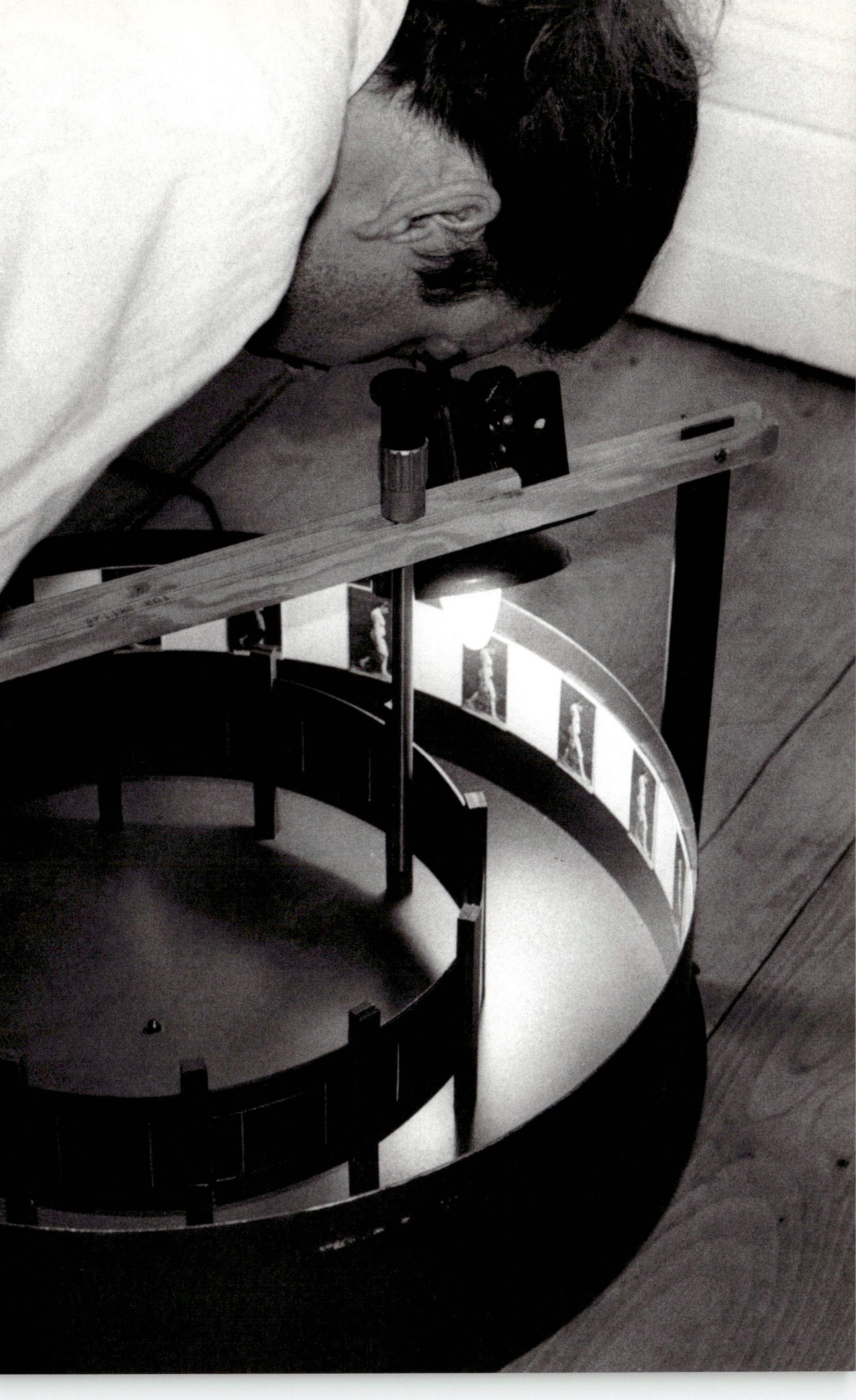

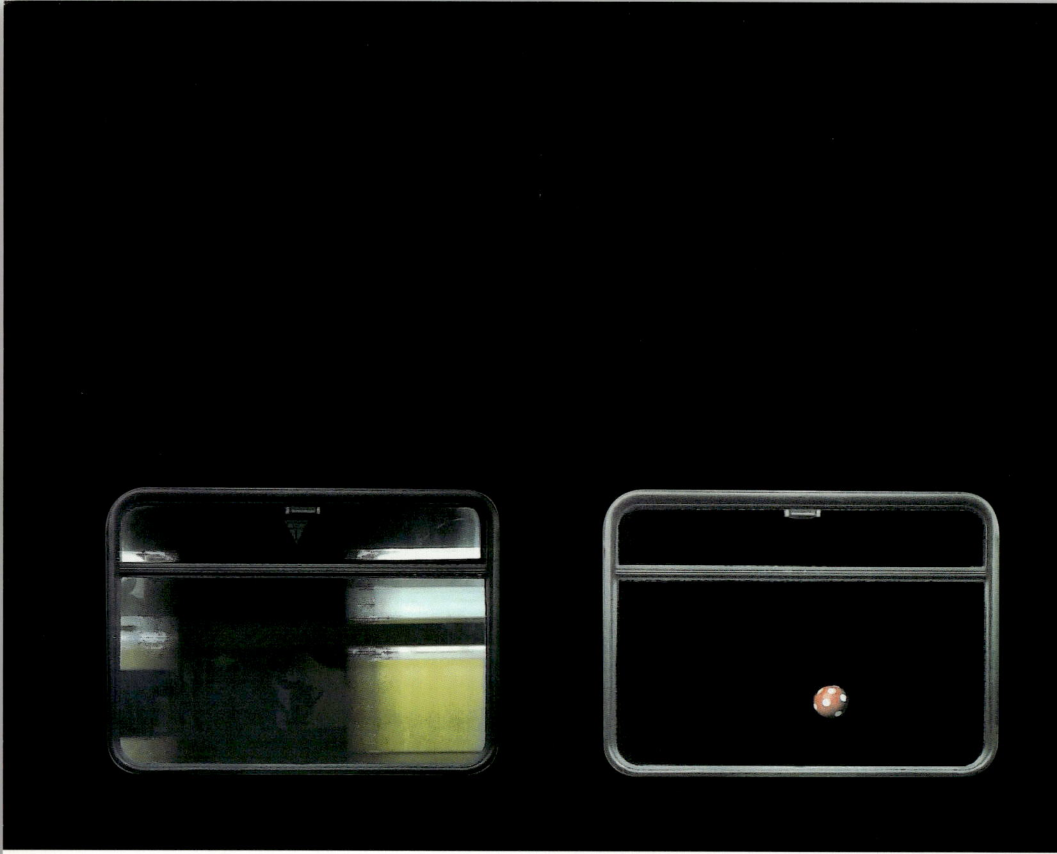

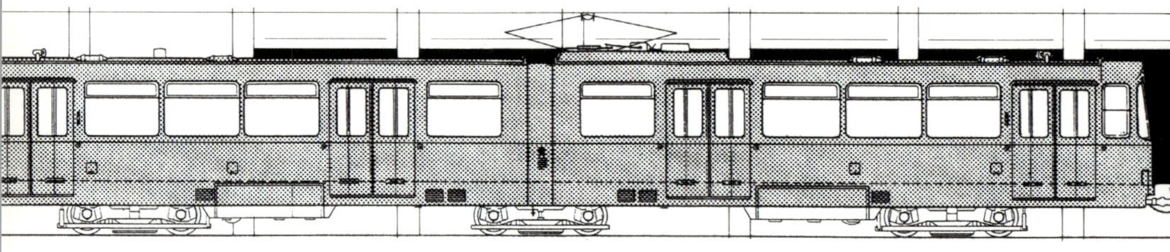

www.christian-moeller.com/a_line

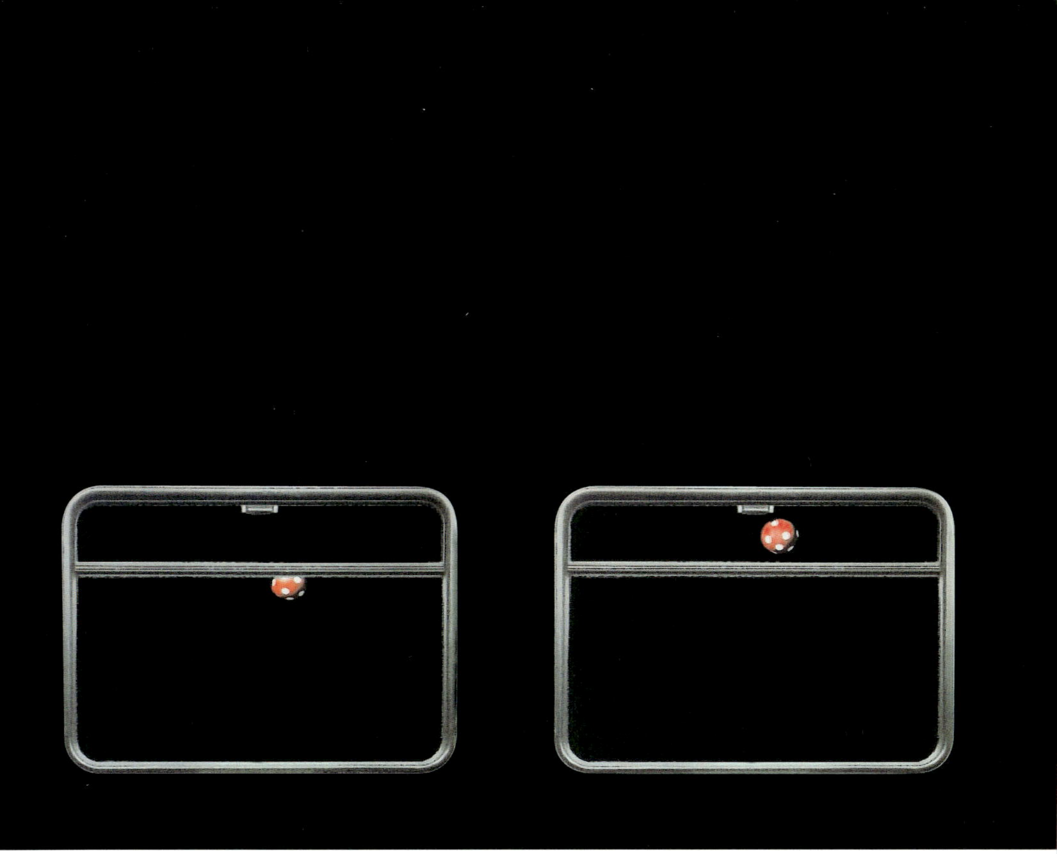

Wall mounted images turn into
an animation as the viewer passes
by train.

Like a zoetrope unrolled, wall mounted
images are installed behind a layer of
shutter panels.

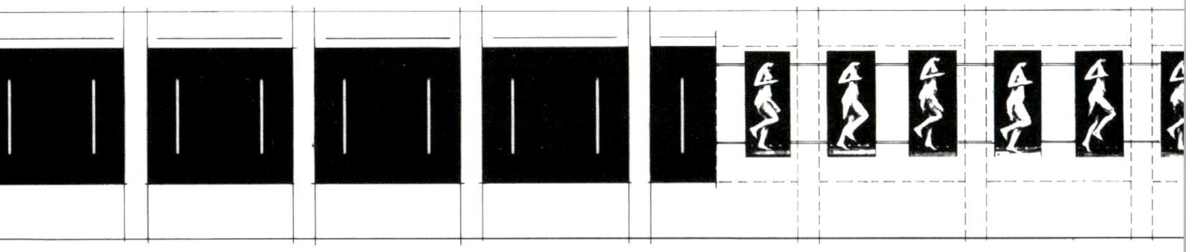

KINETIC LIGHT SCULPTURE

1992
www.christian-moeller.com/kinetic_light_sculpture
Zeilgalerie, Frankfurt/Main
In collaboration with: Rüdiger Kramm and Axel Strigl

Programming: Gideon May
Light design: Christian Bartenbach
Architecture: Kramm & Strigl
Developer: Jürgen Schneider

The “Kinetic Light Sculpture” is an important project from the early stages of my work with electronic media. The year was 1992, and the location was the façade of the Zeilgalerie, a new mall on Frankfurt’s main shopping street. I had met the architect, Rüdiger Kramm, at the metal construction company MBM in Möckmühl. My floor-interface for the installation “Space (Im)Balance” was almost finished and the owner of the company, Peter Müller, invited Rüdiger Kramm and myself to a preliminary inspection of the work and introduced us. Kramm was working on a light installation for the façade of his new building and was looking for the definitive artistic concept for it. Just like that, I received what was then the largest commission yet in my still young career.

We decided to control the constantly changing transparency and color of the resulting light façade by a weather station on the roof of the new building. The façade consisted of a color cluster on the wall varying in position and size, and a horizontal spectrum in the form of a white linear diagram on the upper third of the installation surface. In front of the building, there was a second façade layer made of folded perforated metal panels. In the space between the two layers, 120 HQI spotlights were mounted on catwalks. Each spotlight had a movable lid which we could control by computer in order to vary the emerging light tones from yellow to blue. The data from the weather station on the roof provided us with the outside air temperature, wind speed, wind direction, humidity, and the intensity of the daylight. Outdoor microphones were installed behind the metal screen to pick up ambient sounds from the street. We used the temperature as a parameter for determining the amount of color on the wall. At 0 degree Celsius, the wall was monochrome blue, and as the temperature increased, areas turned yellow. The direction of the wind was responsible for moving these temperature-controlled colors across the wall. The wind in Frankfurt is from a north-easterly direction on 18.2 % of the days of the year, and on 21.6 % of the days, from a south-westerly direction. Believe it or not, there are no other wind directions in Frankfurt, at least according to the meteorological services in Offenbach and at Frankfurt Airport. It turned out that the wind would only blow parallel to the building’s façade, running along our installation either from right to left, or from left to right. We animated the yellow colors across the façade according to the registered wind direction and relative speed. The installation was turned on and off automatically by daylight sensors. At 100 Lux at twilight, the spots went on, and at 20 Lux at dawn, they went off.

At one point during the planning phase, the client asked how long they would be running during the course of a year. A reasonable question, as the likely energy consumption must be calculated, but one that was not easy to answer, and the meteorological office could not help us. So I got the idea of approaching the municipal authority in Frankfurt responsible for having the street lighting turned on and off, and was greatly enlightened. I was surprised to discover that the street lights in the city are still turned on and off manually, and that these times have been registered daily for decades. Without hesitation, the staff at that authority gave me copies of the respective documents relating to the last couple of years. I had

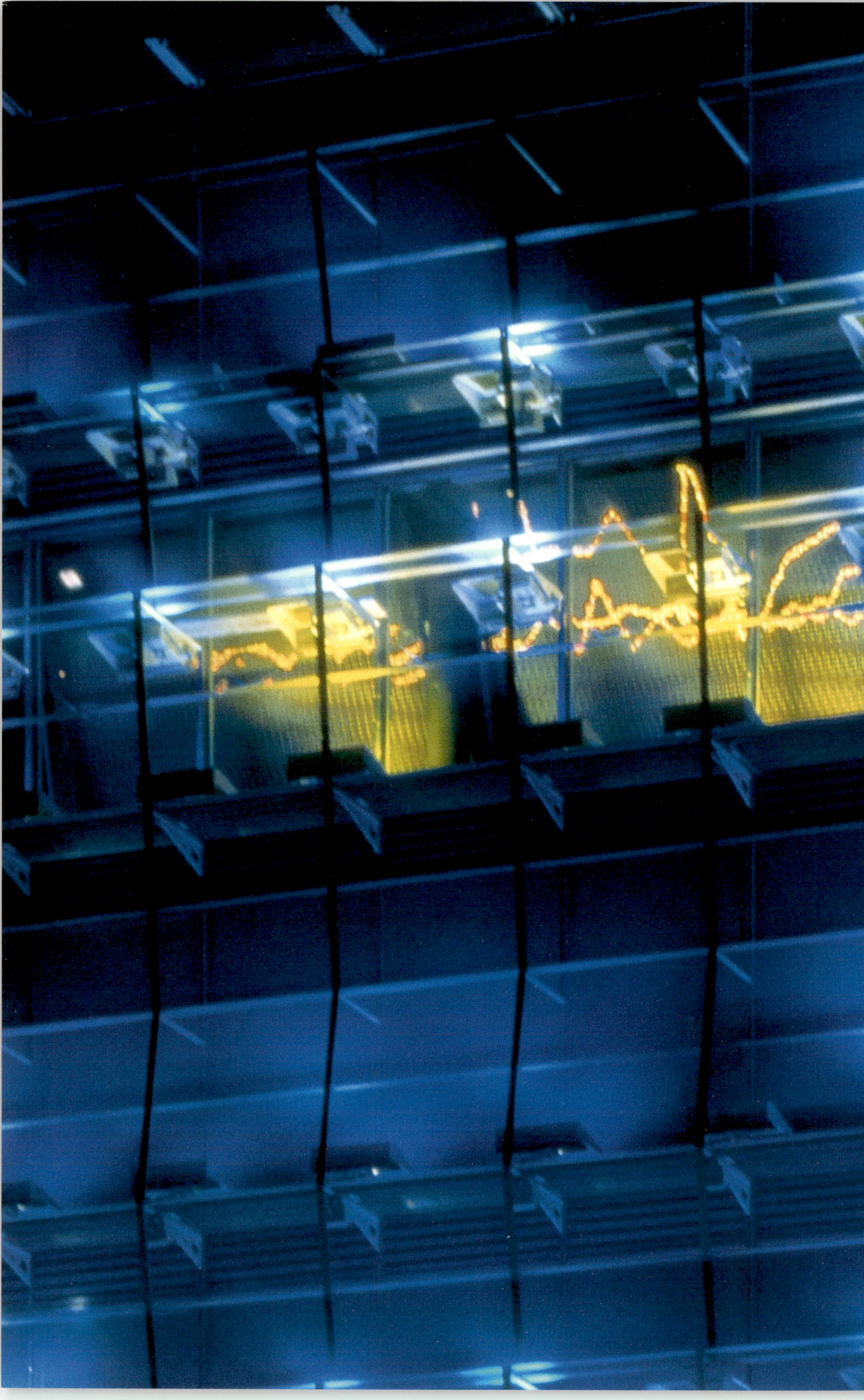

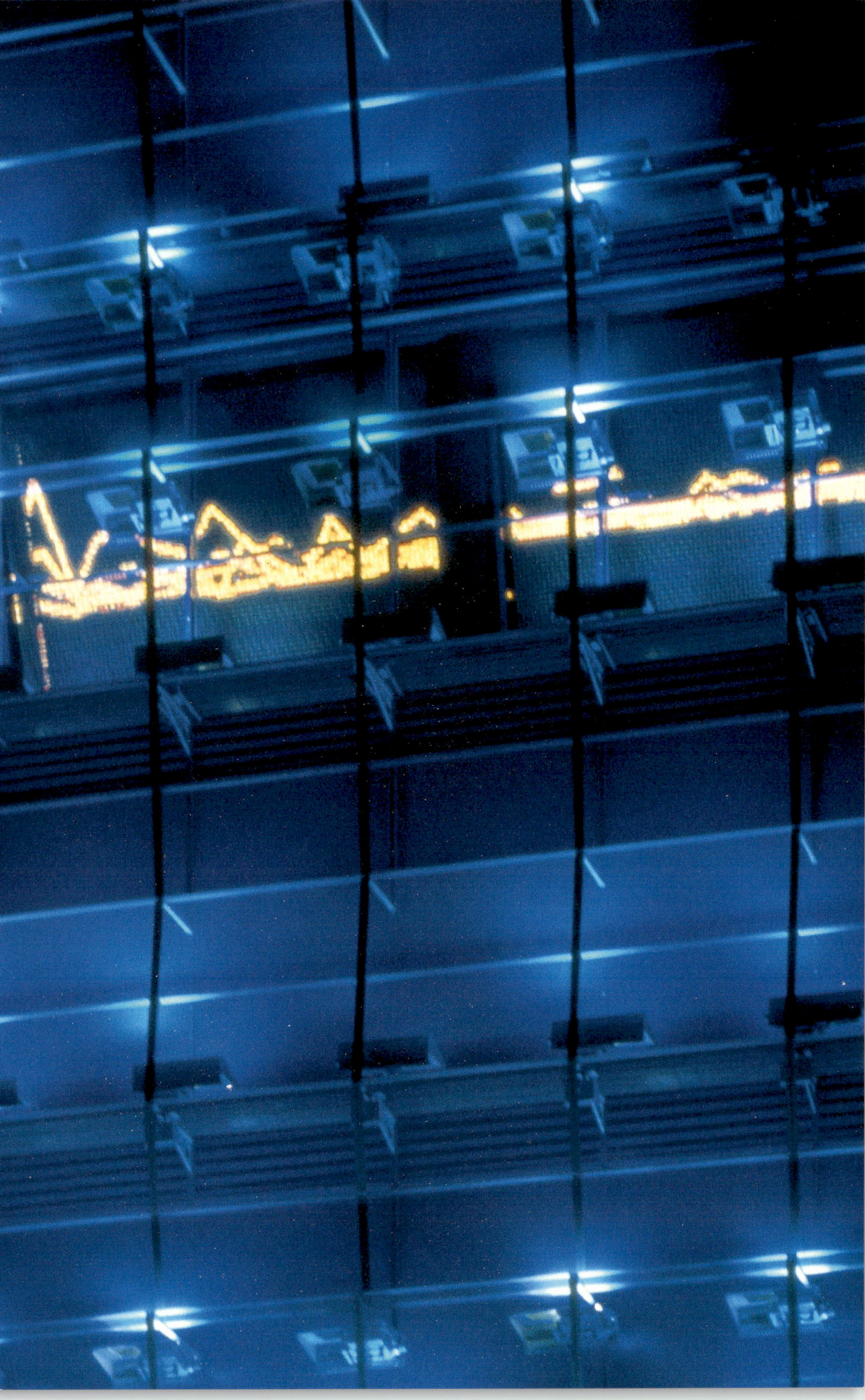

the impression that they were delighted to have finally met someone who was interested in their data. With this in hand, it was easy to outline for the client how long the installation would be lit.
Near the top of the building, we installed a huge LED display measuring 20 meters long and 4 meters high, on which we displayed the oscillating graphical rendering of the ambient sound in the street. This was the first interactive façade installation of this size, and for this alone the developer must be congratulated. Rather than advertising, this display system on the façade of a shopping mall costing millions of DM, showed just a white line moving to the rhythm of the passers-by. A few years later, that same developer, Jürgen Schneider, went bankrupt, causing a scandal of national proportions. The building tycoon was found guilty of fraud and sentenced to jail. He was a fraud, perhaps, but one with a rare appreciation of art, architecture and urban culture.

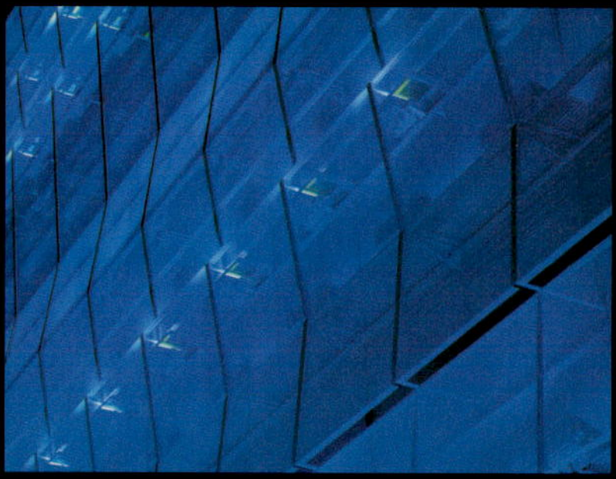

0° C

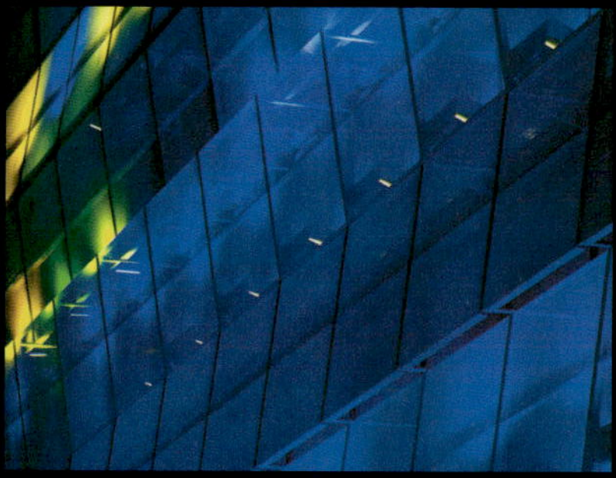

1.5° C

8° C

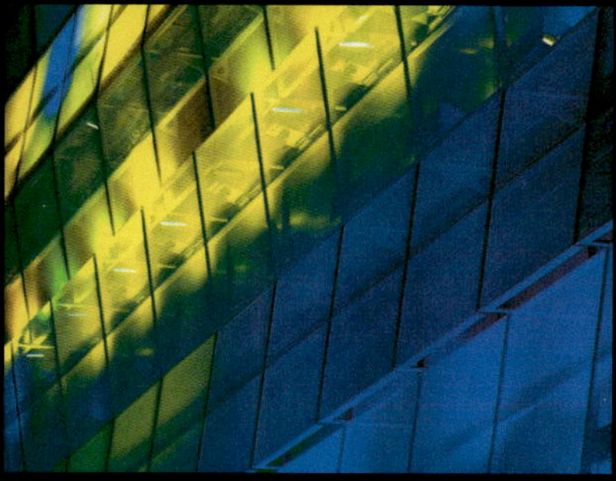

18° C

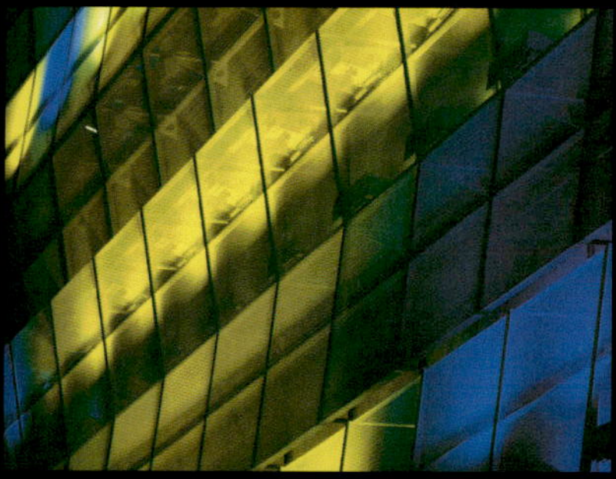

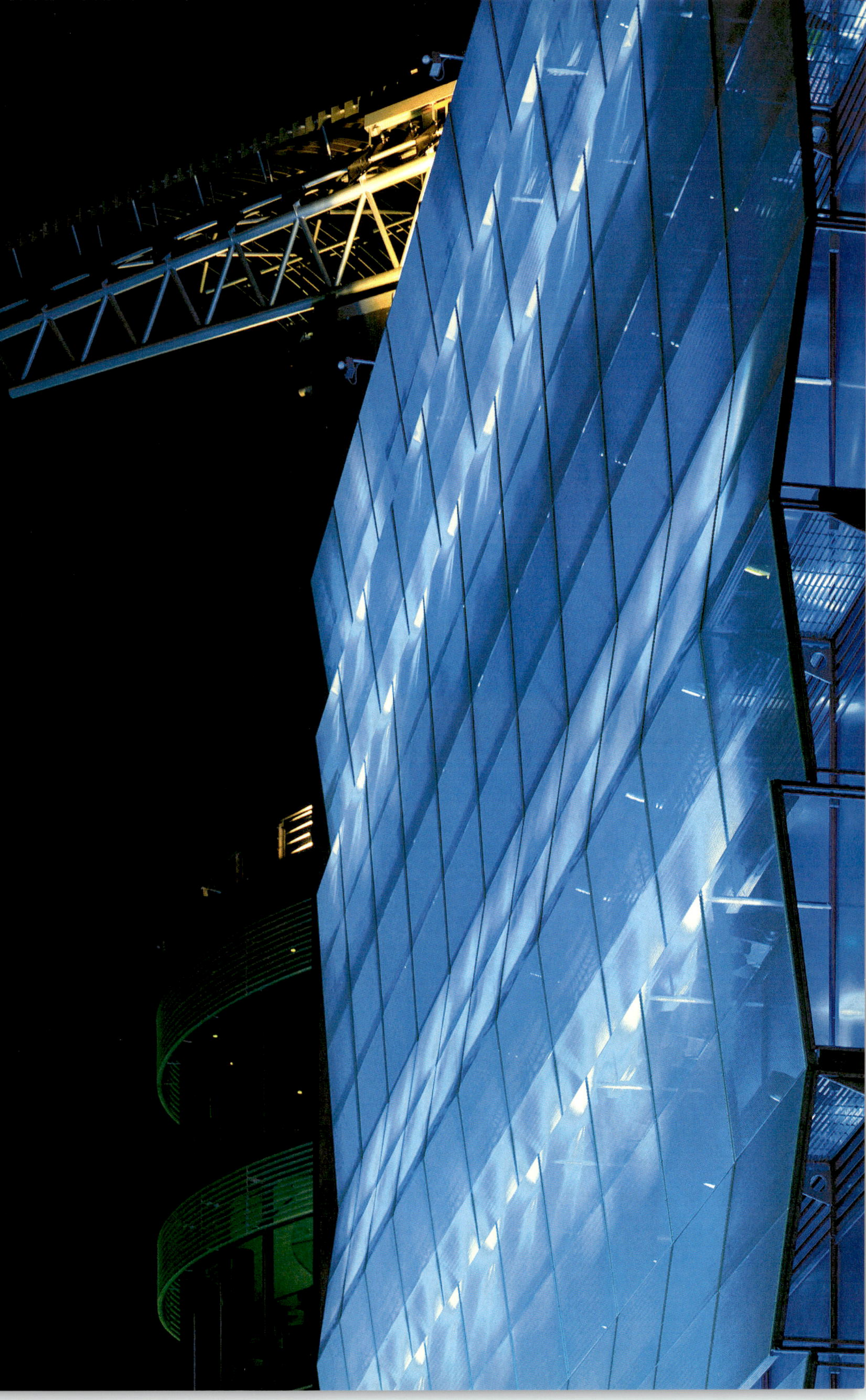

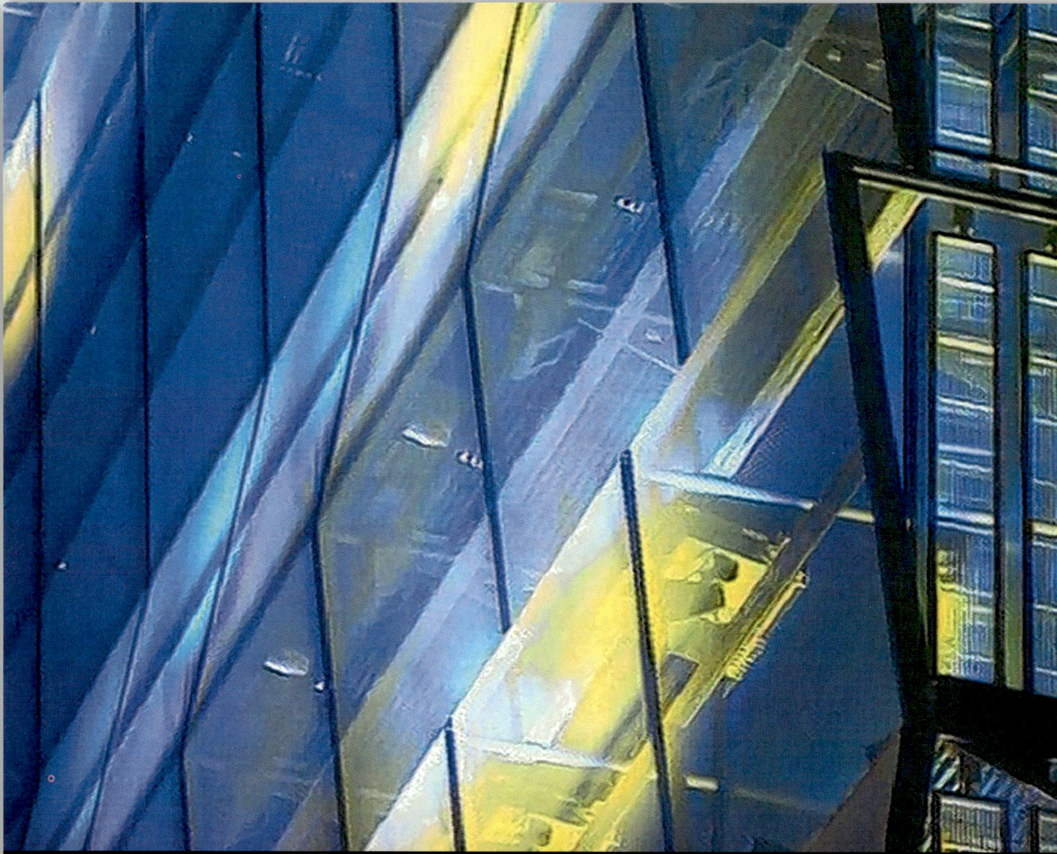

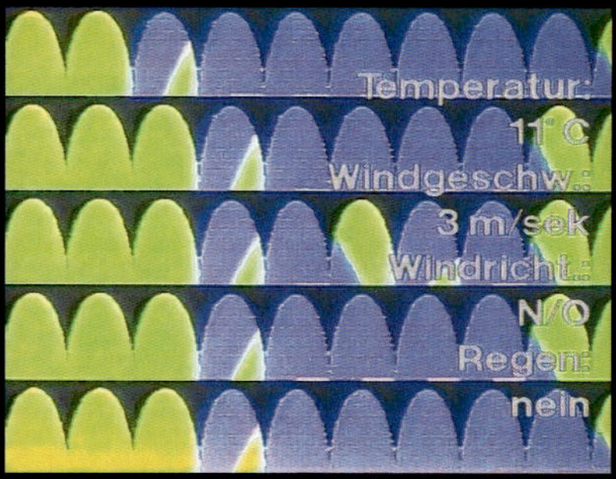

LED screen visualizes street sounds from below.

The software interface controlling the lights.

Flat lights with movable color filters behind aluminum screens change the color distribution on the façade according to weather conditions.

www.christian-moeller.com/kinetic_light_sculpture

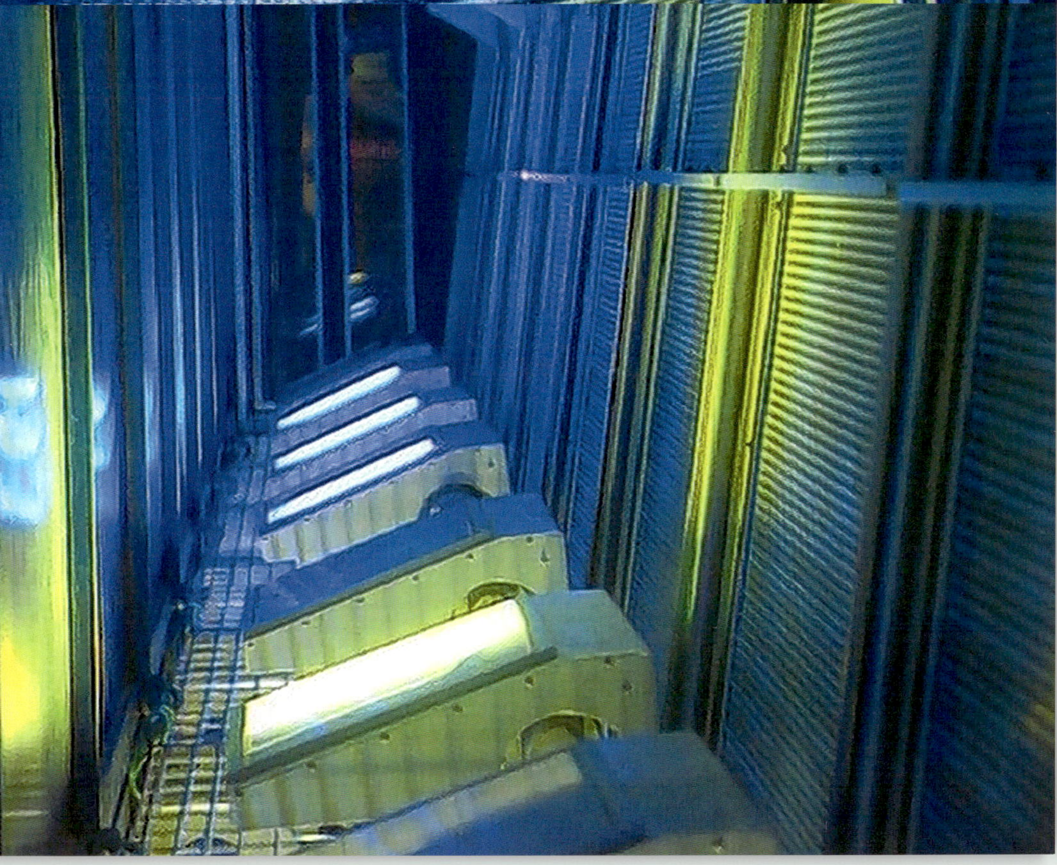

SALA

1993
www.christian-moeller.com/sala
Design Horizonte 1993 at Zeilgalerie, Frankfurt/Main

Producer: Barbara Fuchs
Moderation: Georg Bertsch
Support: Joachim Sauter and Tanja den Broeder

As the years go by, probably every designer takes a more objective stance towards his works. Some mean more to me than others, regardless of how sucessful they may have been with the public. There is one project in particular, actually a concert I organized, which still means a great deal to me today. It was a live performance on the Trautonium **by the ingenious inventor and musician, Oskar Sala.**
Oskar Sala met Friedrich Trautwein in 1930 at the Musikhochschule Berlin, **then under the direction of Paul Hindemith. Trautwein had just invented a new kind of electro-acoustic instrument called the** Trautonium, **an electric oscillating circuit, played using a metal rail, and secured to a board with a wire-covered gut string stretched across it. Sala was so fascinated by the acoustic potential of the** Trautonium **that he devoted much of his life to mastering and further developing this peculiarly beautiful instrument.**
A considerable amount of Sala's music is for cinema. The synthetic bird sounds for Hitchcock's film, The Birds, **is probably his most familiar work. Although he hesitated for quite a while, I succeeded in persuading Oskar Sala to do a concert in Frankfurt in 1993. To transport the Trautonium would be extremely difficult. This irreplacable instrument was the only one of its kind in the world, and Sala's constant companion in his Berlin studio. The nightmare of its getting lost or even damaged in transit, could not have been compensated by any insurance in the world. In the constant company of Sala, the instrument made the journey to Frankfurt. Florian Schneider of Kraftwerk was just one of the people who traveled to Frankfurt especially to attend that memorable concert by this 85-year-old musical pioneer and to hear him play his remarkable music. The performance itself was an urban concert simulcasted on the huge metal screen on the façade of the** Zeilgalerie, **transforming it into what was the largest public TV screen in the public domain to date. Behind it a fantastically** dry **audio system transmitted Sala's Trautonium concert into the open air with a sonic quality close to chamber-music.**
Passers-by stopped to listen, postponing their shopping sprees, and the retail shops along this busy shopping street suffered measurable losses due to the event. Therefore, the very next day, we were prohibited from repeating the event by the threat of a huge fine.

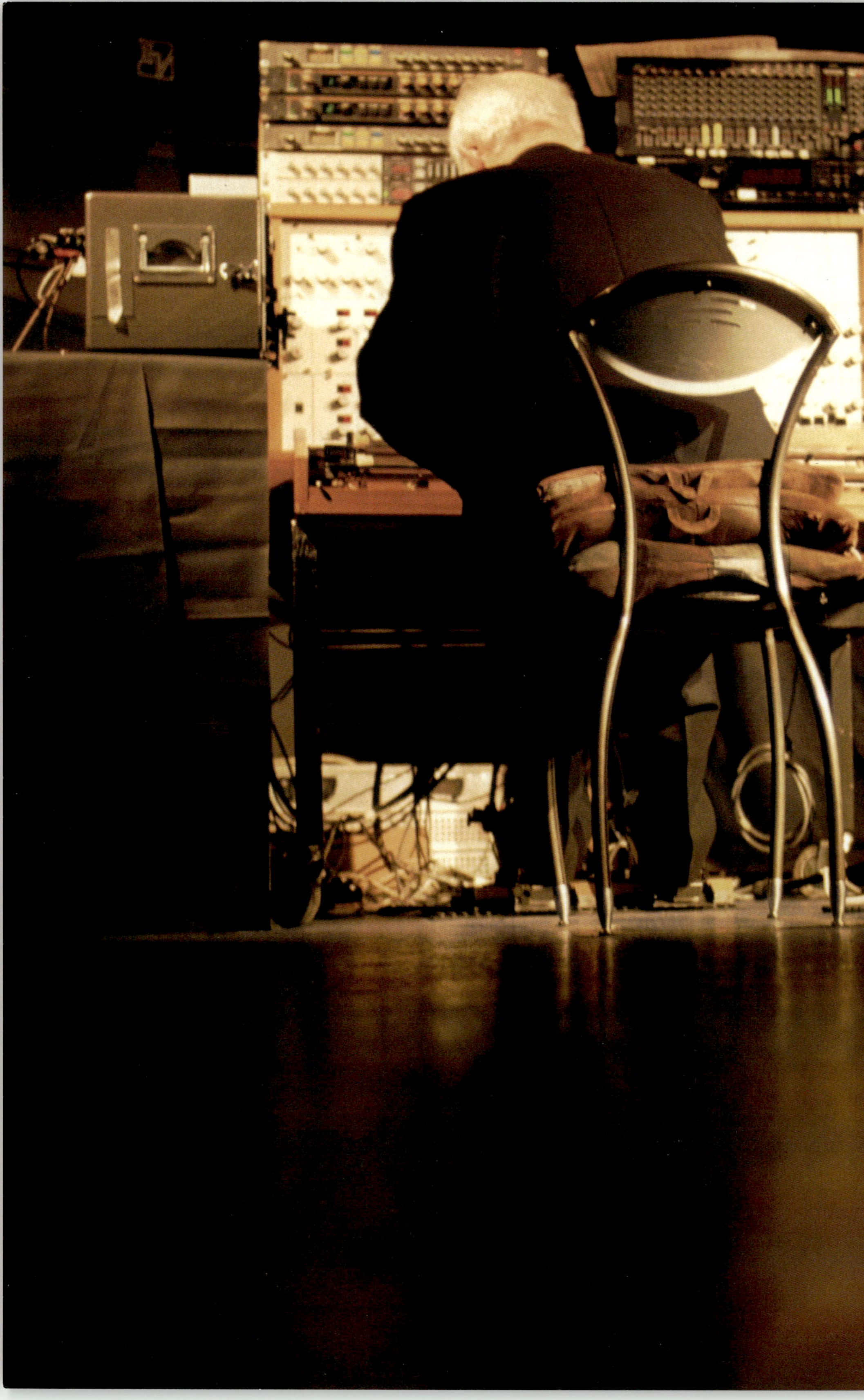

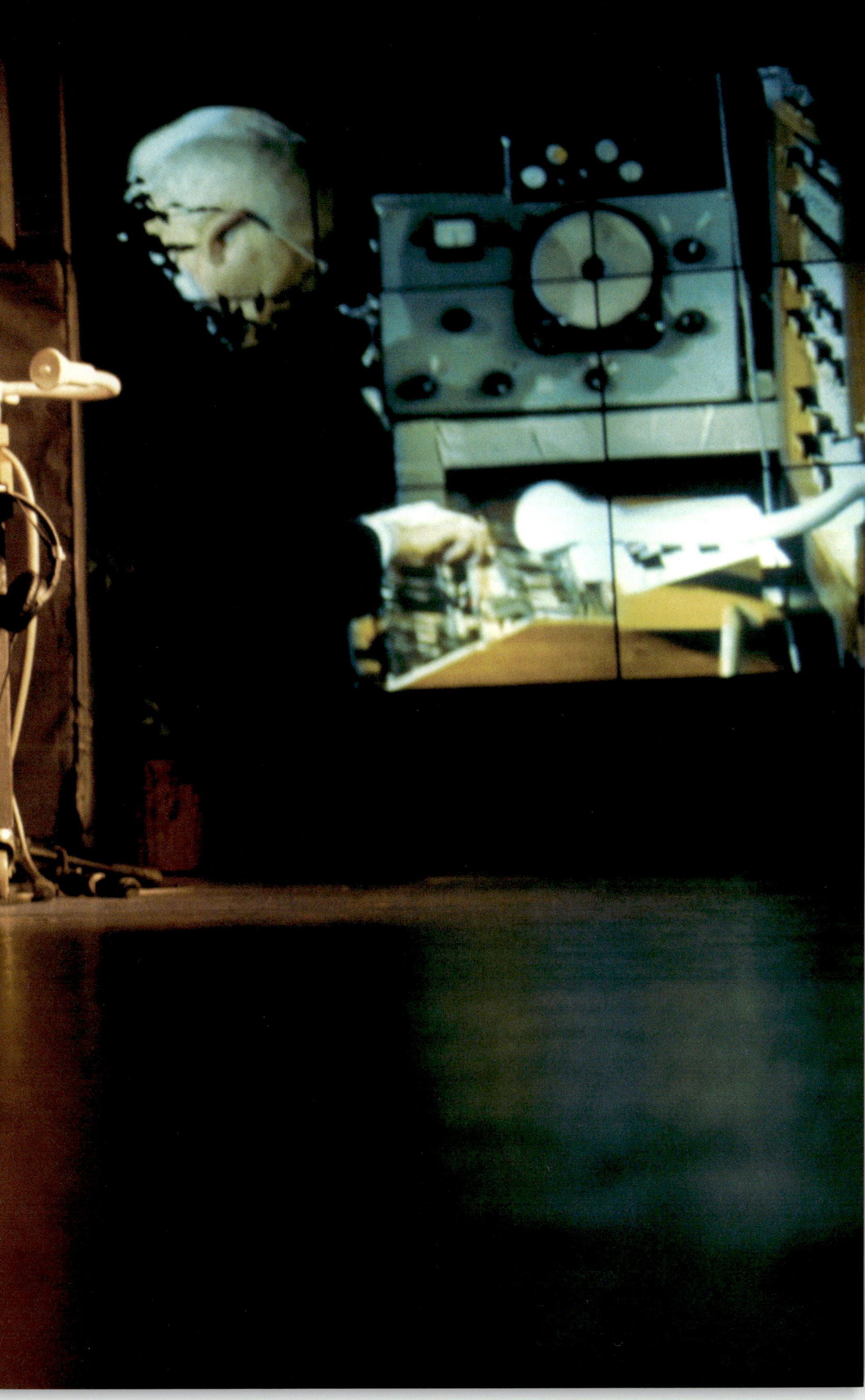

Five-storey live video projection
of Oskar Sala playing the Trautonium.

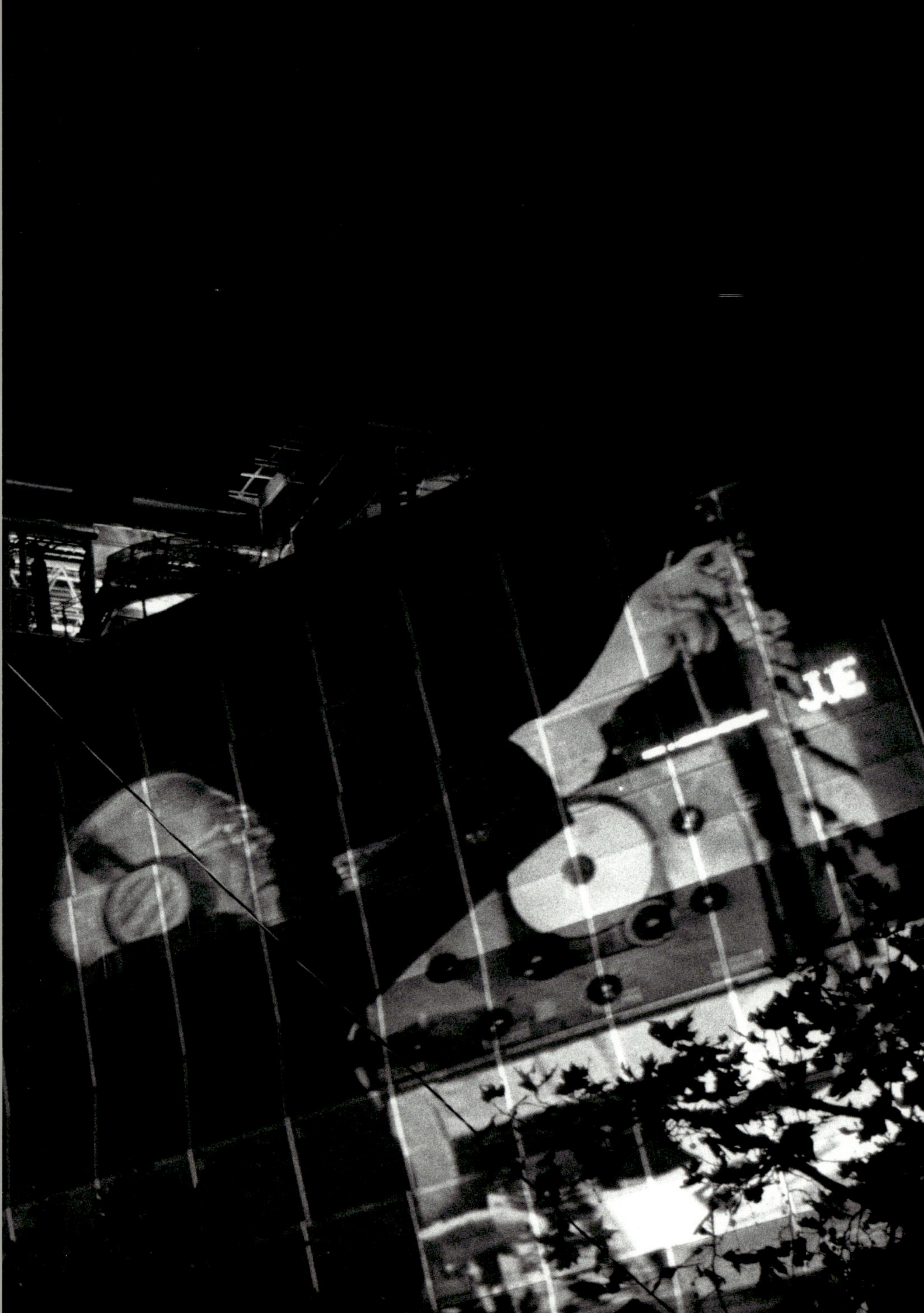

www.christian-moeller.com/sala

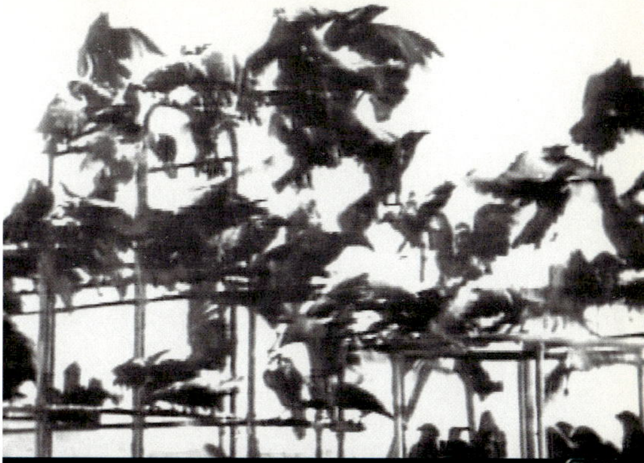

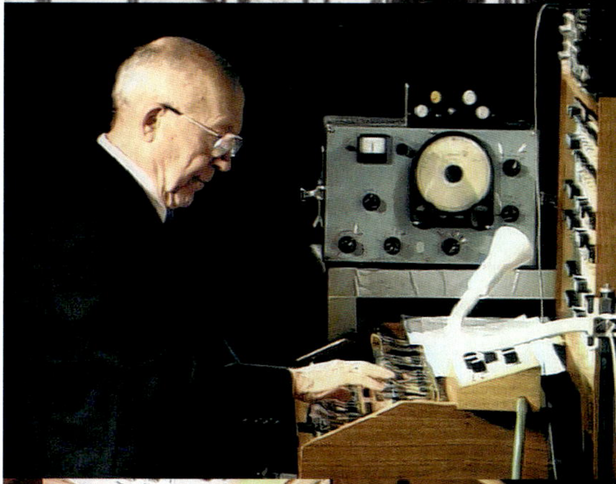

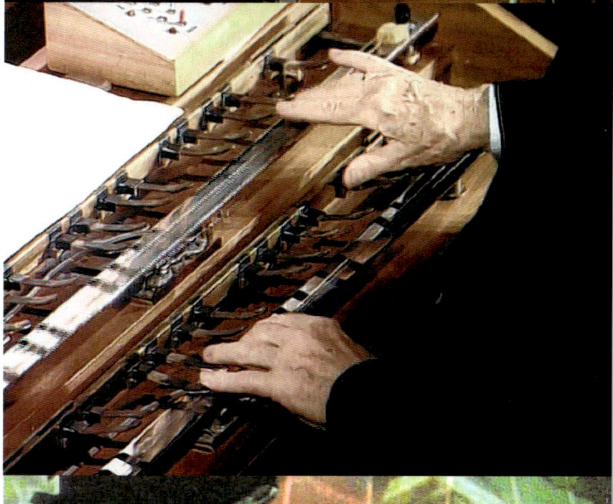

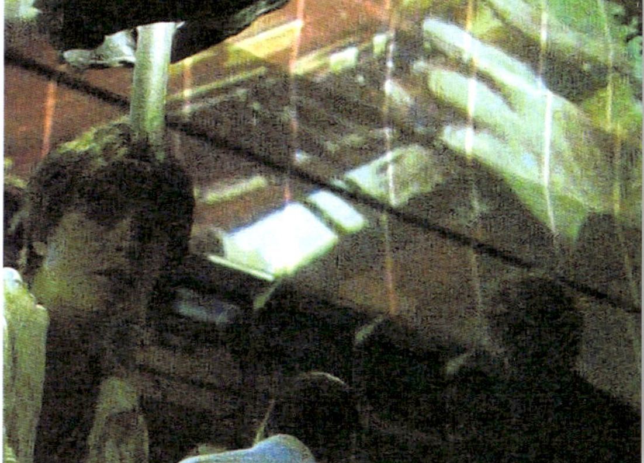

On Bitwalls

Moving images on large displays increasingly overtake and define our cities. But the lack of design skill, or let us simply call it the inconsiderateness of those responsible for these displays, is a corrupting influence. Often the placement of screens is chosen not according to any architectural logic, but only in terms of the number of passers-by likely to see it there. The results can be absurd, and even before the first image starts to flicker, we know that nothing relevant can possibly be transmitted from such an installation. Additionally, the dimensions of those LED displays are always inadequate. Once the viewer is at a distance necessary to see the pixelated images in any reasonable resolution, even large scale installations, like the Jumbotrons by Sony in Shibuja or Leicester Square, look no bigger than the TV screens in our living rooms. Attempts to implement these systems on a satisfactorily architectural scale have so far failed due to the enormous costs involved.

An additional serious problem is the sheer ugliness of the LED display surfaces when they are switched off. This is a problem that also crops up with more conventional light installations, such as animated neon signs. Las Vegas by day makes no sense at all. The appearance of these blackish-grey apparatuses covered with dust is aesthetically unsuitable as a architectural surface.

This fact, plus the desire for quick financial amortization, forces operators of such systems into a perpetual, 24-hour performance. Day and night, the installations flicker in inane self-repetition. They seem to justify themselves not by what they do, but solely by that fact that they do something at all: a huge television set that receives only one obsolete channel and for which no off-switch is at hand.

For some time now I have been working on systems for façades which would function both as an architectonic surface and as image carrier, in both daytime and nighttime. Imagine a surface on which, for days or weeks nothing happens, then when there is something truly relevant to report, it is suddenly transformed into a text display. Real sensations like, "UK adopts the Euro", or, "Swiss football team wins World Cup" are communicated, and then a little later, the system "falls asleep" again.

The costs should be similar to that of a curtain wall façade system which reduces the possible complexity of the display, transmitting only bit-map depictions, and working with low resolutions with pixels sizes up to 30 x 30 cm.

To accomplish this, we developed mechanical pixels, which could switch from black to white quickly and inexpensively. One promising solution was a "hydropixel," an idea by Till Freudenberg. A sheet of perforated black metal floats in a white silicone oil and is pushed against a glass surface, producing a definite black-white contrast which can be switched at a frequency of 20 times per second.

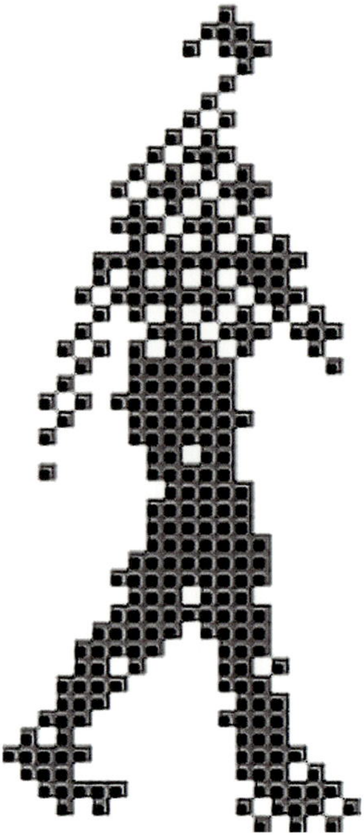

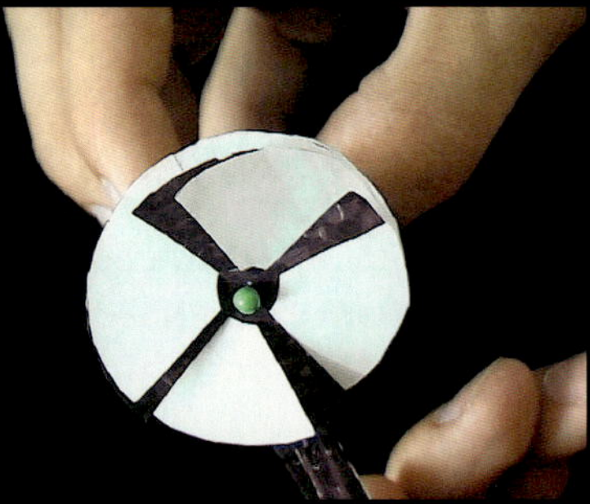

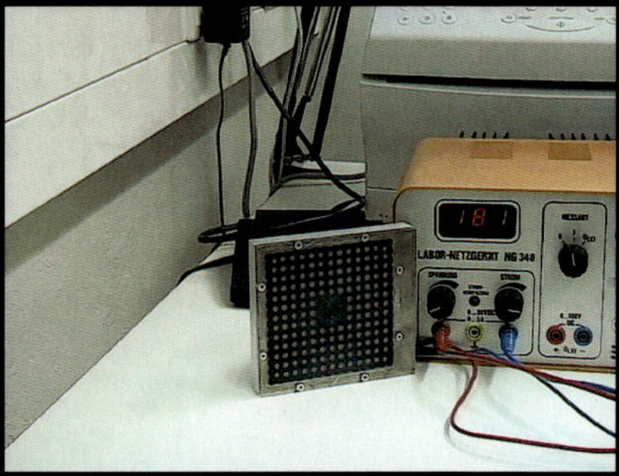

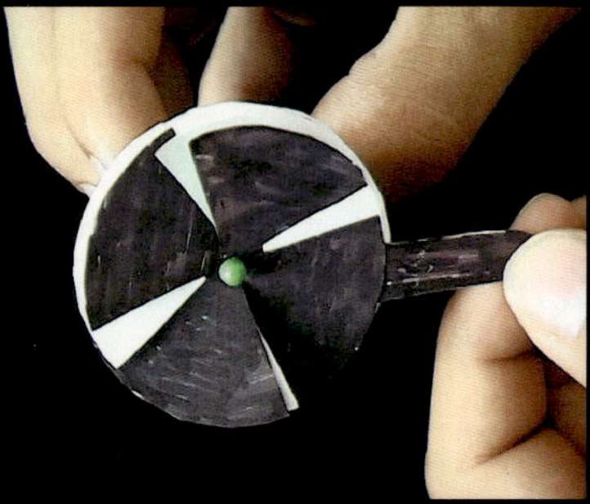

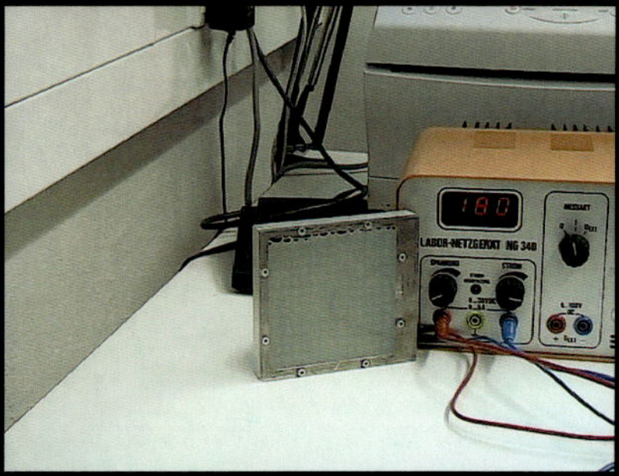

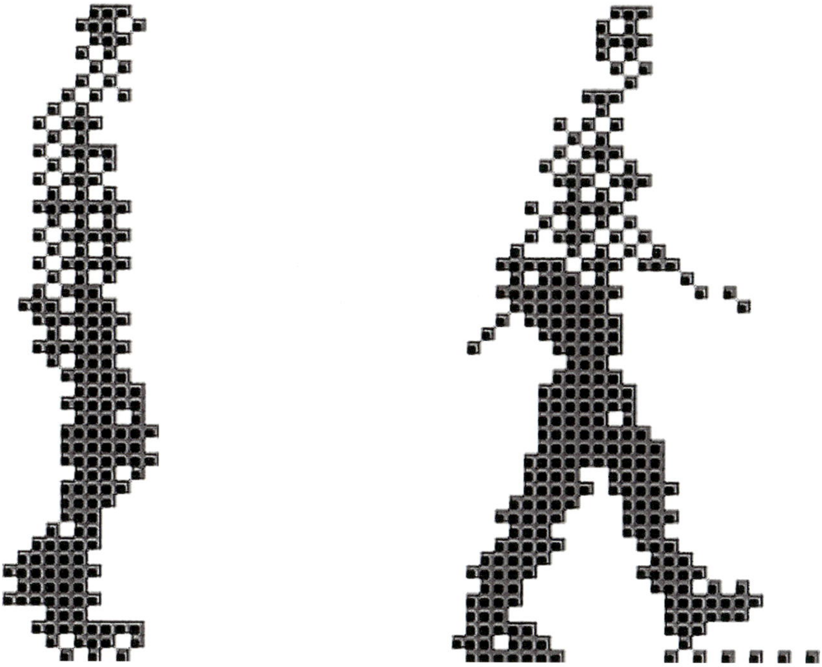

Bitwalls: various experiments with mechanical pixels for use as dynamic graphics on building surfaces.

Mechanical engineering:
Tillmann Freudenberg, Eckhard Schneider and Hans-Jürgen Diekmann

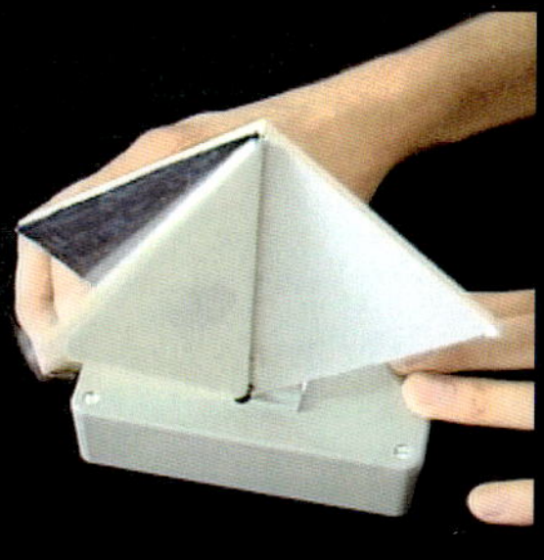

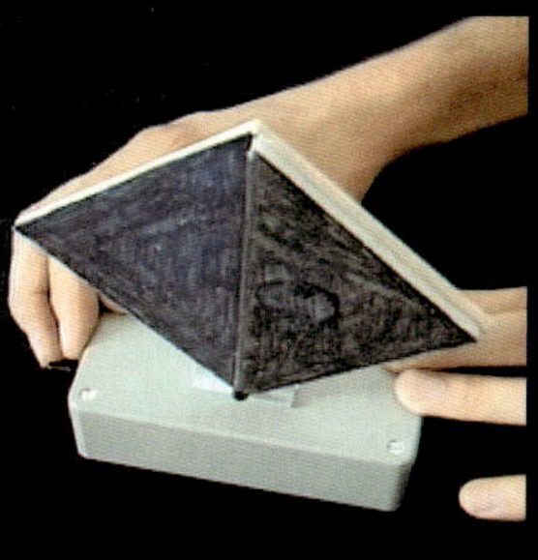

ELBE [BITWALL 1]

2002
www.christian-moeller.com/elbe
BAW, Federal Institute of Hydraulic Engineering, Ilmenau, Germany

Skipper: Herr Füchsel
Programming: Thomas Lauerbach
Display Technology: Sytec
Construction: MBM Konstruktionen
Coordination: Jens Scheiber

The first time we were able to implement a bit-wall system was for a project called Virtual River Bank, Elbe (Bitwall 1). Our experiments with the hydropixel soon exhausted our research budget and could not be taken any further. An alternative was an electro-magnetic hinged pixel. For this, a permanent magnet is embedded into the hinge, and swings on its vertical axis. On the back of each pixel are two electromagnetic coils which flip the hinge 180 degrees by switching their electrical polarities, enabling a maximum image rate of 5 times per second.
For this project, I booked a passage on a cargo boat and, in an uninterrupted sequence of images, digitally photographed 800 km of the banks of the river Elbe, from Prague to Hamburg. With the help of a GPS, the individual images were coded with the exact geographical data on the respective point where they were taken.
With this, we produced a 10-meter high display pillar on which the banks of the Elbe literally unfold, in very crude resolution (7 x 7 cm pixels), at the leisurely speed of a boat on a river. The "virtual" bank of the Elbe is superimposed on the real backdrop of the Thuringian landscape.

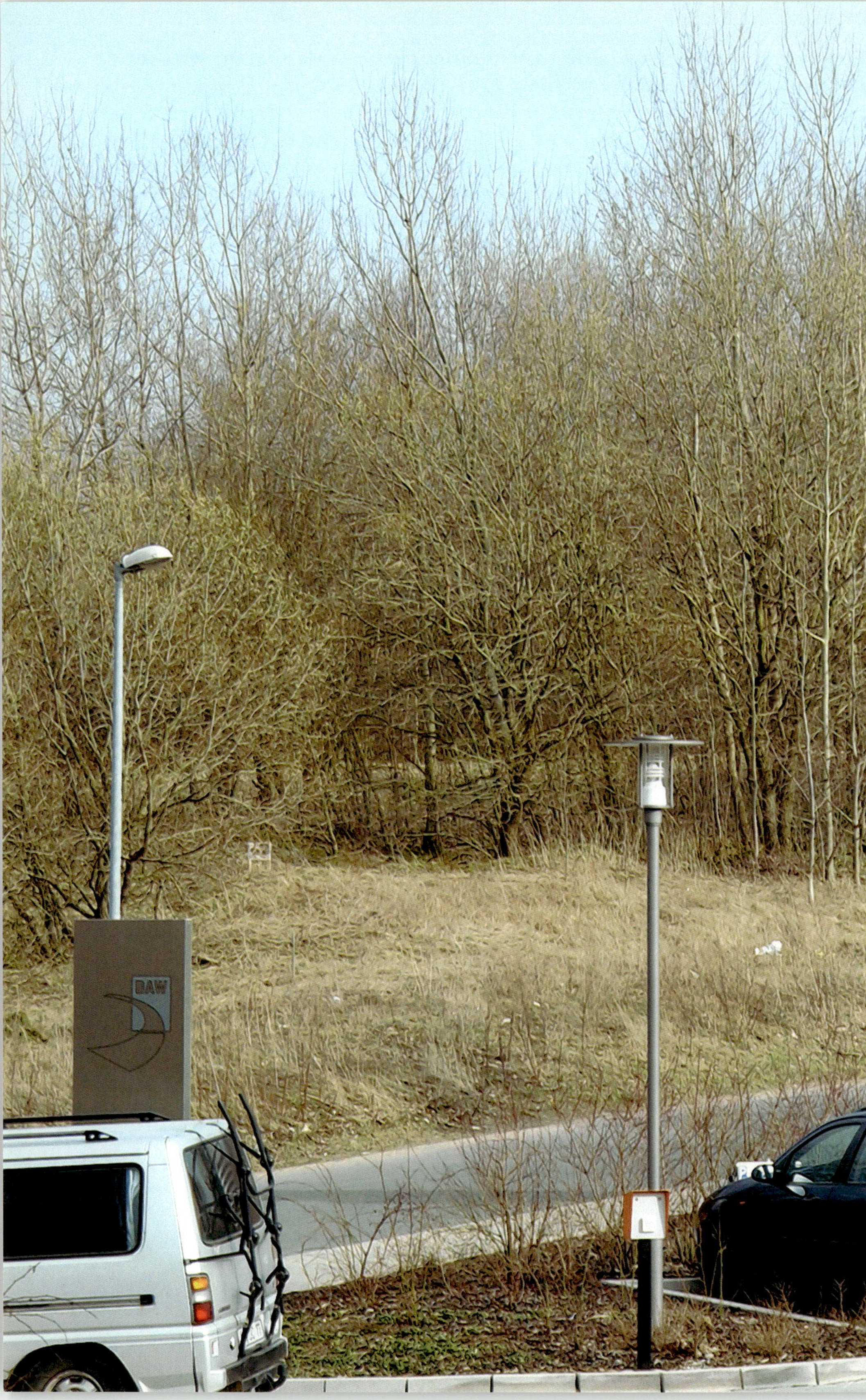
BAW

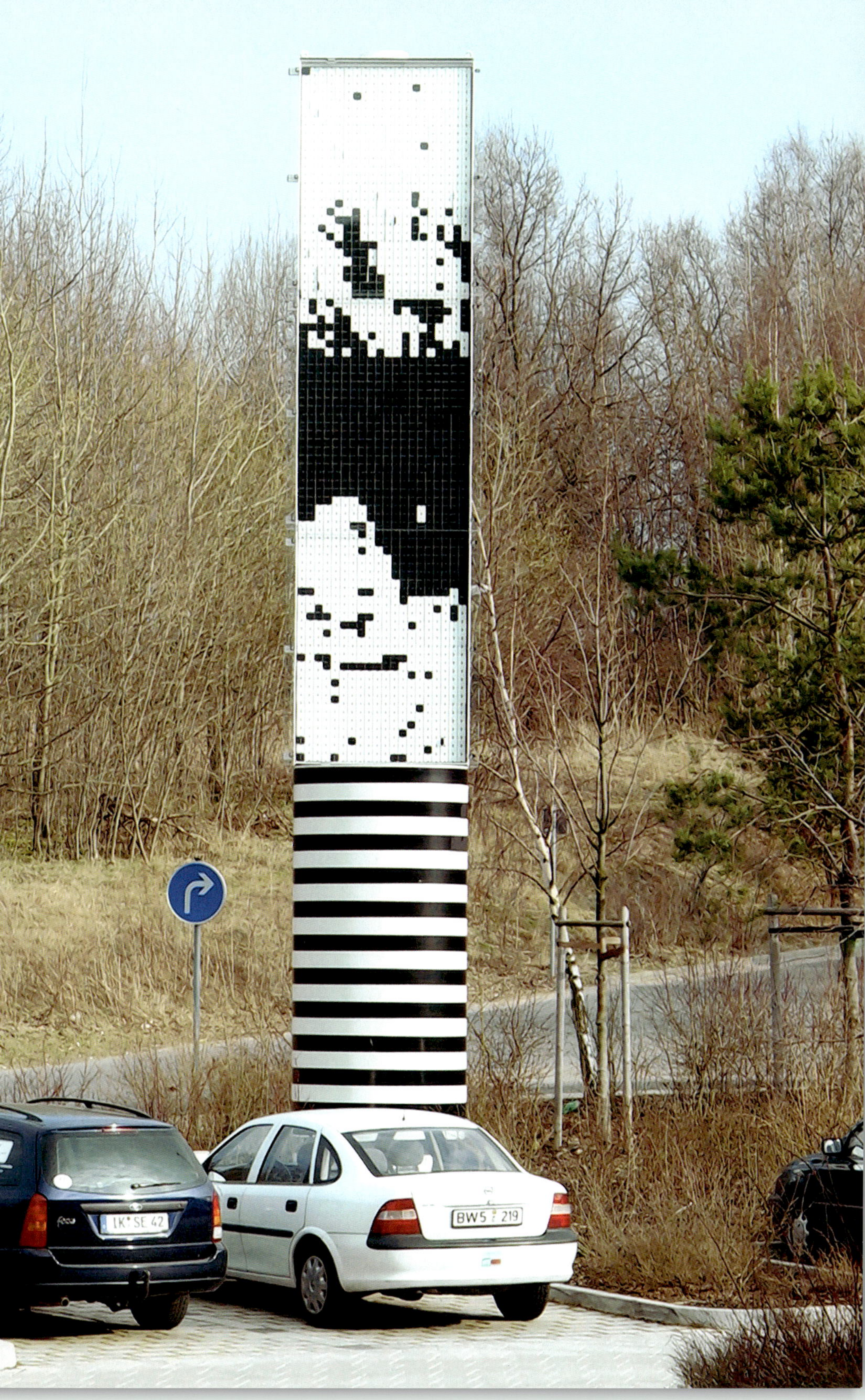
IK SE 42
BW5 219

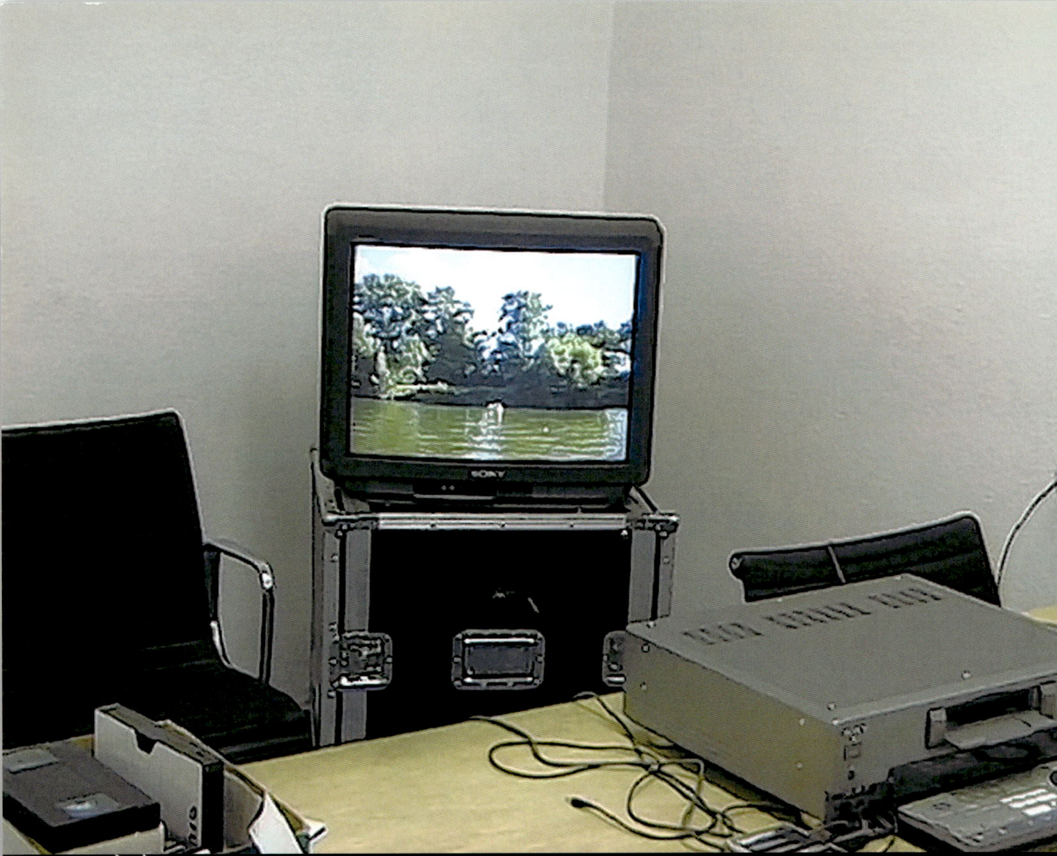

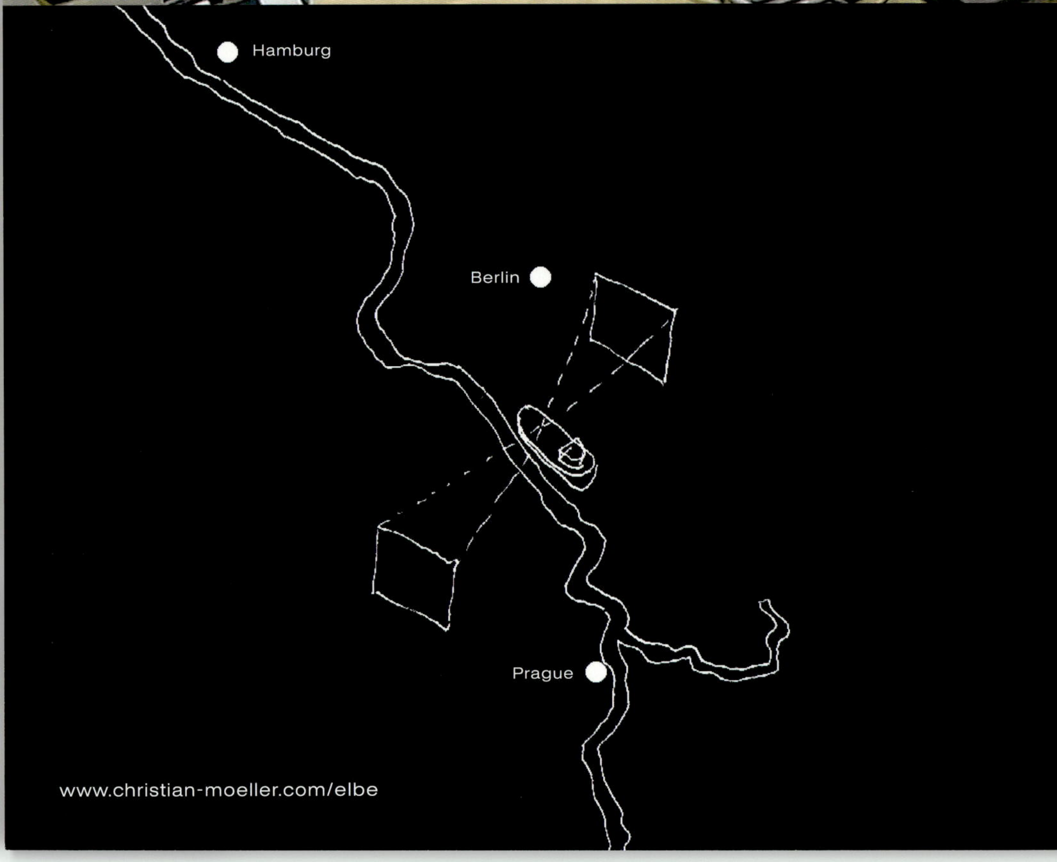

www.christian-moeller.com/elbe

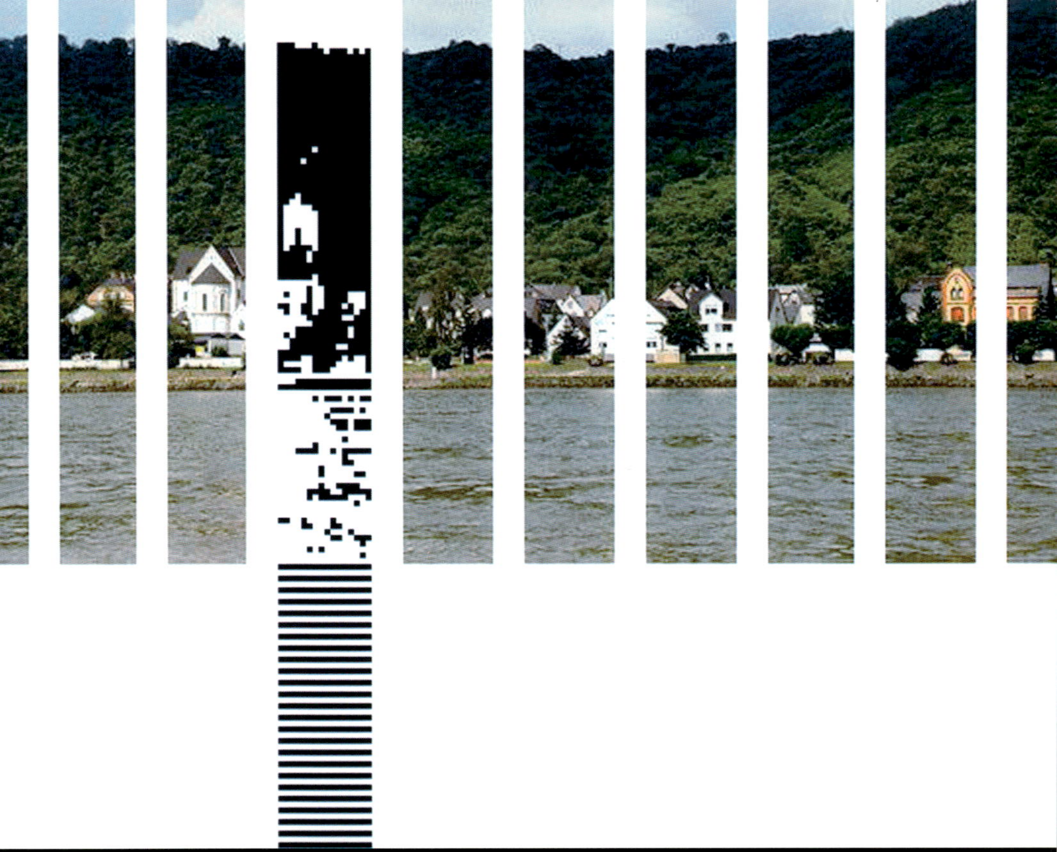

800 km of the Elbe riverside is digitally recorded and translated into bit-mapped graphics.

[BITWALL 2]

2002
www.christian-moeller.com/bielefeld_bitwall2
OWL-Shoping and Trade Fair Center, Bielefeld, Germany

Programming: Thomas Lauerbach
Architecture: Eckhard Gerber

While working on the Elbe Project I received a commission for two façade installations for a hotel and trade fair complex at the main railway station in Bielefeld (Bitwall 2). Unfortunately, this never got beyond the draft stage. A few months after the contract was signed, the investor went bankrupt (again!). What remained were unpaid bills, and some interesting ideas.
The installation area on the entrance façade to the south was approximately 7 x 7 square meters, certainly room for a large image. While this would be too big to install in a conventional museum exhibition space in one piece, as an outdoor installation on the public façade of a building, it would be a lot less impressive in size. In order to seemingly enlarge the area, double it to be precise, my plan was to interrupt the image matrix at regular intervals. I called this procedure "virtual stretching." The result is a ladder-like object made up of horizontal rows totalling 18.4 meters high and 5.6 meters wide.
One can only see how "virtual stretching" works in the moving image (see URL below). The eye of the observer fills in the missing parts, interpolating the transitions from image strip to image strip and eliminating the optical gaps.
A practical side-effect of the ladder technique is that it doesn't hide the view from behind the glass façade, so that one can look out of the building from within.
A video camera was to survey the entrance area outside the building and present the approaching visitors in the installation in the form of huge portraits.

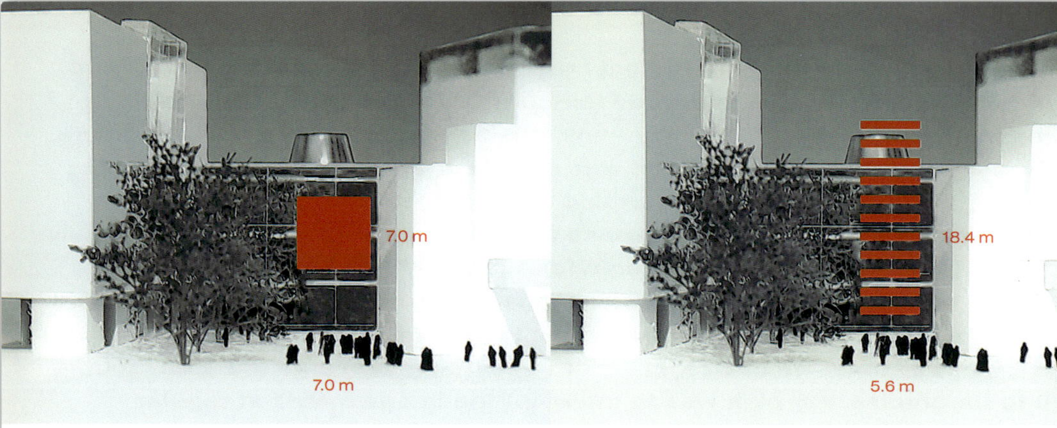

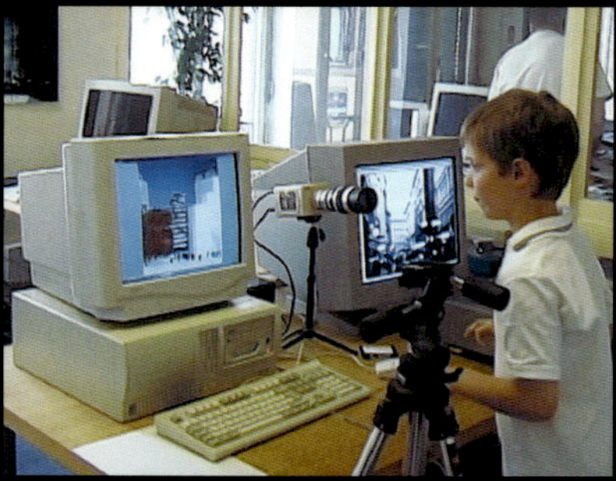

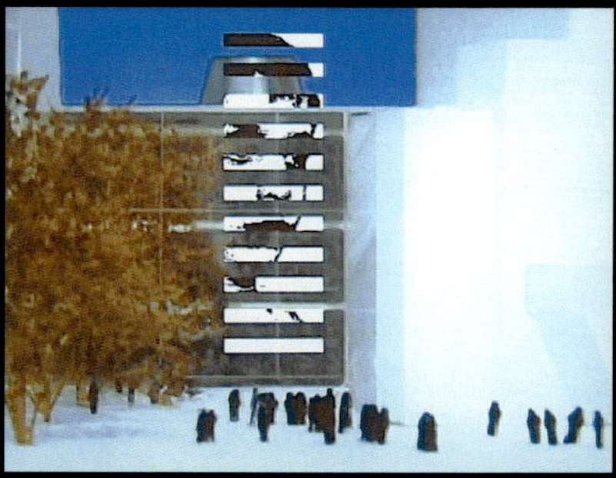

The eye fills in the gaps: “video stretching” increases the physical display dimensions by interweaving empty spaces into the moving image.

www.christian-moeller.com/bielefeld_bitwall2

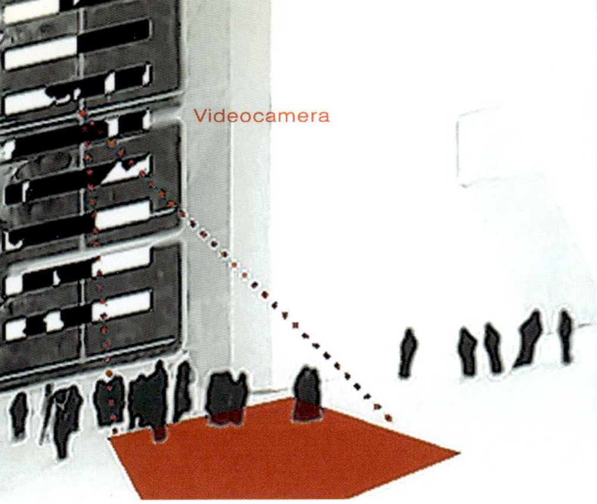
Videocamera

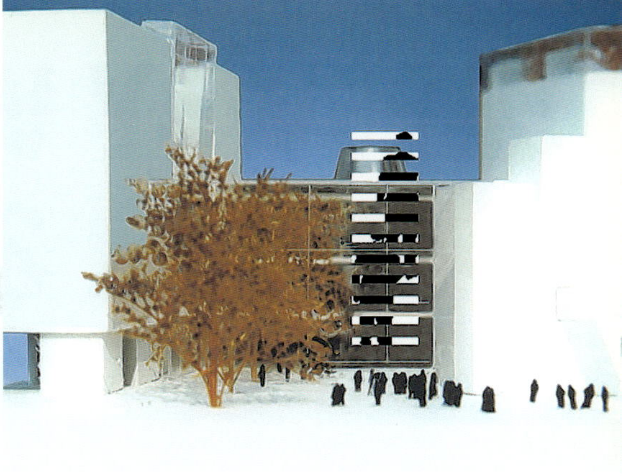

FREEWAY WALLS [BITWALL 3]

2001–
www.christian-moeller.com/freeway_walls
Freeway L 605/Südtangente, City of Karlsruhe, Germany

Research and design: Petra Trefzger
Coordination (City of Karlsruhe): Gerhard Schönbeck

Within a few days of successfully presenting this project to the Bielefeld City Council, and under the working assumption that it would be built, I had a chance meeting with the documentary filmmaker, Lothar Spree, in an Italian restaurant in Karlsruhe. He was with the mayor of the city, Heinke Salisch, and introduced me as an architect and installation artist who was planning huge black-and-white pictorial installations along the fast-train line at the railway station in Bielefeld. Before my meal was even served, I had received a new and very interesting commission. The City of Karlsruhe was to build a huge number of sound proofing walls along a stretch of highway, and I was to work on a design study for it. Because of the amount of surface area involved, such sound proofing measures are rather expensive, but from the aesthetic viewpoint the finished result is usually quite unsatisfactory.

I came up with the idea of a relief system in which the necessary sound absorbers would run as horizontal slats. This structure would be interrupted at certain sections in the wall. In the direct sunlight the shadows cast by the slats onto the wall surface would form legible bit-map graphics. Seen close up, i.e., by a passing car driver, these images would remain abstract, but for a person out walking and seeing these walls from a distance, the shadows would merge to produce huge portraits in the surrounding landscape. To select the images, we have devised a simple procedure. Shortly before the project will be realized, we will, in conjunction with the Karlsruhe Hall of Records, appeal to the city's oldest citizens to make their portraits available for this work. Preliminary plans were completed in 2001 and received a positive response from the City Council. Meanwhile, the first prototypes have been made, in concrete, at a 1:1 scale. The first section of the wall is to be built in the years 2004–2005.

While the working models were being made, an unexpected context for the Bitwalls presented itself. Hellmut Seemann, Director of the Kunsthalle Schirn in Frankfurt, visited me in my studio and found the model that we had made the previous day for Karlsruhe so convincing that he ordered a similar work for the outer façade of his museum, done in the same resolution as the planned motorway walls.

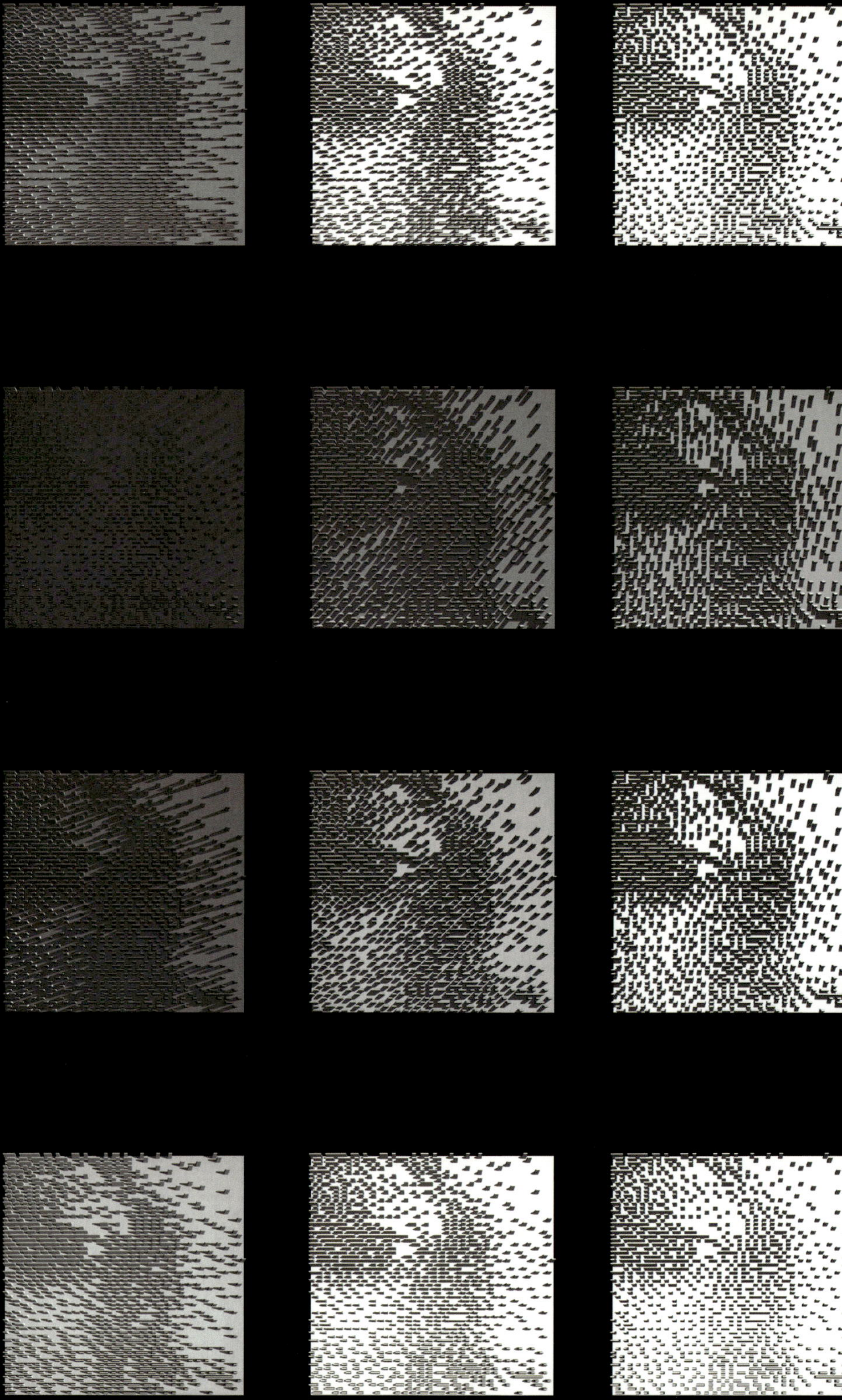

08:00 10:00 12:0

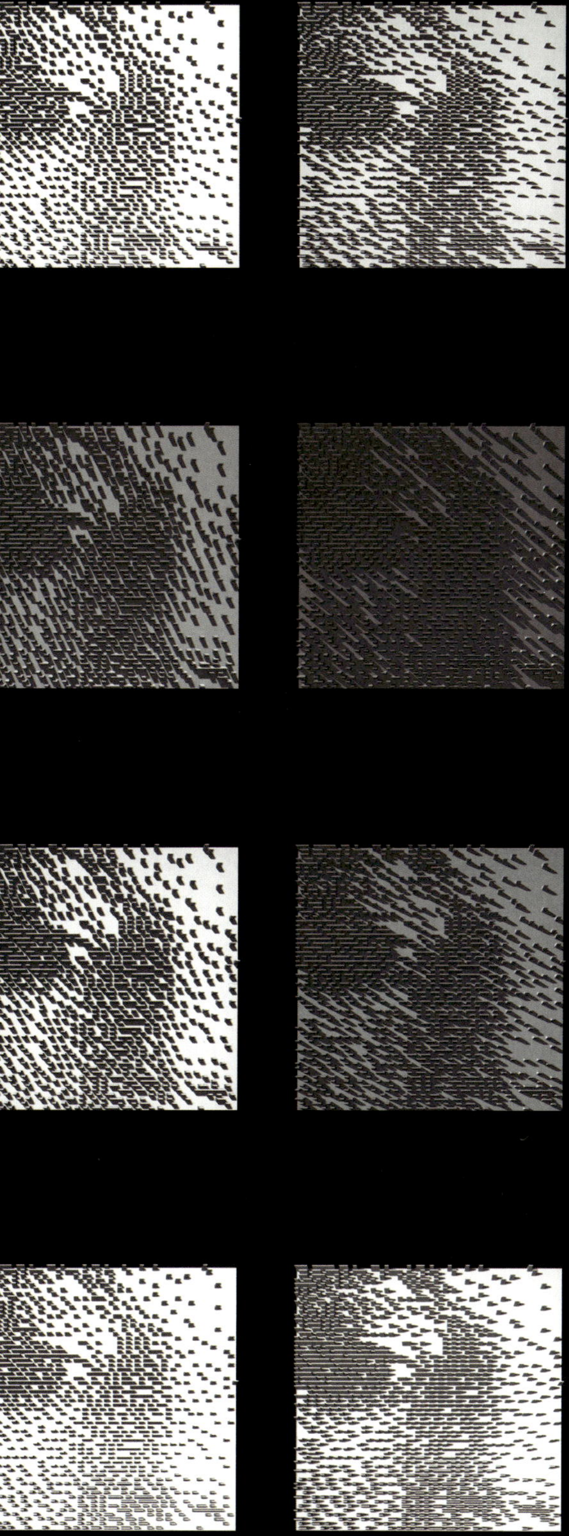

Simulation of various shadow textures produced at different times of the year.

March

June

September

December

14:00

16:00

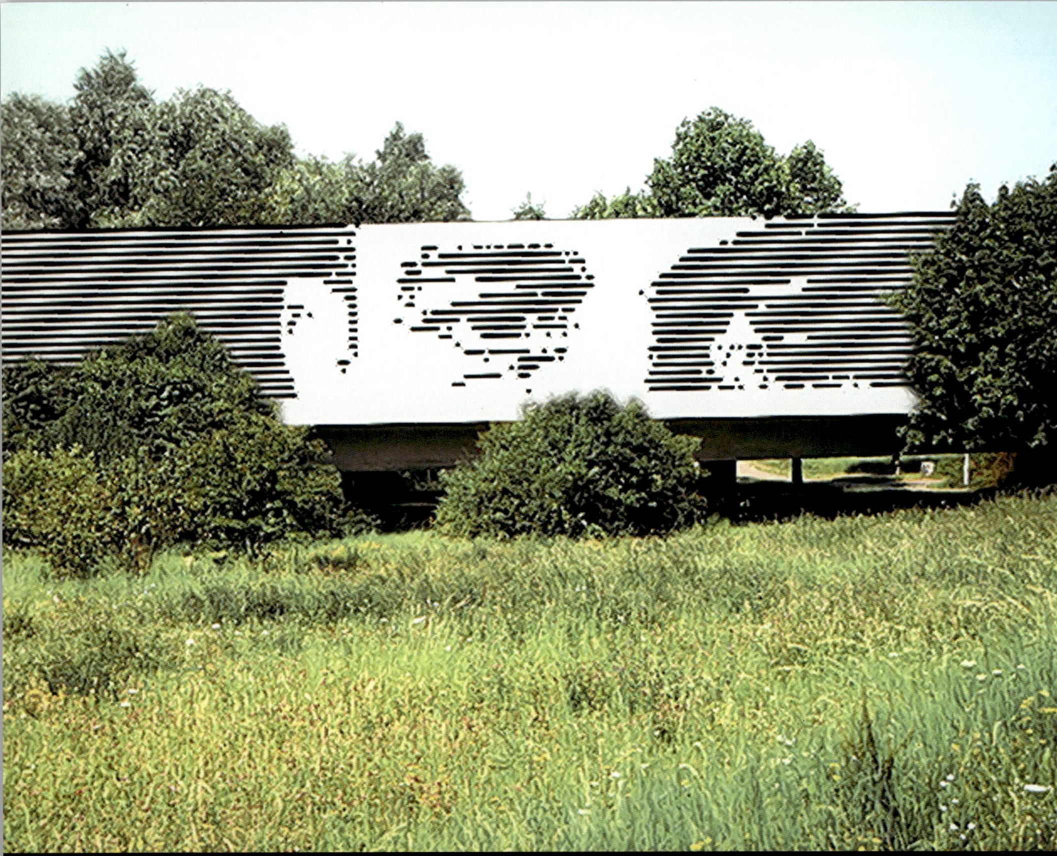

Study for freeway walls: visualization
of a bit-wall embedded in the landscape.

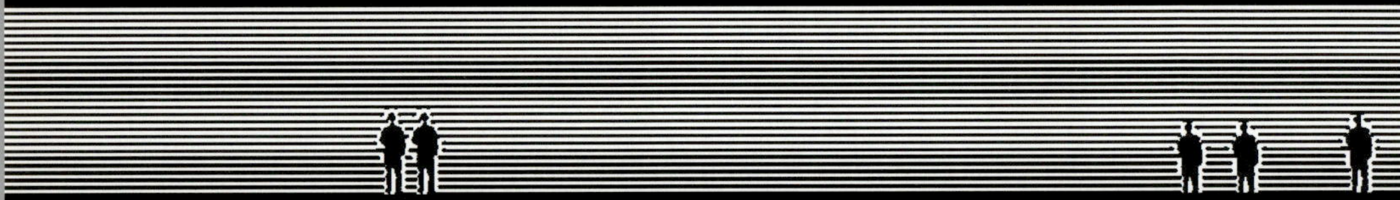

www.christian-moeller.com/freeway_walls

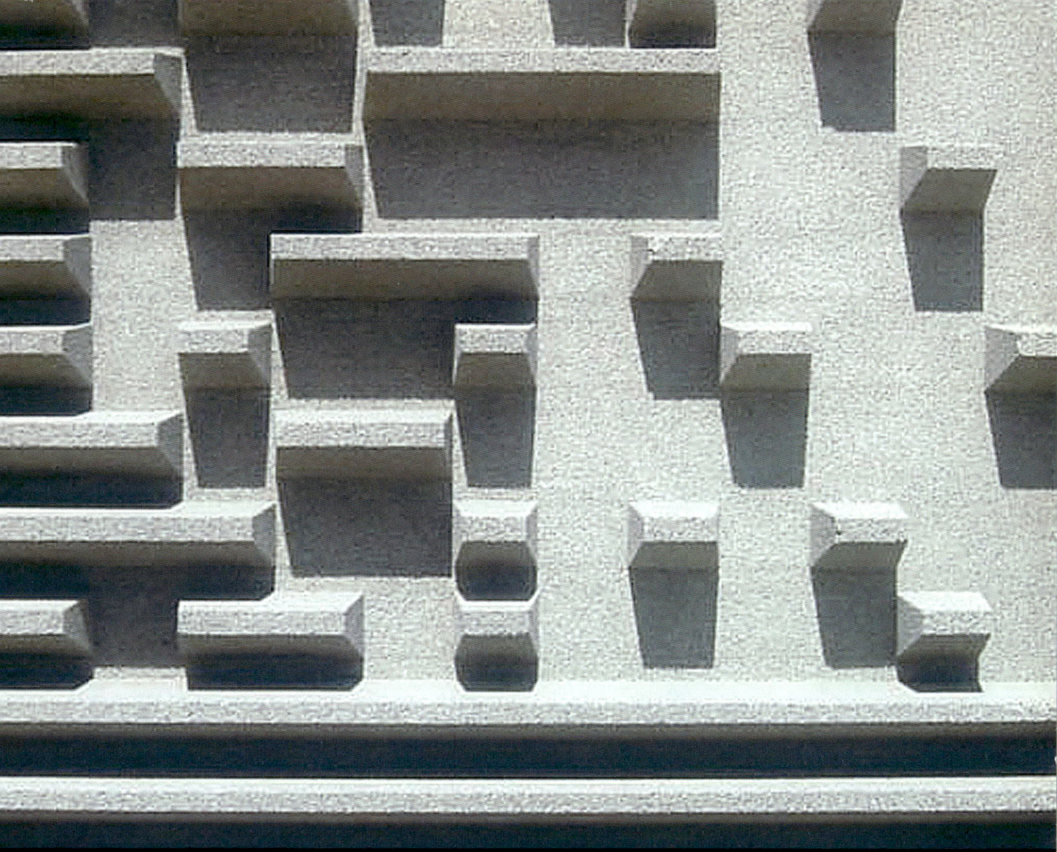

Close-up of a fabricated concrete wall element.

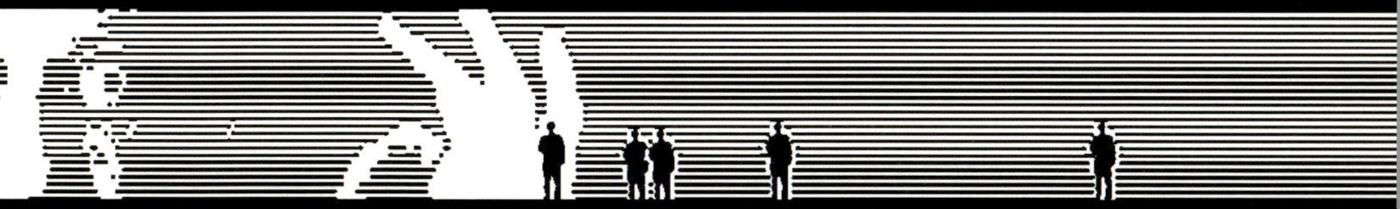

Bitwall portrait of a homeless person
at Kunsthalle Schirn, Frankfurt.

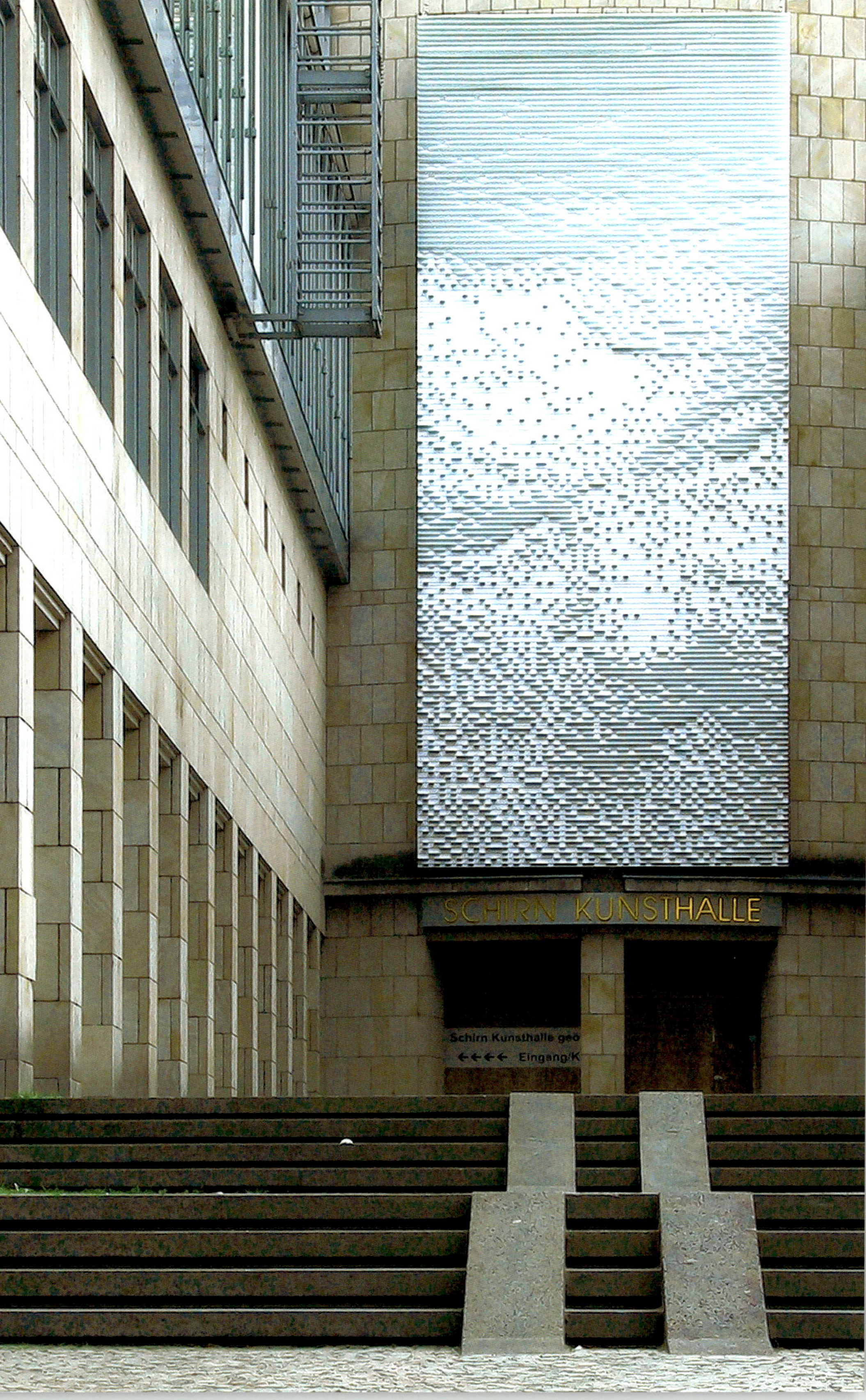
SCHIRN KUNSTHALLE
Schirn Kunsthalle geö
←←←← Eingang/K

DE-PICTURED [BITWALL 4]

2001
www.christian-moeller.com/de_pictured
De-Pictured at Williamson Gallery Art Center College of Design, Pasadena

Curator: Stephen Nowlin
Portrait phorography: Harald Schröder
Programming: Sven Thöne
Construction management: Julian Goldwhite

De-Pictured is the last project to date in the Bitwall series, and the first in my new home, Los Angeles. At the Willamson Gallery in the Art Center College of Design in Pasadena, we installed a wall relief showing 15 portraits of male prisoners cast and photographed in a German jail. Software translates the selected portraits into binary graphics from which the exact positions of the pixels can be read and determined. It took more than three weeks to put the reliefs together, involving a total of 60 000 parts.

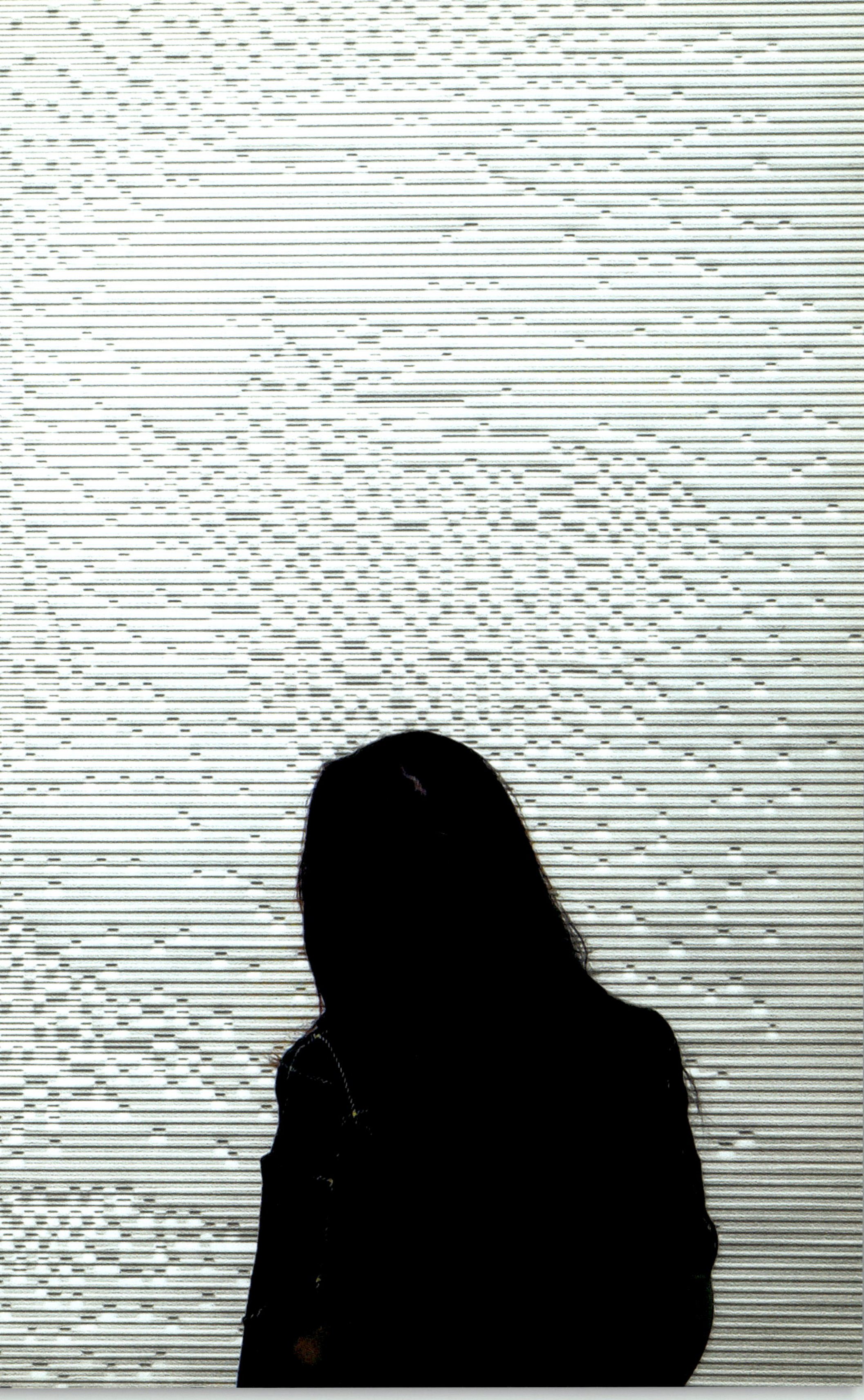

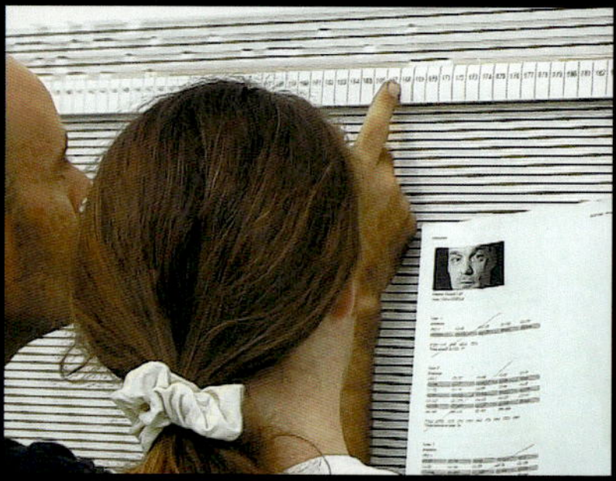

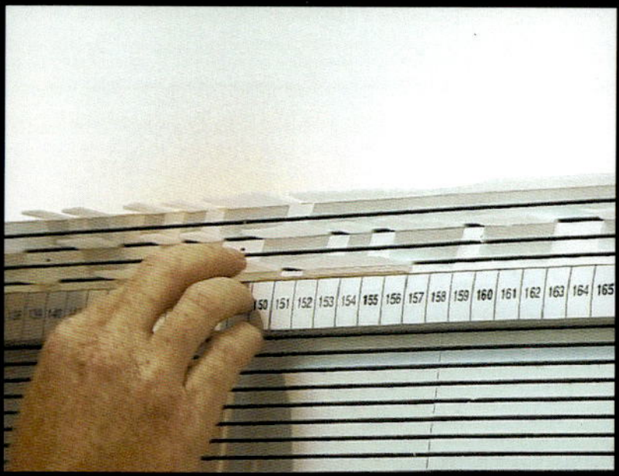

Based on printouts of planned pixel coordinates, plastic chips are installed by hand.

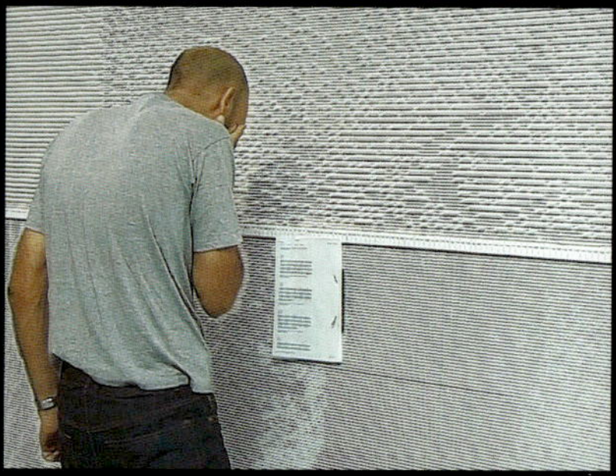

www.christian-moeller.com/de_pictured

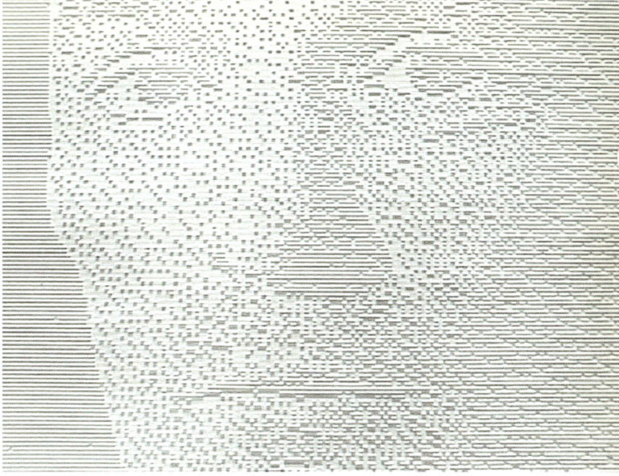

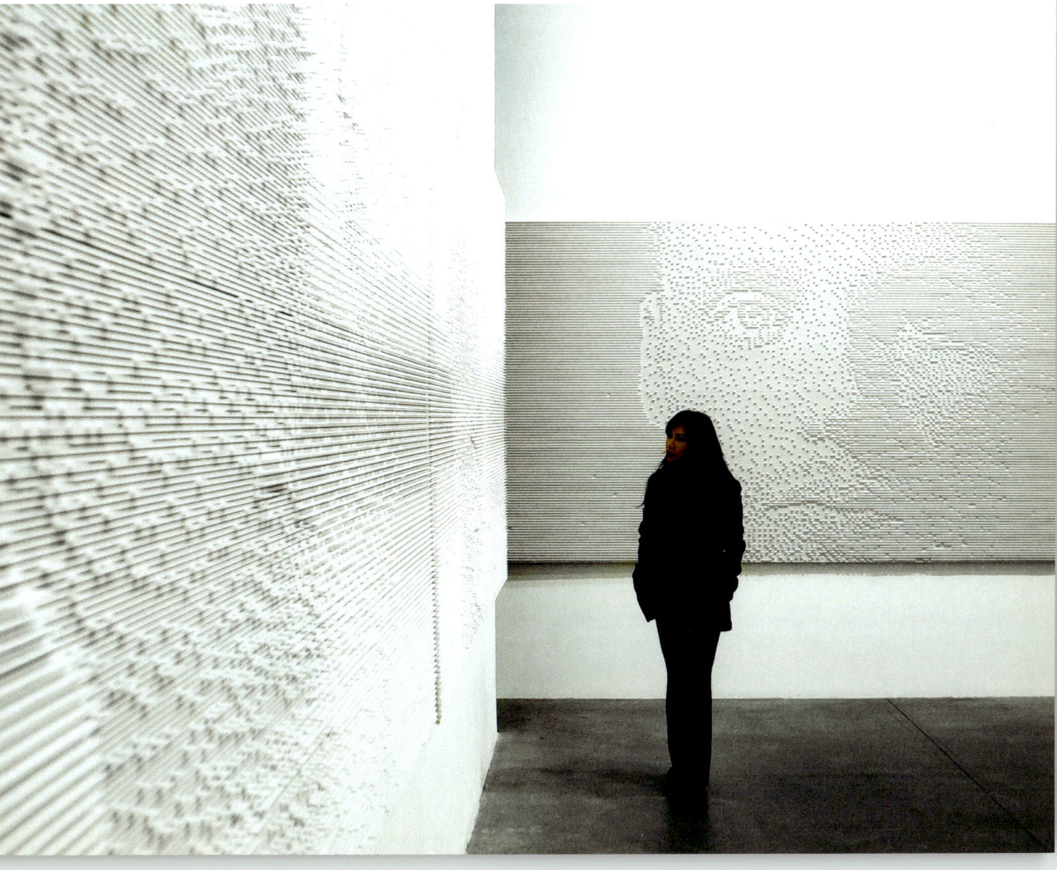

TOWER OF BABEL

2003
www.christian-moeller.com/tower_of_babel
The Tower of Babel, Origin and Diversity of oral and written languages,
Kunsthistorisches Museum Vienna, at Eggenberg Castle, Graz.
In collaboration with: Pete Conolly and Wilfried Seipel

Design: Pete Conolly
Coordination (KHM): Gabriele Stöger
Surveying: Heinz Karner
Construction management (Artex): Gerhard Veigel
Construction: Dekorationsbau Winter

Tower of Babel was an exhibition at Castle Eggenberg, curated by Kunsthistorishen Museum Vienna as part of the European Cultural Captial Graz 2003. Wilfried Seipel asked me to design an installation for the outdoor areas of the castle.
With focus on "the origin and diversity of oral and written language", from the Biblical "confusion of tongues" to contemporary communications media, the project showed the historical tradition and cultural reception of the five thousand year old myth of the "Tower of Babel".
Together with Pete Conolly, I developed word sculptures in the park of the castle which are configured out of 56 rectangular panel elements, some as tall as 18 ft.
Readable only from particular perspective positions along the pathway towards the main entrance, the seemingly abstract arrangement of panels literally configures **the German words "Turm," "zu" and "Babel" ("Tower of Babel.")**

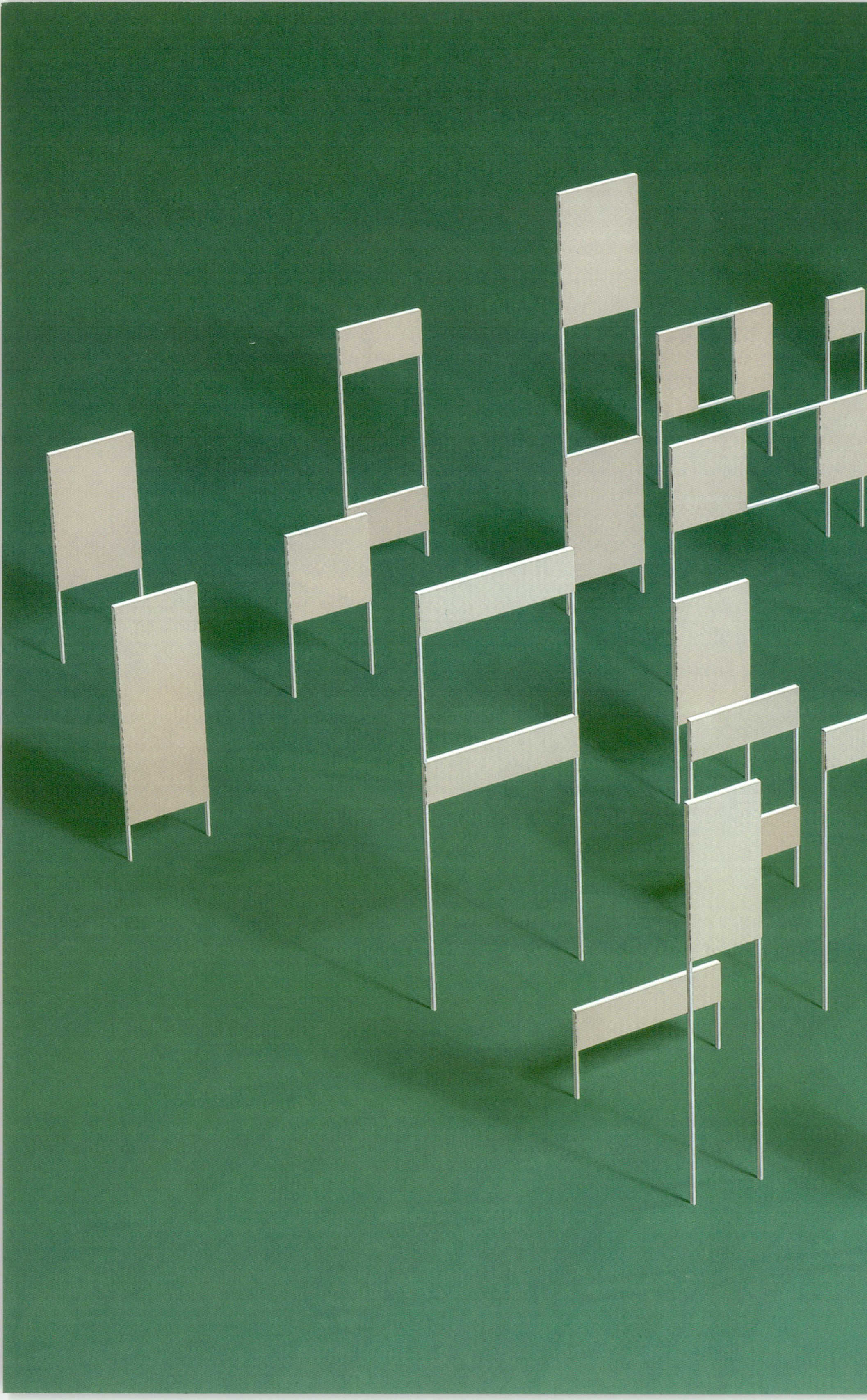

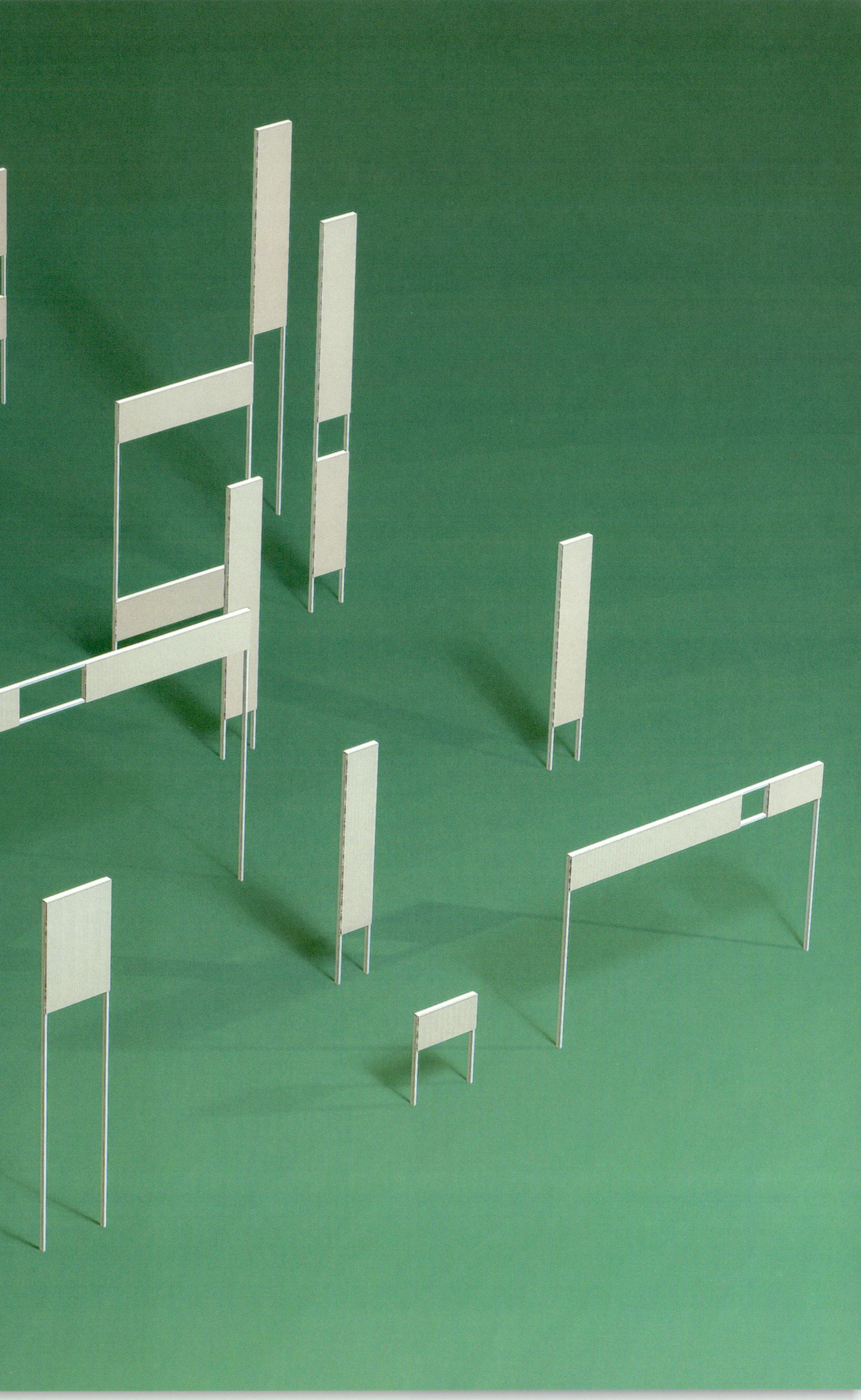

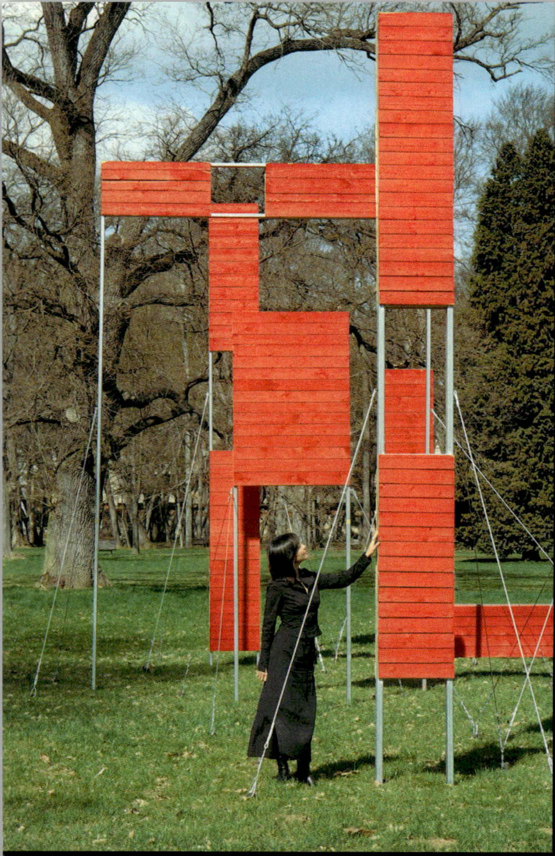

www.christian-moeller.com/tower_of_babel

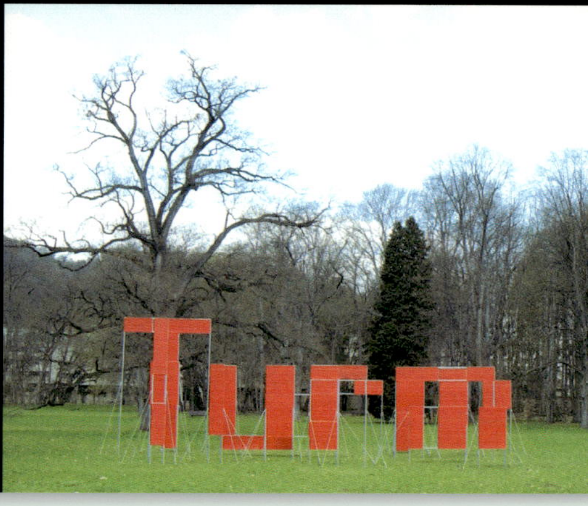

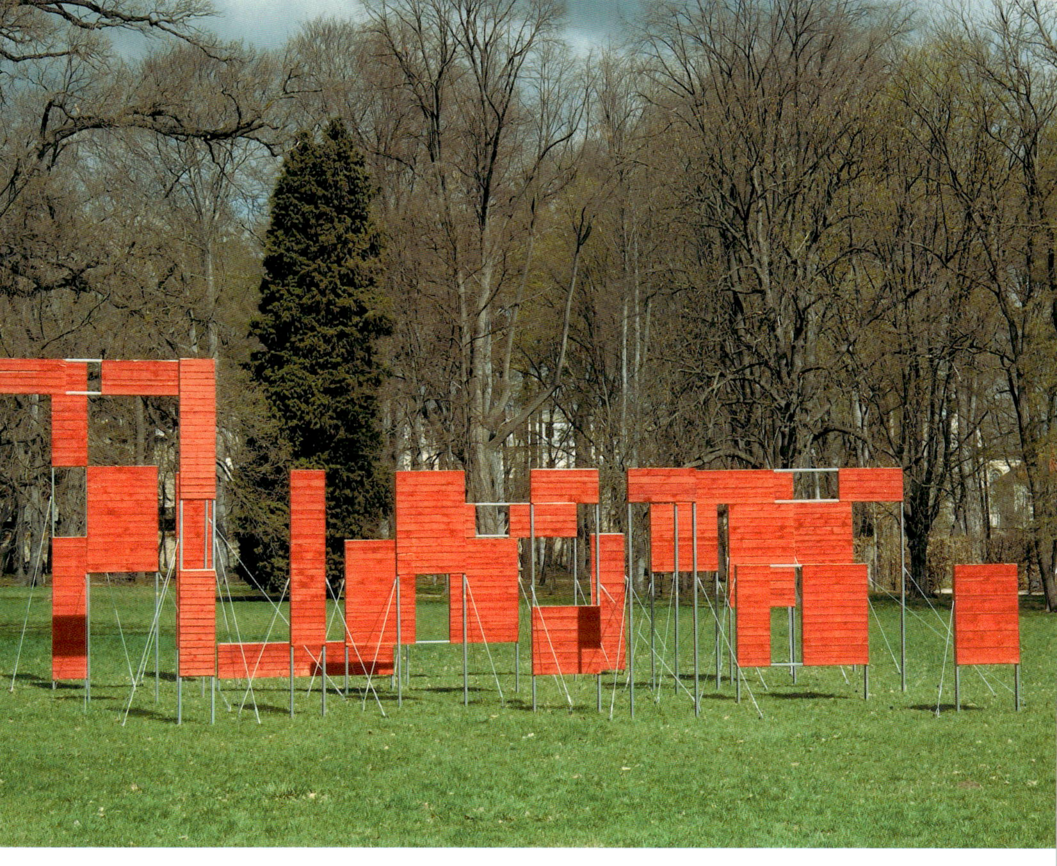

Seen from a particular perspective, wooden panels turn into readable words “Turm zu Babel” (“Tower of Babel”).

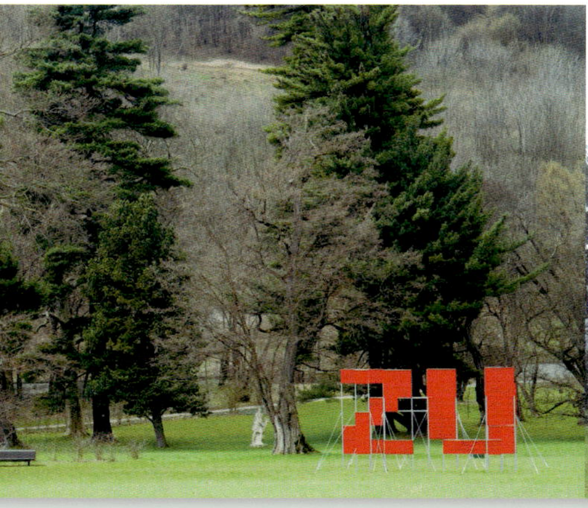

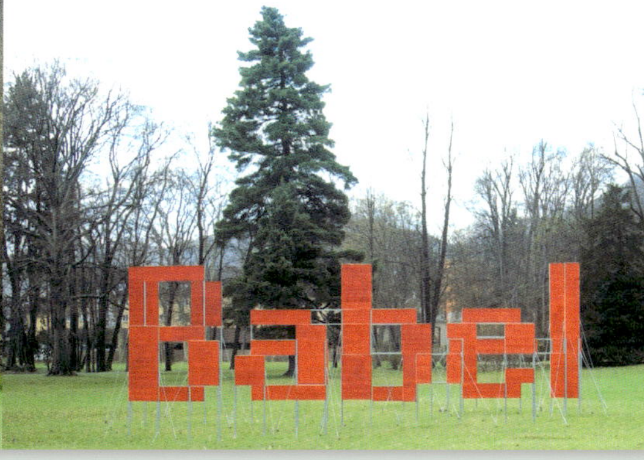

ON AIR

2003

www.christian-moeller.com/on_air

The Tower of Babel, Origin and Diversity of oral and written languages,
Kunsthistorisches Museum Vienna, at Eggenberg Castle, Graz.
In collaboration with: Wilfried Seipel

Programming: Sven Thöne
Hardware: Wolfgang Schemmert
Coordination (KHM): Gabriele Stöger
Construction management (Artex): Gerhard Veigel
Construction: Dekorationsbau Winter

The first concepts for the exhibition, “Tower of Babel,” started in the late 1990s. The Kunsthistorisches Museum Vienna moved the exhibition date several times. When the decision was made to realize “Tower of Babel” in April 2003, no one could have known that the actual Babylon (in Iraq) would be under the siege of war.
The plan was to create an other installation in the inner courtyard of Castle Eggenberg that represents the confusion of languages in the myth of the Tower of Babel. I used once again the touch-sensitive interface developed first for the Audio Grove installation in Tokyo, this time with fewer but larger poles.
By touching any of the 44 steel poles, each representing the country of origin of a broadcast signal, visitors can listen to the different languages currently “on air”, those receivable via satellite in the Northern Hemisphere: Albanian, Bosnian, Bulgarian, German, English, French, Georgian, Greek, Italian, Croation, Kurdish, Macedonian, Dutch, Polish, Romanian, Russian, Serbian, Slovakian, Slovenian, Spanish, Turkish, Chechnyan, Hungarian, Arabic, Armenian, Bengali, Cantonese, Mandarin, Farsi, Hindi, Japanese, Korean, Malaysian, Pakistani, Tamil and Thai.
The tragic main attraction in this installation became the pole standing in for the state television channel from Iraq. While bombs were falling around the Euphrates and Tigris, uncanny music and war propaganda from this pole dominated the ambience of the Castle Eggenberg. April 6, 2003, the day after the opening of the exhibition, the pole of Iraq fell silent.

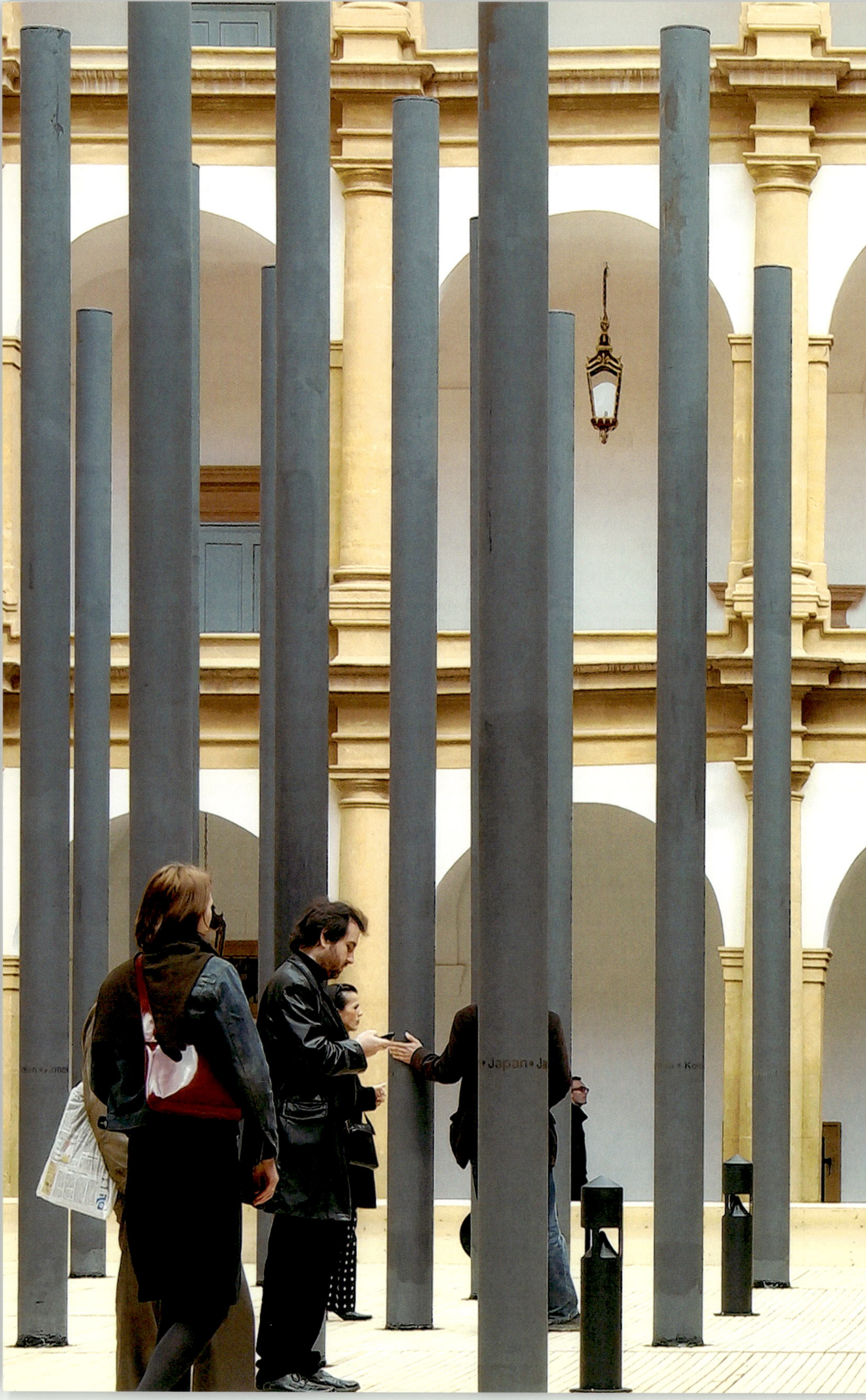
Japan

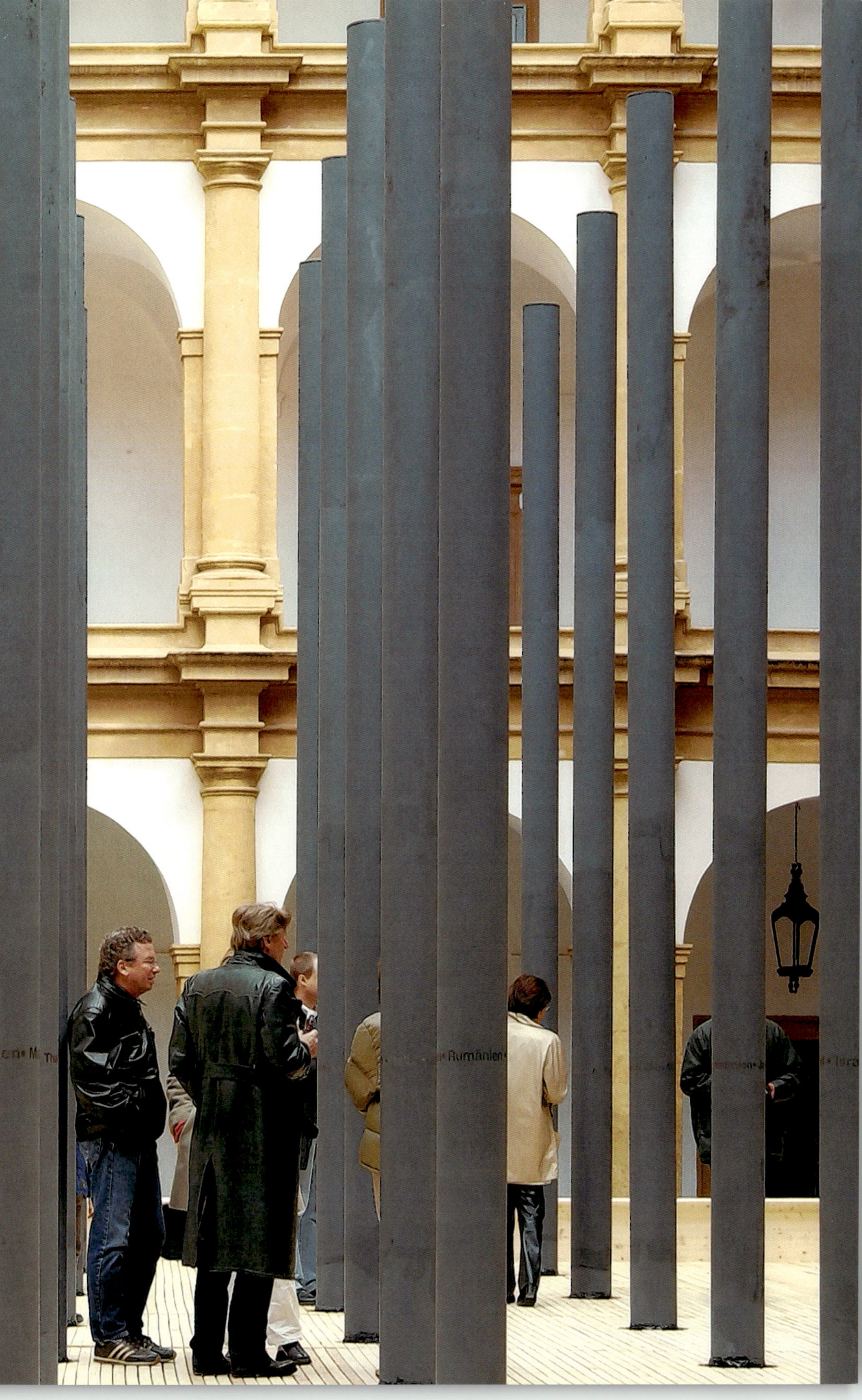
Rumänien

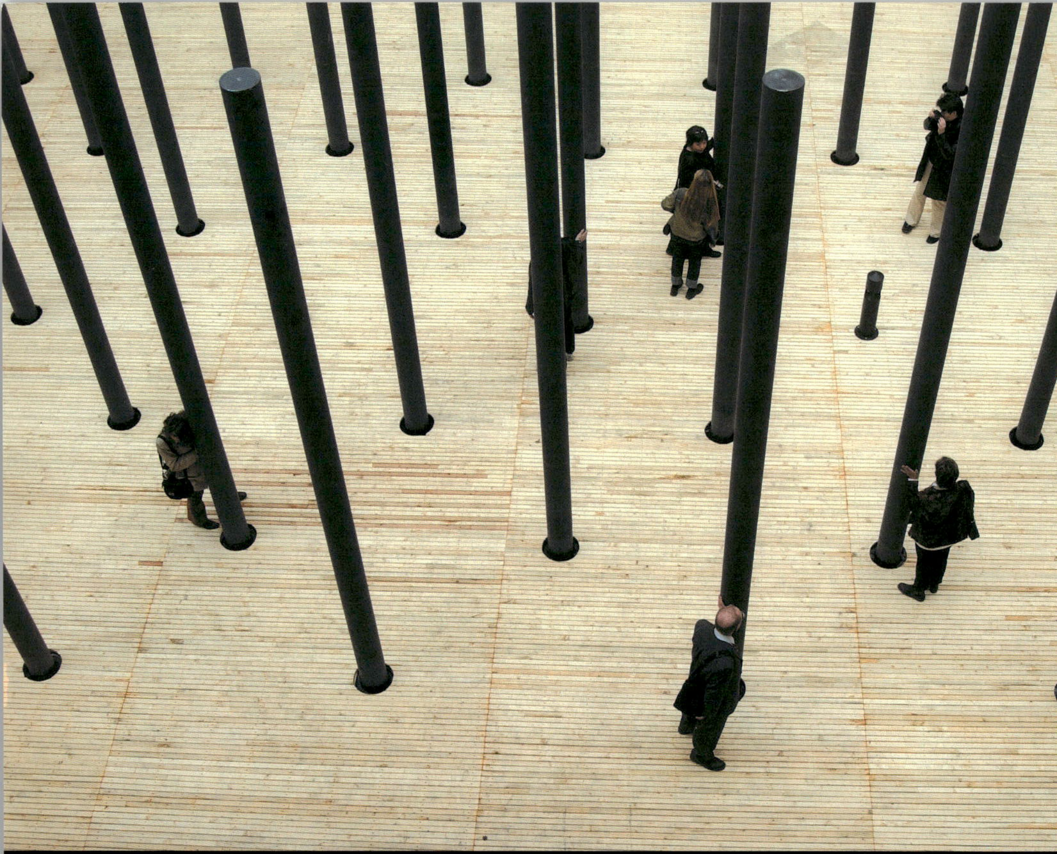

www.christian-moeller.com/on_air

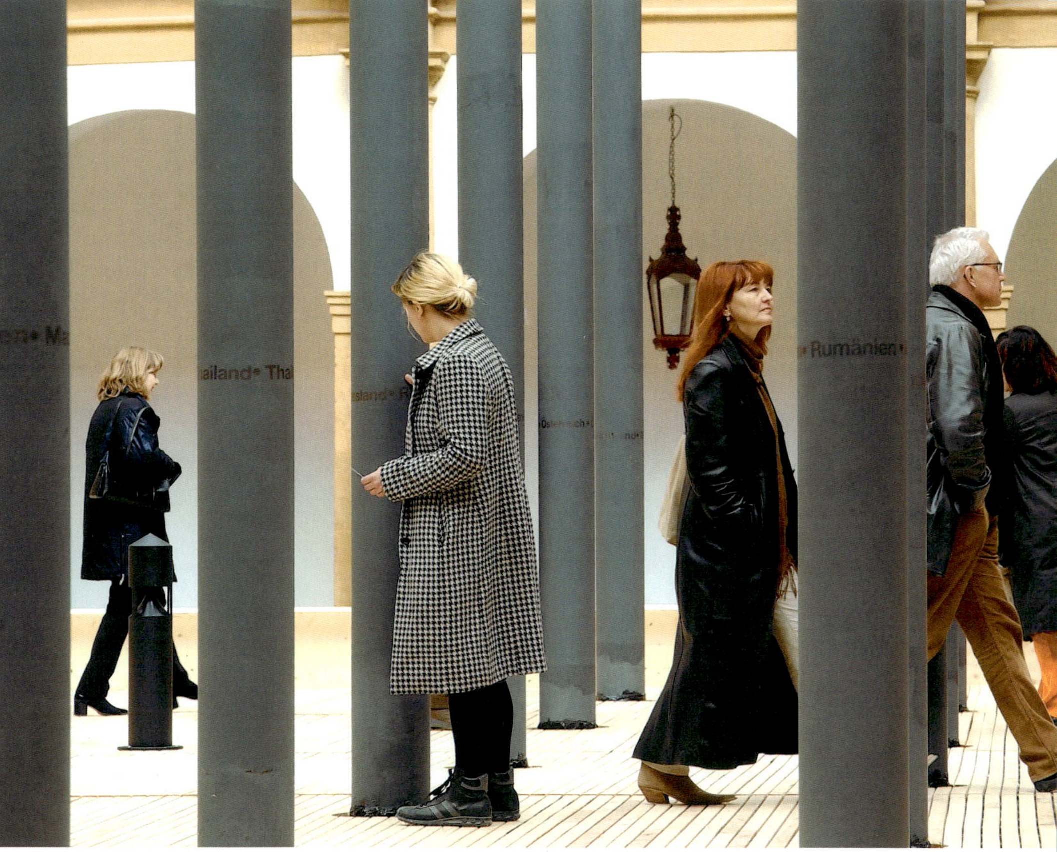

Visitors select and hear live playback of
broadcasts in 44 different languages
by touching steel poles in the courtyard
of Castle Eggenberg.

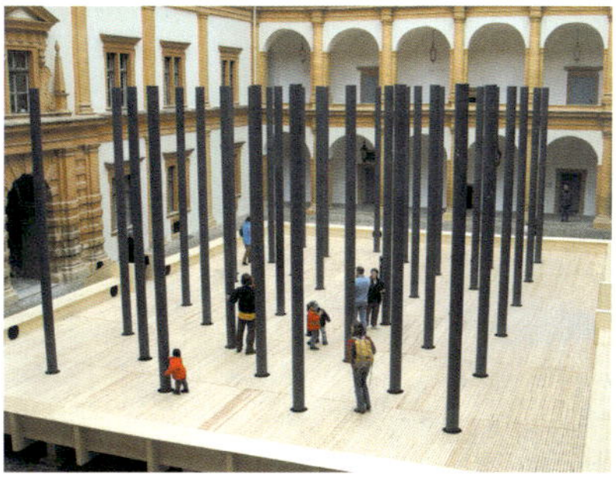

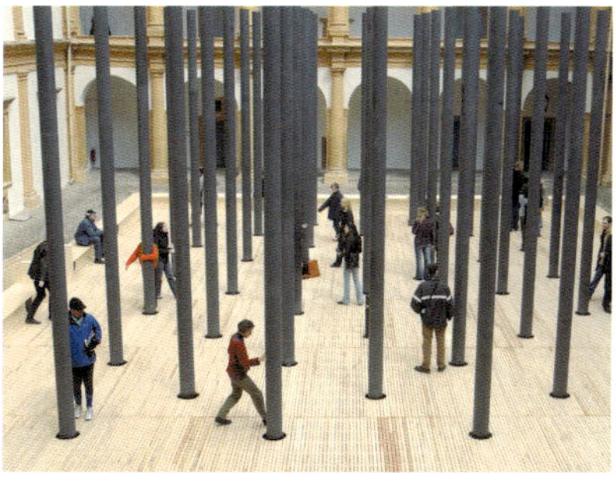

CHEESE

2003
www.christian-moeller.com/cheese
Neuro, in cooperation with Caltech (California Institute of Technology)
at Williamson Gallery Art Center College of Design, Pasadena
In collaboration with: Pietro Perona

Curator: Stephen Nowlin
Programming: Sean Crowe
Video technique: Pierre Moreels and Maroun Harb
Actresses: Laura Clumeck, Natasha Desai, Susan Marshall,
Kyra Locke, Cameo Cara Martine, Melissa Berger
Make up: Kehli O'Byrne
Casting: Katharine Wright
Construction management: Julian Goldwhite
Construction: Tim Quin
Software: Javier Movellan, Marni Bartlett, The Machine Perception Laboratory
at the University of California San Diego's Institute for Neural Computation.

In the year 2002 I received an invitation from Pietro Perona, Director of the Center for Neuromorphic Systems Engineering at California Institute of Technology in Pasadena, who, along with Stephen Nowlin from Art Center College of Design, had plans for an exhibition of commissioned works which would be created in cooperation between artists and scientists.

Perona's institute is researching applications of human visual perception phenomena for the design of machines. Among their projects is a robot to be sent to Mars that instead of being controlled remotely from Earth, will be sufficiently intelligent to explore the planet's terrain on its own. An important constraint is that such a machine must also have very complex visual perception capabilities.

The robot has an imaging sensor far more sophisticated than automatic focus and exposure. It has an intelligence capable of understanding its environment and choosing what will make an interesting and valuable picture.

In the shadow of this work, "Cheese" is an experiment in the architecture of sincerity. It was developed in co-production with the Machine Perception Laboratories of the University of California, San Diego. Inspired by the omnipresent friendly, smiling faces of my new world in Hollywood, I decided to use the theme of "emotion recognition". More than 800 young actresses answered a small advertisement I placed in an entertainment industry trade magazine: "looking for actress, news anchor type, for a series of video portraits."

We created a sort of human-computer interaction scenario in which the computer took the dominant position. On camera, six actresses each tried to hold a smile for as long as they could, up to one and a half hours. Each ongoing smile was scrutinized by the computer's perception system, and whenever the display of happiness fell below a certain threshold, an alarm alerted the actress to show more sincerity.

An increasingly terrifying situation was created in which the reality of their emotional discomfort, camouflaged by their convincing performances, was only apparent during the intermittent breaks necessary to soothe their exhausted faces.

Displayed in the gallery on six flat panel monitors, sequenced adjacent to each other along the wall, the piece created a concert of alert signals within an ambience of forced friendliness and irritating melancholy.

The performance of sincerity is very hard work.

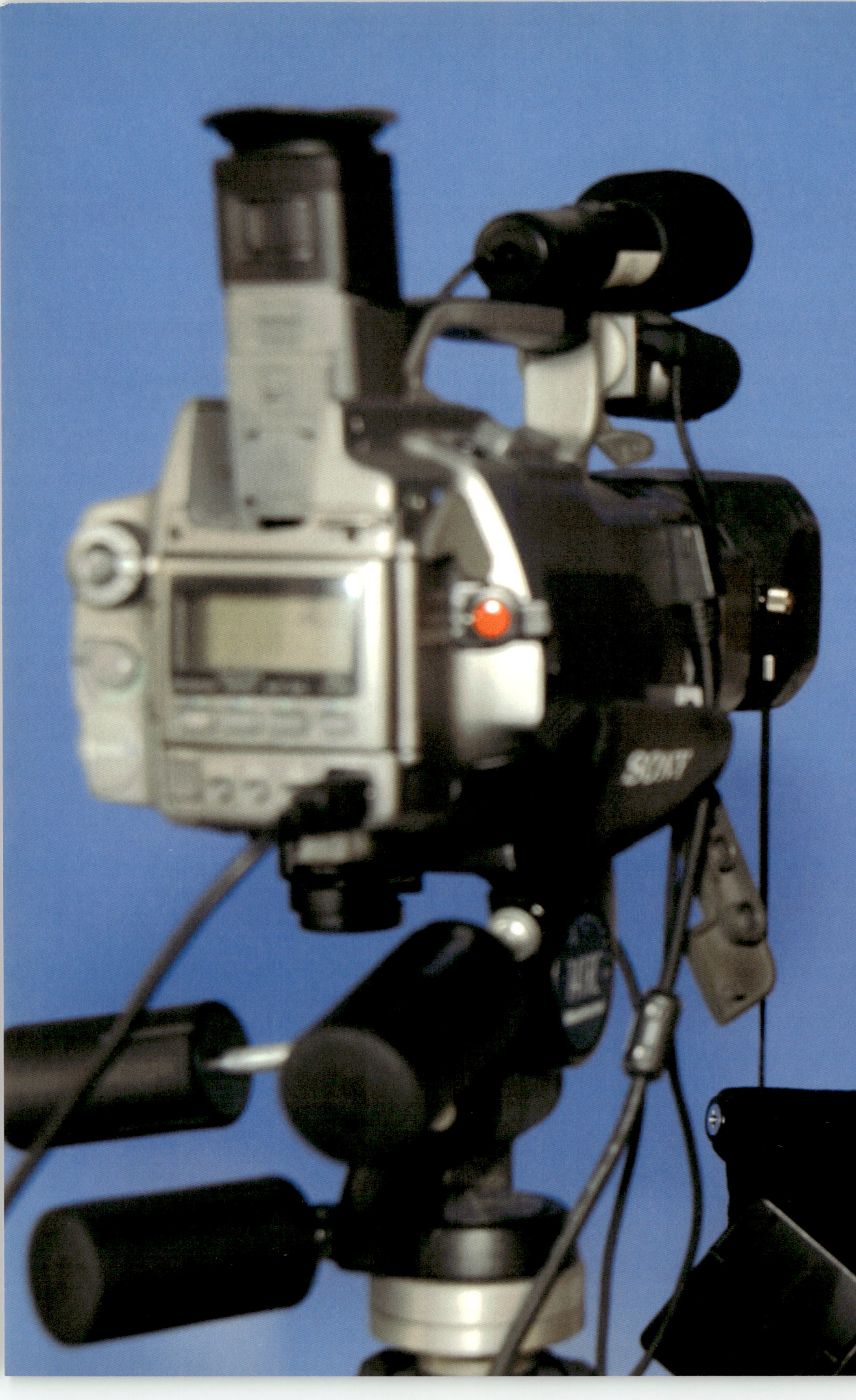
SONY

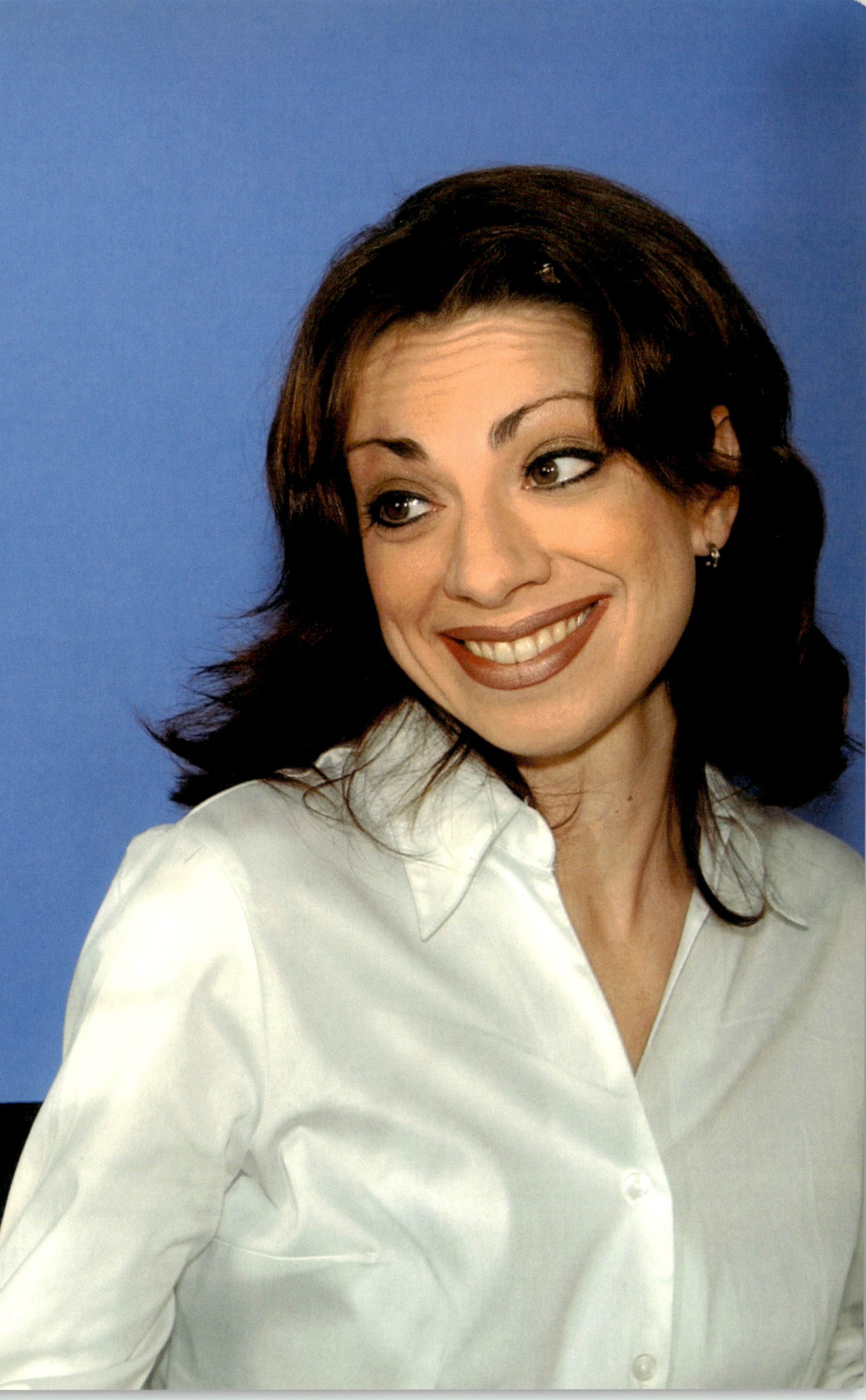

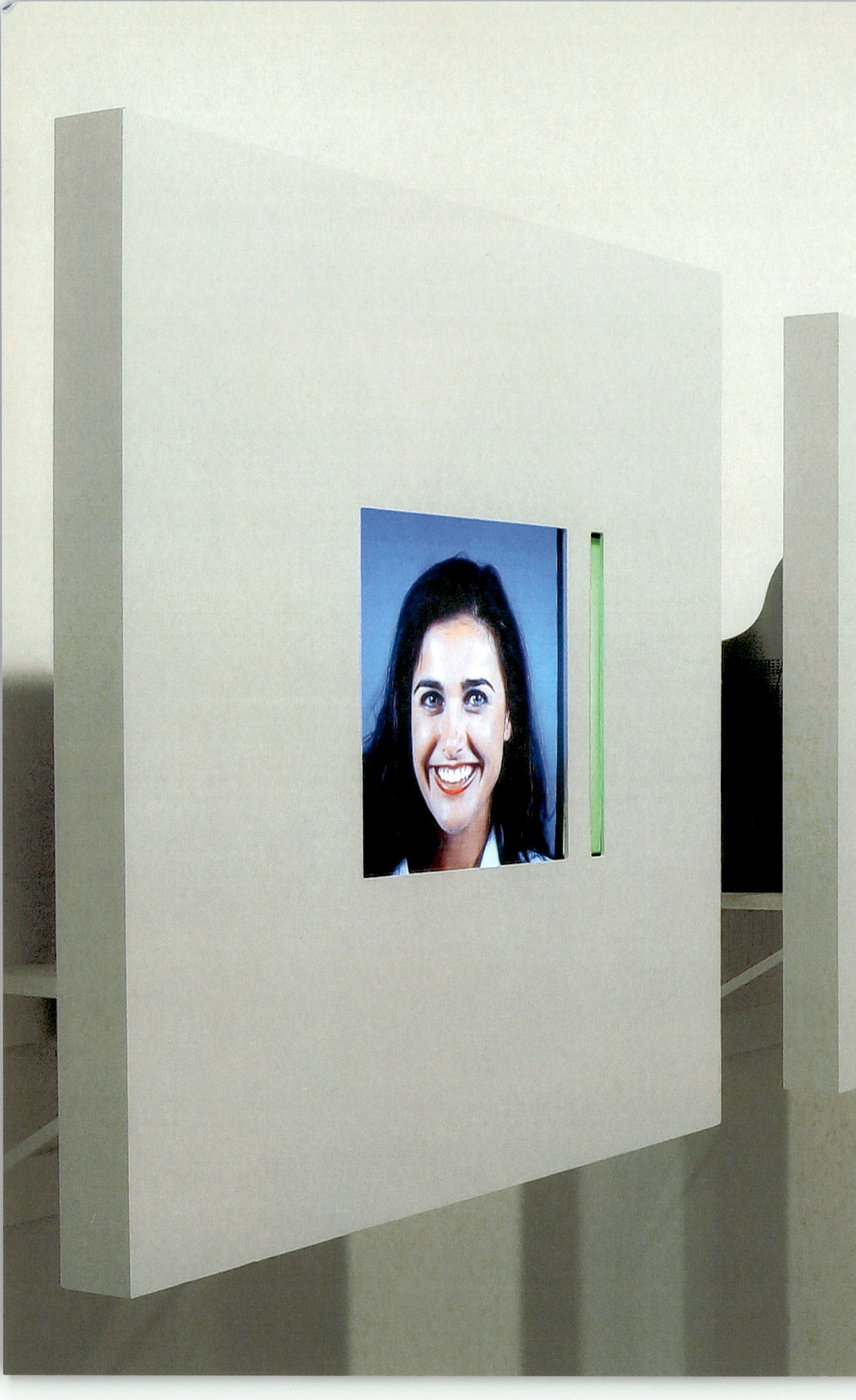

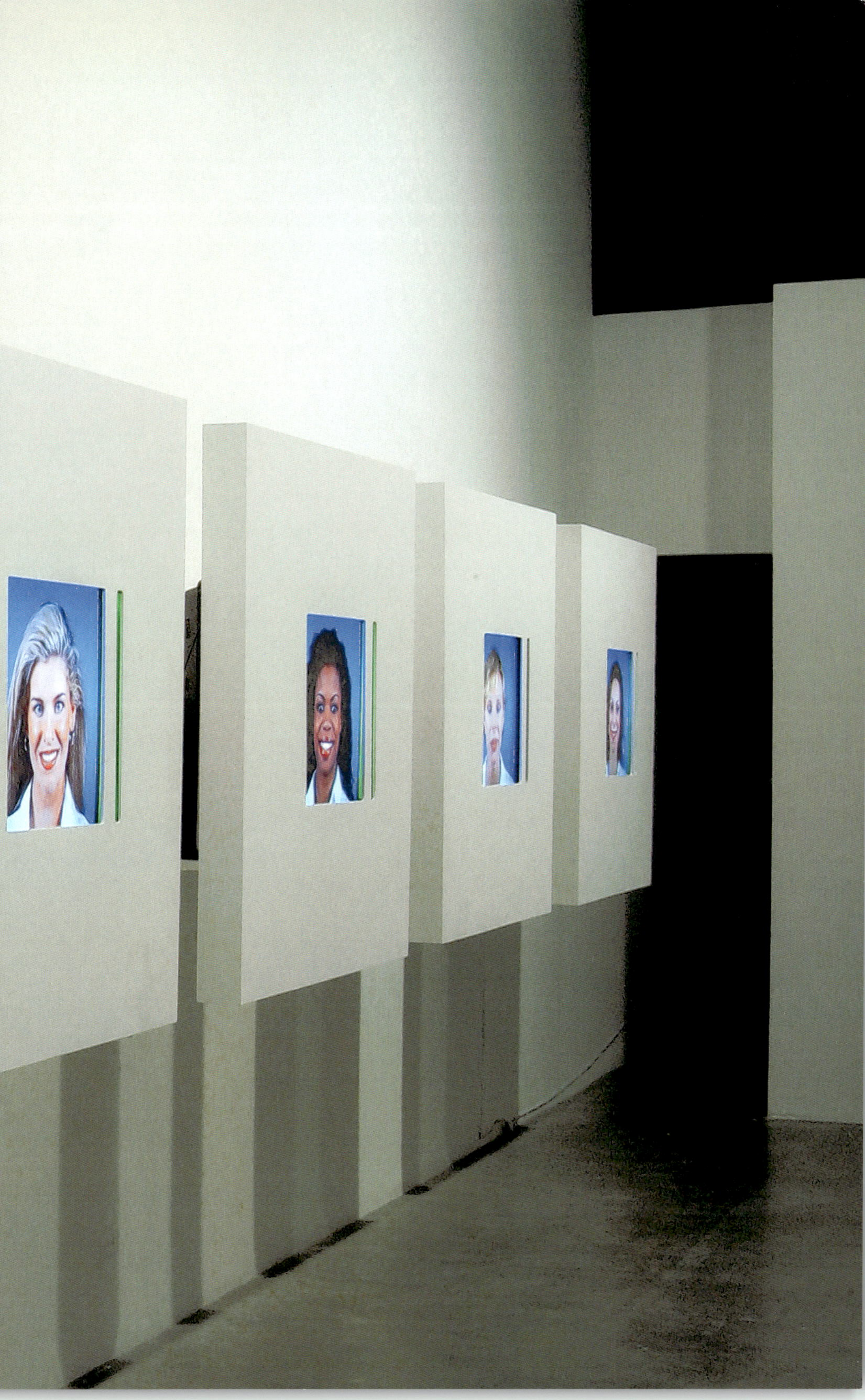

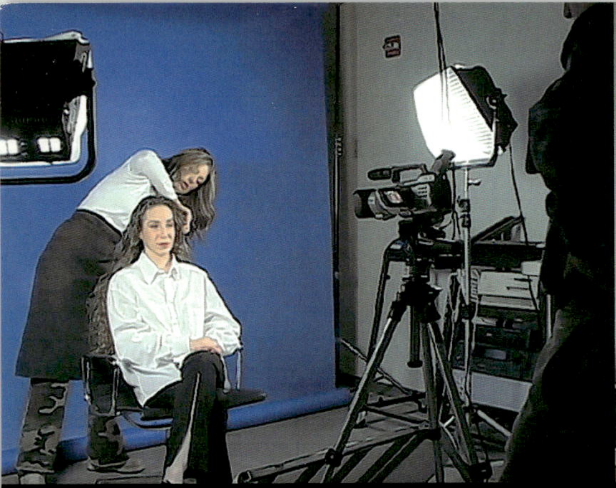

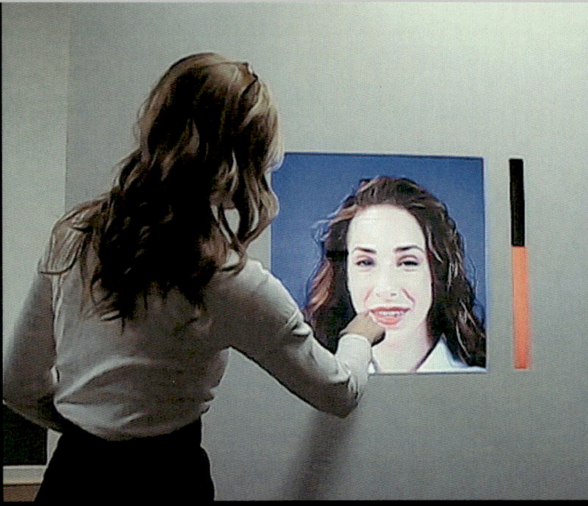

Preparation of a recording session
in the studio.

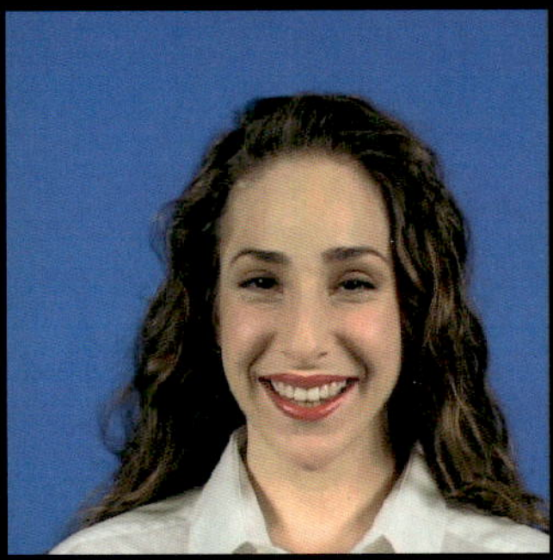

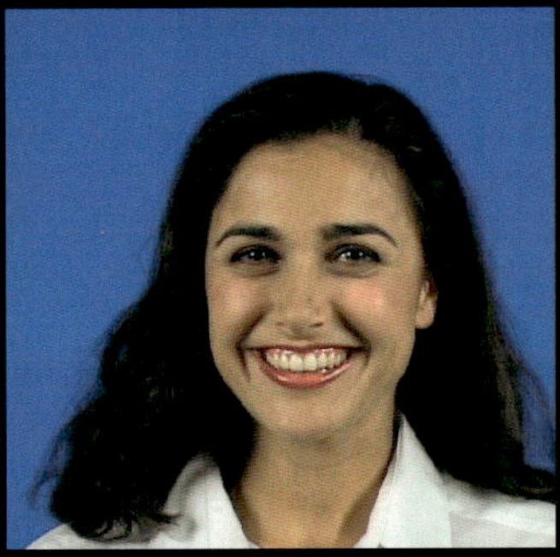

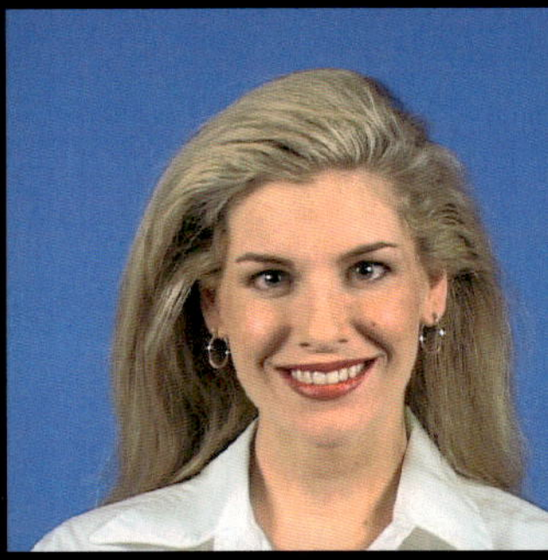

www.christian-moeller.com/cheese

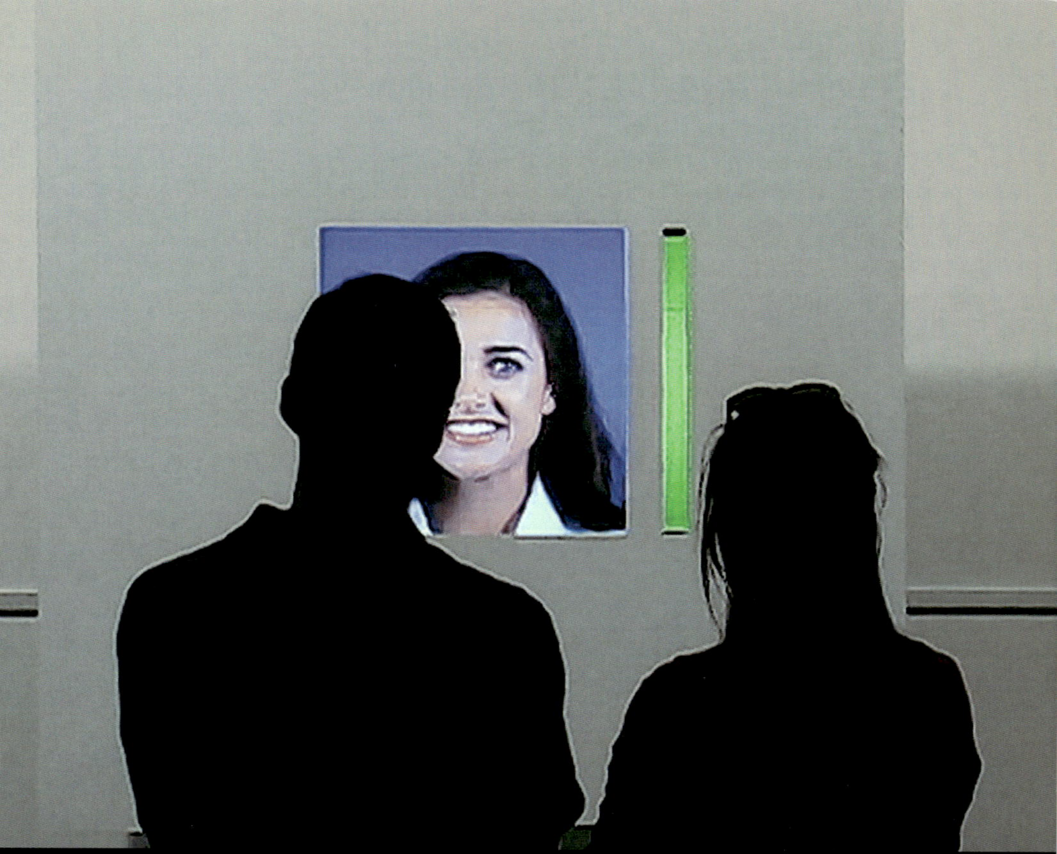

The emotional recognition system observes each face, and displays the level of sincerity on a vertical bar, switching from red to green.

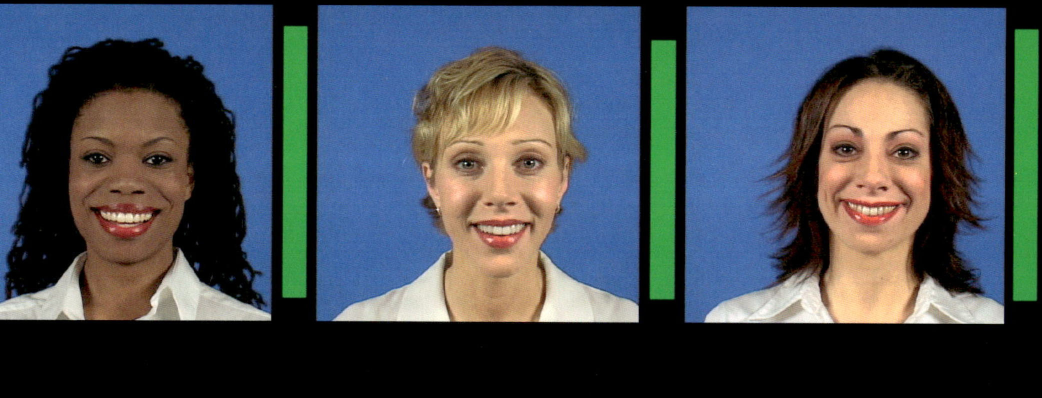

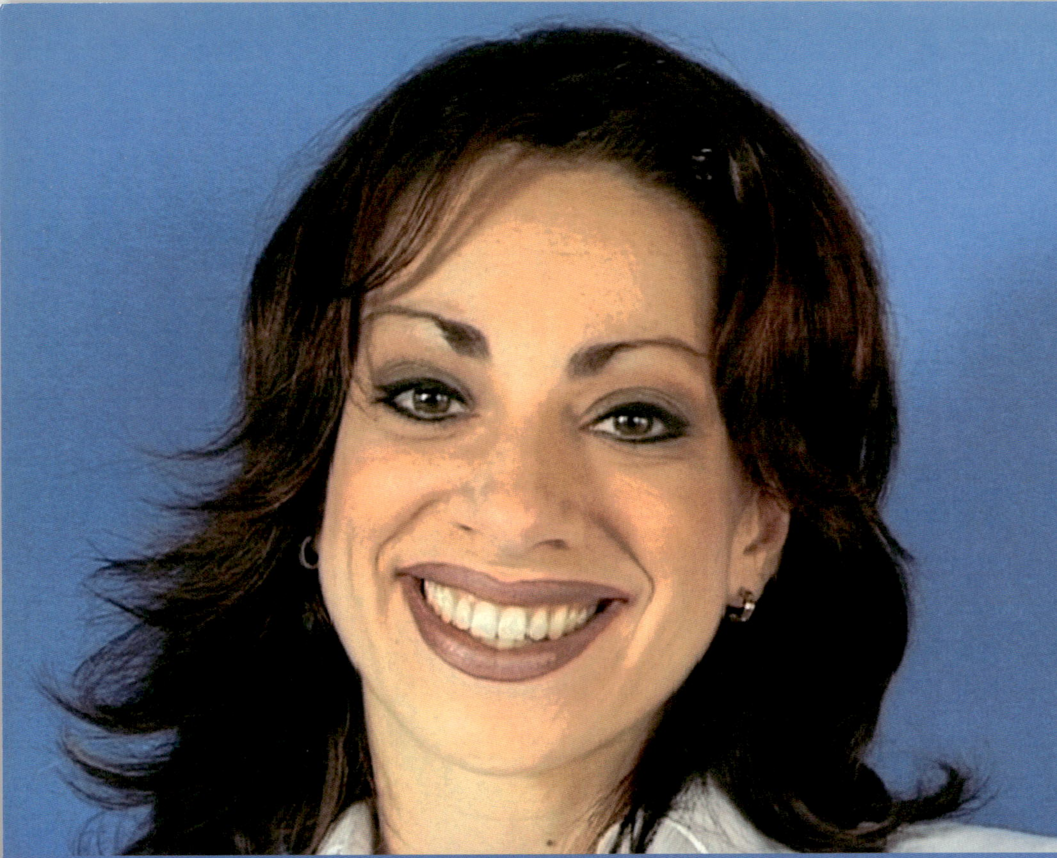

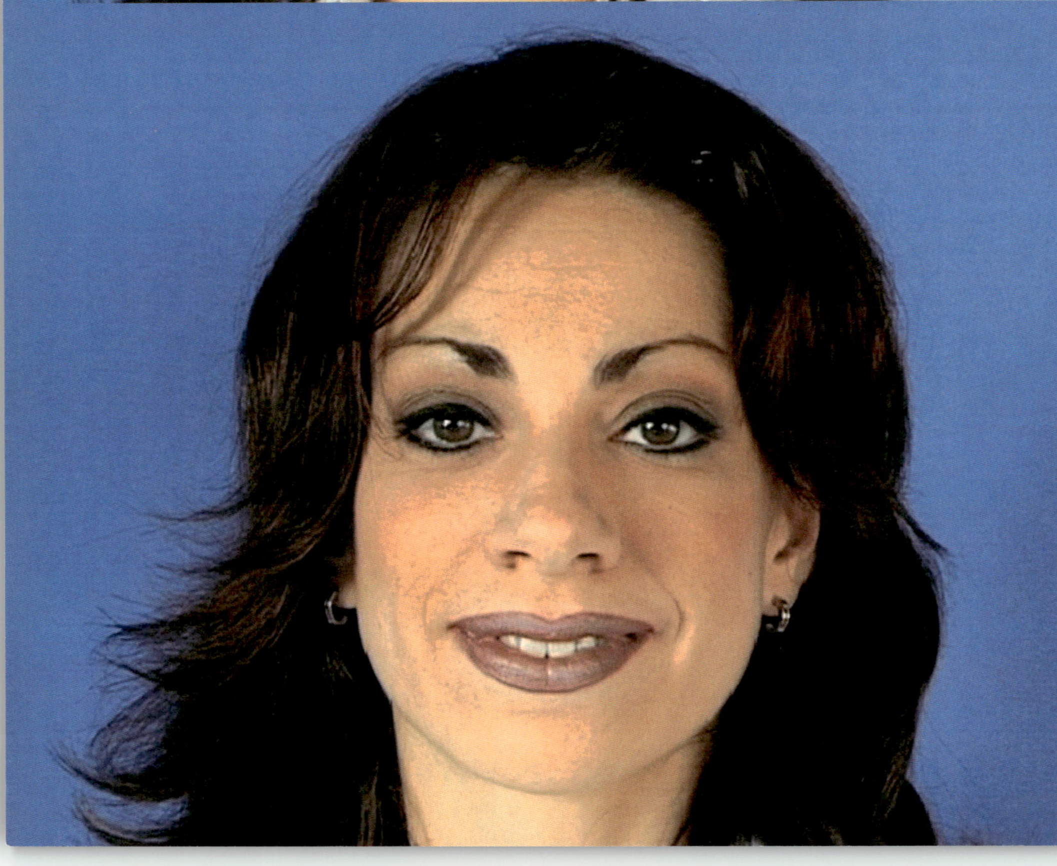

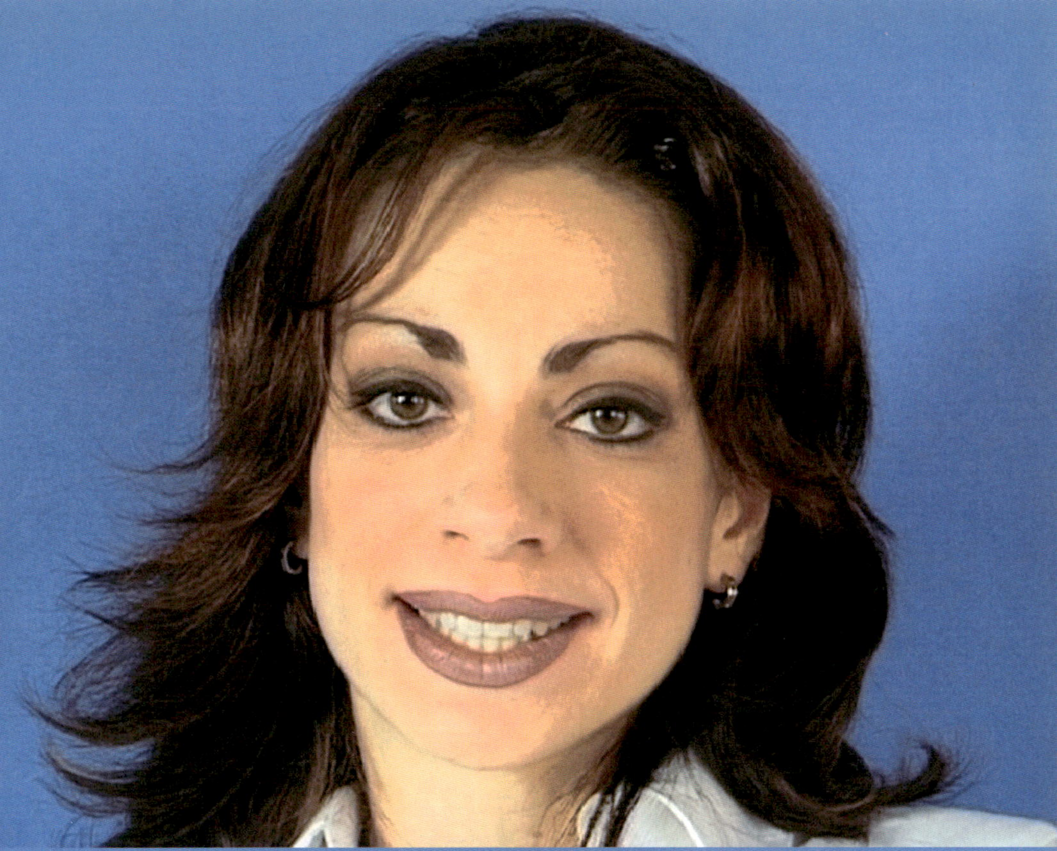

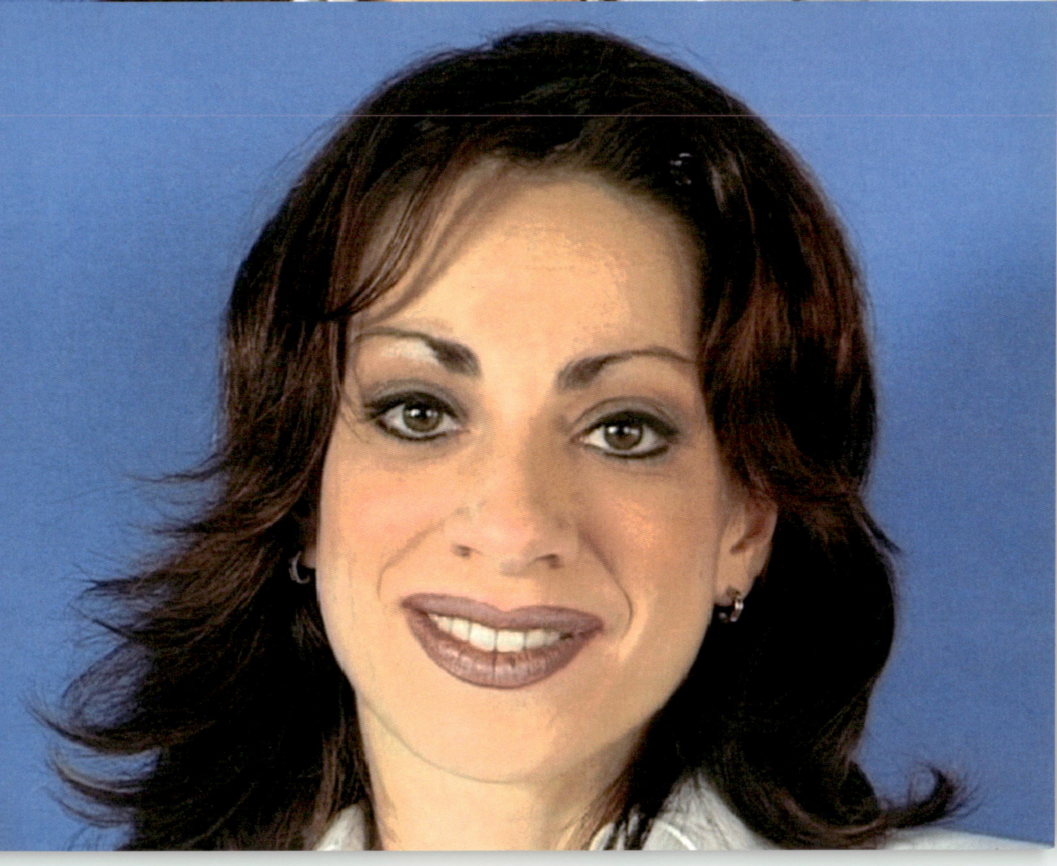

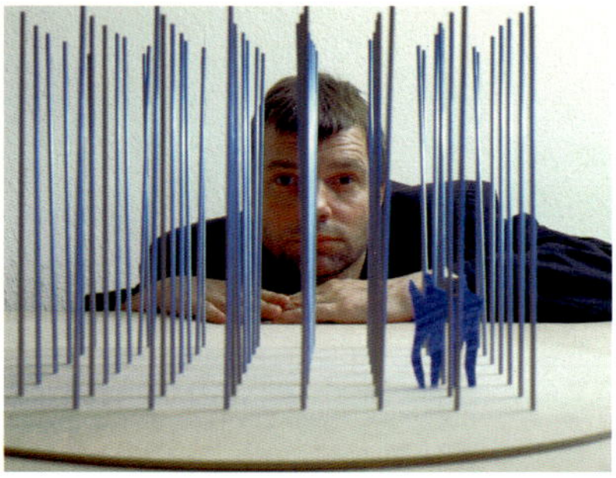

Biography

Christian Moeller was born in 1959 in Frankfurt/Main. He studied architecture at the College of Applied Sciences in Frankfurt and at the Academy of Fine Arts in Vienna. In 1990 he joined Peter Weibel's Institut für Neue Medien **and founded his own studio and media laboratory in Frankfurt. From 1995 to 1997 he headed the ARCHIMEDIA Research Institute at the College of Design in Linz. He was a Professor at the State College of Design in Karlsruhe until he moved to the United States in the year 2001. Currently he is a Professor in the Department of Design | Media Arts at UCLA (University of California Los Angeles) and operates his studio in Hollywood, California.**

Projects and Exhibitions

1991
A-Line – Cinematoscope Installation, Frankfurt.

1992
Space (Im)Balance, Bucknerhaus, ARS Electronica'92, **Linz, Austria.**
Kinetic Light Sculpture, together with Rüdiger Kramm, at Zeilgalerie, Frankfurt.

1993
The Virtual Cage, at the TAT, Theater am Turm in Frankfurt.
Electronic Mirror, in "The Intrinsic World of Apparatuses", Institute for New Media, Frankfurt.
Stations of the Image – Chapter III, in the Carmelite Monastery, Frankfurt.
Chronolyze, in the Linden Tunnel, Berlin.
Surfaces of Variable Visibility, in the Stadtpark Gallery, Krems, Austria.
Algorithmic Habitat, for Peter Weibel's "On Justifying the Hypothetical Nature of Art and its Non-Identity with the Object World," Gallery Tanja Grunert, Cologne and SIGGRAPH'93, **Los Angeles.**
Light Blaster, Design Horizonte'93, **Naxos Hall, Frankfurt.**
Sala, Audiovisual Project with Trautonium, together with Oskar Sala, Design Horizonte'93 **at Frankfurt.**

1994
Interactive Architecture, in the Aedes Gallery, Berlin.
Electro Clips, at the TAT, Theater am Turm in Frankfurt and at the ARS Electronica'94 **in Linz.**
Electronic Mirror 2, ARS Electronica'94, **Design Center, Linz.**
Networked Skin, together with Joachim Sauter, ARS Electronica'94, **Landesmuseum Oberösterreich, Linz.**
Musical Pendulums, ISEA'94, **Helsinki, Finland.**

1995
Electro Clips, at Dance 95 in Munich.
Electronic Mirror, Press Enter-Between Seduction and Disbelief, in the Power Plant Gallery, Toronto.
Audio Park – The Party Effect, Openair Audiosculpture, in the Museumpark, Rotterdam.
Archimedia, Prototyps and Projects, Innovatives Oberösterreich, Design Center Linz.
Fugue for Piano, KV 385k = 154, in the Figarohaus, Vienna.

1996
Autonomous Mirror, VISA, **in Le Manège, Maubeuge and** EXIT, **Maison des Arts, Paris.**
Backbone, in Wunschmaschine Welterfindung, Kunsthalle Vienna.
Autonomous Mirror, in Wunschmaschine Welterfindung, Kunsthalle Vienna.

The third dimension of Ritratto di Gentiluomo and Fugue for Piano, KV 385k = 154, The Bridge, Museum of Contemporary Arts, SIGGRAPH'96, **New Orleans.**
Kamera Musik, with Adelhard Roidinger, in Projects'96, **ARCHIMEDIA Gallery, Linz.**
Variable Objects with Helmuth Gsoellpointner in Projects'96, **ARCHIMEDIA Gallery, Linz.**
Virtual Sensations, (The Virtual Touch, Text Space and Immersive Audio) 3 VR-Stations at the ARS Electronica Center, Linz.
Backbone, Object Video, Landesmuseum Oberösterreich, Linz.
The Expanded Chamber, at the exhibition Botschaft der Musik, Kunsthistorisches Museum Vienna, Palais Harrach, Vienna.

1997
Sound garden with Audio Grove, Camera Musik and Virtual Train at Spiral/Wacoal Art Center, in Tokyo.
Virtual Cage, ARTLAB-Prospect 2, at Tochoji Auditorium P3, Tokyo.

1998
The Voice of the People, at the exhibition "1848 Aufbruch zur Freiheit", Schirn Kunsthalle, Frankfurt.
Audio Grove, at Cyber 98, **Centro Cultural de Belem, Lisbon**

1999
Downlights, at Centro Cultural Candido Mendes, Rio de Janeiro, Brasil.

2000
Insound Out and Particles, at the Science Museum, London.

2001
De-Pictured – Bitwall 4, at Alyce de Roulet Williamson Gallery, Art Center College of Design, Pasadena.

2002
Elbe-Bitwall 1, at the Federal Institute of Hydraulic Engineering, Ilmenau, Germany.
Polylog, Wörgl, Austria.

2003
Turm zu Babel, Der Turmbau zu Babel, Kunsthistorisches Museum Vienna, at Castle Eggenberg, Graz.
On-Air, Der Turmbau zu Babel, Kunsthistorisches Museum Vienna, at Castle Eggenberg, Graz.
Cheese, at the exhibition Neuro, Alyce de Roulet Williamson Gallery, Art Center College of Design, Pasadena.

Aknowledgements

I would like especially thank Peter Weibel, for first introducing me to media technology; Peter Müller, for his unwavering support for the realization of my projects; and Sven Thöne, Nathan Thompson and Wolfgang Schemmert, for their enduring collaboration.

Over the past 13 years, I have had the pleasure to work with great people, without whom, this work would never have been accomplished. While this list is inevitably incomplete, I would like to especially thank the following people for their generosity and intelligence.

Kazunao Abe, Alex Adriaansen, Volker Albus, Marni Bartlett, Jytte Basler, Dieter Beck, Michael Behrendt, Georg Bertsch, Willi Bopp, Klaus Bollinger, Benjamin H. Bratton, Tanja den Broeder, Ludger Brümmer, Lucy Bullivant, Richard Castelli, Alexandra Chun, Paul Claessen, Pete Conolly, Susanne Craemer, Sean Crowe, Pauline Cumbers, Louis Philippe Demers, Hans-Jürgen Diekmann, Louise Dompierre, David Dunn, Rolf Engel, Alexander von Fersen, Hartmut Florin, Raquel Francois, Tillmann Freudenberg, Barbara Fuchs, Jeremy Gaines, Stephen Galloway, Hermann Gruber, Katharina Gsöllpointner, Christian Gusenbauer, Maroun Harb, Dick Hebdige, Monika Heinisch, Hans Hoffer, Ottmar Hörl, Shinobu Ito, Ronald Kammer, Heinz Karner, Derrick de Kerckhove, Norman Klein, Klaus Klemp, Heinrich Klotz, Rüdiger Kramm, Machiko Kusahara, Hans-Jürgen Kubina, Herbert Lachmayer, Roland Lambrette, Thomas Lauerbach, Harlan Lee, George Legrady, Barbara Luecke, Peter Lunenfeld, Dirk Lüsebrink, Hubert Machnik, Sang Mah, Miltos Manetas, Roger Mann, Lev Manovich, Gideon May, Rebeca Mendez, Christoph Meyer, Vasa Mihich, Diane Mills, Pierre Moreels, Stephan Morgenstern, S. Joy Mountford, Javier Movellan, Fred Moske, Mutare Ensemble, Pete Namlook, Stephen Nowlin, Bob O'Kane, Simon Penny, Pietro Perona, Falk Petry, Elsa Prochazka, Tim Quin, Hannah Redler, Adelhard Roidinger, Oskar Sala, Anna Saup, Michael Saup, Joachim Sauter, Ulrich Schaaf, Hermann Schaefer, Jens Scheiber, Ulrike Schiedermair, Thecla Schiphorst, Daniel Schmitt, Eckhard Schneider, Harald Schröder, Ulla Schuch, Hellmut Seemann, Gabriela Seifert, Wilfried Seipel, Maurizo Seracini, Yukiko Shikata, Wolfgang Soeder, Edith Spiegl, Rejanne Spitz, Jennifer Steinkamp, Gerfried Stocker, Götz Stöckmann, Gabriele Stöger, Axel Strigl, Tom Stromberg, Fumihiko Sumitomo, Petra Trefzger, Rui Trindade, J. E. Weidinger, Gerhard Veigel, Victoria Vesna, Maria Vogiatzis, Hans Walchhofer, Arnd Wesemann, Christopher Winter, Thomas Wollenzien, Katharine Wright, Siegfried Zielinski, Stefan Zimmermann, Hans-Joachim Zinner

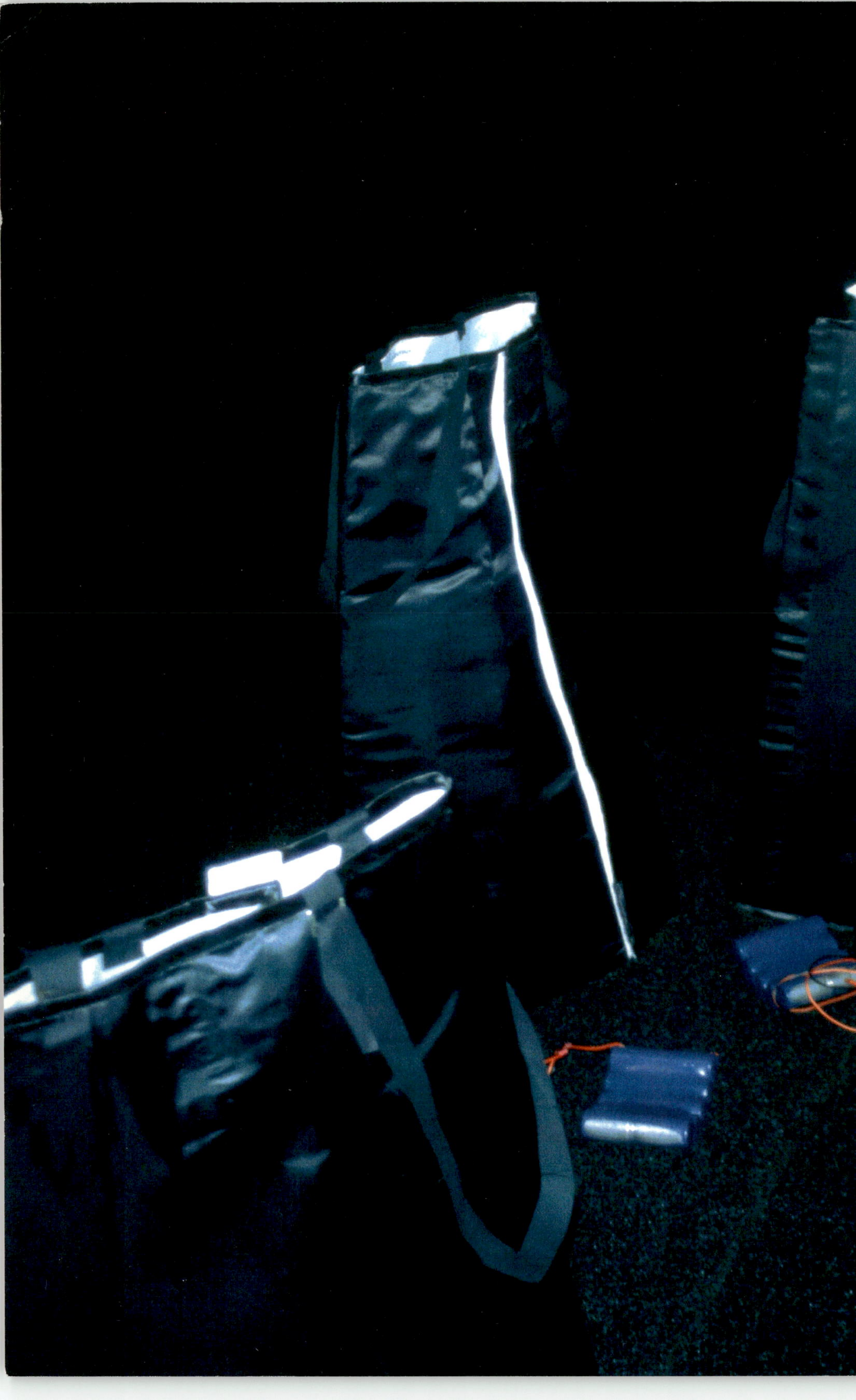

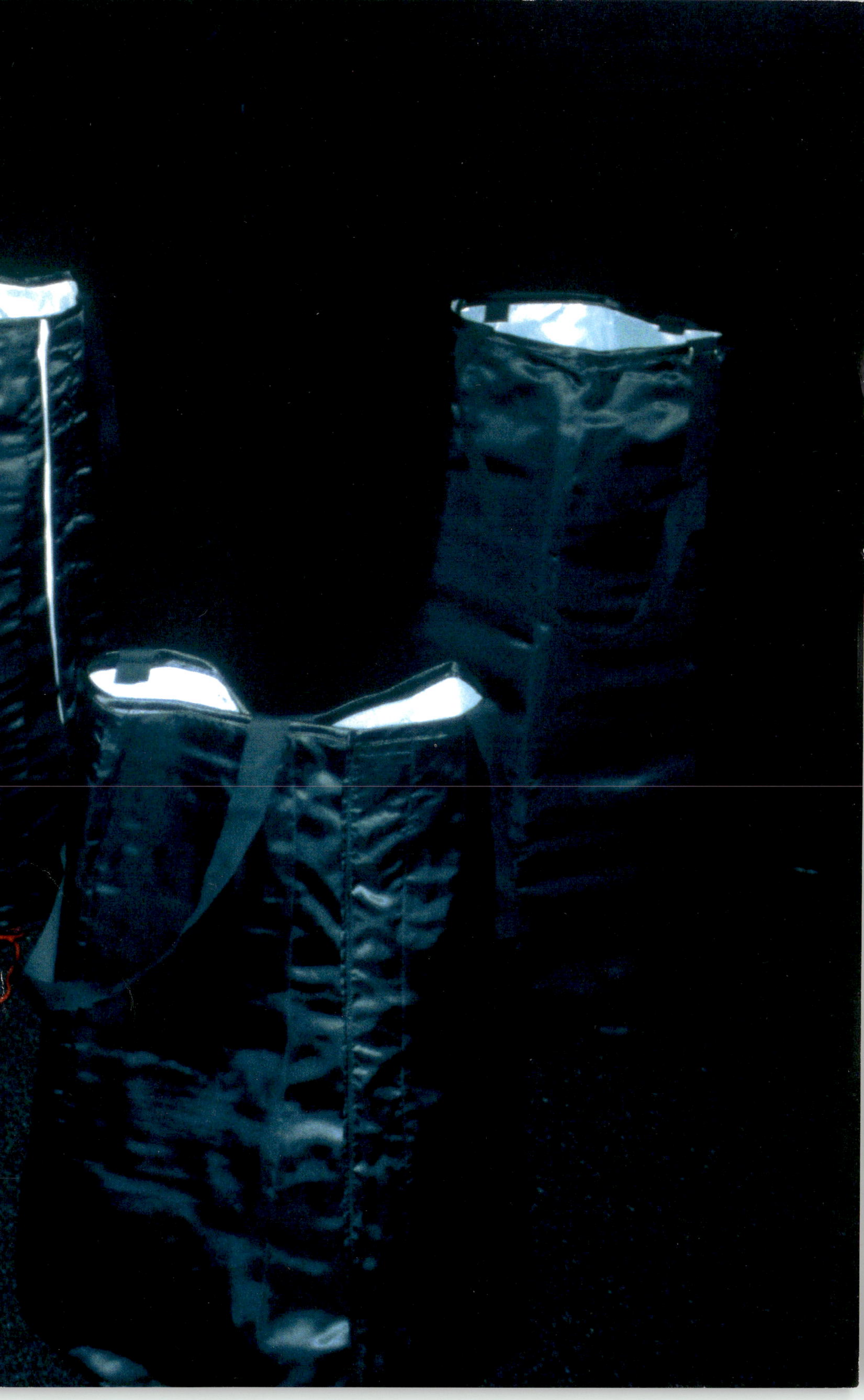

A Time and Place
Christian Moeller
Media Architecture
1991–2003

Concept: Christian Moeller and Lars Müller
Editorial Direction: Benjamin H. Bratton
Editorial Assistance: Daniel Sauter,
Katharine Wrigth, Sean Crowe, Yean-Ling Tang
First Reader: Hannah Redler
For the Title "A Time and Place": Pete Conolly
Translation: Pauline Cumbers
Proofreading English: Michael Robinson

Design: Integral Lars Müller/Lars Müller
and Daniele Barbiero
Typography: Gabriela König
Printing: Vetsch & Co., CH-Köniz
Binding: Buchbinderei Burkhardt, CH-Mönchaltorf

Design of http://www.christian-moeller.com: Daniel Sauter

Printed in Switzerland

ISBN 3-907078-91-8

Lars Müller Publishers
5401 Baden/Switzerland
www.lars-muller-publishers.com

Distributed in North America by
D.A.P./Distributed Art Publishers, Inc.
155 Sixth Avenue, 2nd Floor
New York, NY 10013
www.artbook.com